# BANKING SECTOR IN INDIA

:: Author ::

**DR. GAURANGKUMAR C. BAROT**

(M.Com., M.Phil., G-SET., Ph.D)

**Assistant Professor in Commerce & Accountancy**
**Silvassa College (Govt. College), Silvassa**
**U.T. of Dadara & Nagar Haveli- 396230**

**PUBLISHED BY**

Hemchandracharya International Publishing House
HQ. At & Po. Chaveli., Ta- Chansma,
Dist- Patan, North Gujarat, India, Asia.
www.iphouseindia.com

**BANKING SECTOR IN INDIA**



First Publication: 1st MARCH, 2015



ISBN:- 978-15-08949-72-5

Price: Rs.750/- INDIA

$ 15 OUTSIDE INDIA

**PUBLISHED BY**

**Hemchandracharya International Publishing House**

**HQ. At & Po. Chaveli., Ta- Chansma,**

**Dist- Patan, North Gujarat, India, Asia.**

**www.iphouseindia.com**

***Dedicated***
***to***
***my***
***Parents***

# INDEX

# CHAPTER -1

# BANKING IN INDIA

## 1.1 Introduction

Banking was started in the modern sense originated in the last decades of the 18th century. The first banks were Bank of Hindustan (1770-1829) and The General Bank of India, established 1786 and since defunct.

The largest bank, and the oldest still in existence, is the State Bank of India, which originated in the Bank of Calcutta in June 1806, which almost immediately became the Bank of Bengal. This was one of the three presidency banks, the other two being the Bank of Bombay and the Bank of Madras, all three of which were established under charters from the British East India Company. The three banks merged in 1921 to form the Imperial Bank of India, which, upon India's independence, became the State in 1955. For many years the presidency banks acted as quasi-central banks, as did their successors, until the Reserve Bank of India was established in 1935.

In 1969 the Indian government nationalised all the major banks that it did not already own and these have remained under government ownership. They are run under a structure know as 'profit-making public sector undertaking' (PSU) and are allowed to compete and operate as commercial banks. The Indian banking sector is made up of four types of banks, as well as the PSUs and the state banks; they have been joined since the 1990s by new private commercial banks and a number of foreign banks.

Banking in India was generally fairly mature in terms of supply, product range and reach-even though reach in rural India and to the poor still remains a challenge. The government has developed initiatives to address this through the State Bank of India expanding its branch network and through the National Bank for Agriculture and Rural Development with things like microfinance.

Indian Banking Industry currently employs 1,175,149 employees and has a total of 109,811 branches in India and 171 branches abroad and manages an aggregate deposit of ₹67504.54 billion (US$1.1 trillion or €840 billion) and bank credit of ₹ 52604.59 billion (US$870 billion or €650 billion). The net profit of the banks operating in India was ₹1027.51 billion(US$17 billion or €13 billion) against a turnover of ₹9148.59 billion (US$150 billion or €110 billion) for the fiscal year 2012-13.

## 1.2 History

In ancient India there is evidence of loans from the Vedic period (beginning 1750 BC). Later during the Maurya dynasty (321 to 185 BC), an instrument called adesha was in use, which was an order on a banker desiring him to pay the money of the note to a third person, which corresponds to the definition of a bill of exchange as we understand it today. During the Buddhist period, there was considerable use of these instruments. Merchants in large towns gave letters of credit to one another. There is difference of opinion in this regards. According to some authorities, the word "Bank" itself is derived from the world "Branches" or "Banque that is a bench. The early bankers transacted their business on benches in the market place. When a banker failed his banco was broken up by the people, when the word 'bankrupt'. As early as 2000 B.C., the Babylonians has developed a banking system. There is evidence to show that the temples of Babylon were used as banks and such great temples as those of Ephesus and of Delphi were the most powerful of the Greek banking institutions. But the spread of irreligion soon destroyed the public sense of security in depositing money and the priests were not longer acting as financial agents. The Romans did not organize state banks as did the Greeks But their minute regulation were calculated to create the utmost confidence in it.

There are others who are of the opinion that the word 'Bank' is originally derived from German word 'Bank' meaning a joint stock fund, which was Italianized into "Bank" when the Germans were masters of a great part of Italy. This appears to be more possible. But "Whatever be the origin of the word "Bank", as Professor Ramchandra Rao says it would trace the history of banking in Europe from the Middle Ages. Bank is a financial institute which mobilizes funds from the people for the purpose of lending to the required people or institute and industry. With the end of the civilization of antiquity, and as a result of administrative, decentralization and demoralization of the government authority, with its inevitable counterpart of commercial insecurity, Banking degenerated for a period of some centuries into a system of financial make shits. But that was not the only cause. In India, the ancient Indus scriptures refer to the money lending activities in the Vedic period. In India during the

Ramayana and Mahabharata eras, banking had become a full fledged business activity and during the smriti period which followed the Vedic period and Epic age, the business of banking was carried on by the members of the vaishyas community. Manu, the great law giver of the time, speaks of the earning of interest as the business of Vaishyas. The banker of smriti period performed most of those functions which banks perform in modern time such as the accepting of deposit, granting secured and unsecured loans, granting loans, to kings in times of grave crisis, acting as the treasure rank banker to the state and issuing and managing the currency of the country.

### 1.3 Pre-Independence era

During the period of British rule merchants established the Union Bank of Calcutta in 1829, first as a private joint stock association, then partnership. Its proprietors were the owners of the earlier Commercial Bank and the Calcutta Bank, who by mutual consent created Union Bank to replace these two banks. In 1840 it established an agency at Singapore, and closed the one at Mirzapore that it had opened in the previous year. Also in 1840 the Bank revealed that it had been the subject of a fraud by the bank's accountant. Union Bank was incorporated in 1845 but failed in 1848, having been insolvent for some time and having used new money from depositors to pay its dividends.

The Allahabad Bank, established in 1865 and still functioning today, is the oldest Joint Stock bank in India. It was not the first though. That honour belongs to the Bank of Upper

India, which was established in 1863, and which survived until 1913, when it failed, with some of its assets and liabilities being transferred to the Alliance Bank of Simla. Foreign banks too started to appear, particularly in Calcutta, in the 1860s. The Comptoir d'Escompte de Paris opened a branch in Calcutta in 1860, and another in Bombay in 1862; branches in Madras and Pondicherry, then a French possession, followed. HSBC established itself in Bengal in 1869. Calcutta was the most active trading port in India, mainly due to the trade of the British Empire, and so became a banking centre. The first entirely Indian joint stock bank was the Oudh Commercial Bank, established in 1881 in Faizabad. It failed in 1958. The next was the Punjab National Bank, established in Lahore in 1895, which has survived to the present and is now one of the largest banks in India.

Around the turn of the 20th Century, the Indian economy was passing through a relative period of stability. Around five decades had elapsed since the Indian Mutiny, and the social, industrial and other infrastructure had improved. Indians had established small banks, most of which served particular ethnic and religious communities.

The presidency banks dominated banking in India but there were also some exchange banks and a number of Indian joint stock banks. All these banks operated in different segments of the economy. The exchange banks, mostly owned by Europeans, concentrated on financing foreign trade. Indian joint stock banks were generally undercapitalized and lacked the experience and maturity to compete with the presidency and exchange banks. This segmentation let Lord Curzon to observe, "In respect of banking it seems we are behind the times. We are like some old fashioned sailing ship, divided by solid wooden bulkheads into separate and cumbersome compartments."

The period between 1906 and 1911, saw the establishment of banks inspired by the Swadeshi movement. The Swadeshi movement inspired local businessmen and political figures to found banks of and for the Indian community. A number of banks established then have survived to the present such as Bank of India, Corporation Bank, Indian Bank,Bank of Baroda, Canara Bank and Central Bank of India.

The fervour of Swadeshi movement lead to establishing of many private banks in Dakshina Kannada and Udupi district which were unified earlier and known by the name South Canara ( South Kanara ) district. Four nationalised banks started in this district and also a leading private sector bank. Hence undivided Dakshina Kannada district is known as "Cradle of Indian Banking".

During the First World War (1914–1918) through the end of the Second World War (1939–1945), and two years thereafter until the independence of India were challenging for Indian banking. The years of the First World War were turbulent, and it took its toll with banks simply collapsing despite the Indian economy gaining indirect boost due to war-related economic activities. At least 94 banks in India failed between 1913 and 1918 as indicated in the following table:

**Table No. 1.1 Banking Data regarding failed to collect Authorized Capital**

| Years | No. of banks that failed | Authorised Capital (₹ Lakhs) | Paid-up Capital (₹ Lakhs) |
|---|---|---|---|
| 1913 | 12 | 274 | 35 |
| 1914 | 42 | 710 | 109 |
| 1915 | 11 | 56 | 5 |
| 1916 | 13 | 231 | 4 |
| 1917 | 9 | 76 | 25 |
| 1918 | 7 | 209 | 1 |

## 1.4 BEFORE 1950

Banking on European lines started in India when two British managing agencies namely agency (I) Ferguson & Co. (II) Alexander & Co. setup three banks. The first joint stock bank was established in 1786 in the name of General bank of India [Bank of Hindustan] it is continue only up to 1806 while other two banks had failed earlier. Then in 1809, the first presidency bank was established under the heading of pre independence era.

**Table No. 1.2 Improvement of Banking in India Table:-**

| | | |
|---|---|---|
| 1 | 1786 – 1806 | Bank of Hindustan (General Bank of India) |
| 2 | 1809-1920 | Presidency Bank |
| 3 | 1840 | Bank of Bombay |
| | | Bank of Madras |
| 4 | 1895 | Punjab National Bank |

| 5 | 1906-1913 | Banks Like |
|---|---|---|
| | | Bank of India |
| | | The Central Bank of India |
| | | Bank of Baroda |
| | | People Bank of India |
| 6 | 1913-17 | Failure of Indian Bank due to world war – I |
| 7 | 1919-25 | Failure of Indian Banks due to inexperience of Indian Bankers in conducting banking in European style. |
| 8 | 1939-1945 | Boom period for Indian banks during world war – II. |
| 9 | 1947 | Partition gave a jolt and created heap of problems of Indian Banks. |

## 1.5 Post-Independence (After 1950)

In those initial days, the need of the hour was to re-organize and to consolidate the prevailing banking net work keeping in view the requirements of the economy. The first stop taken to that end was the enactment of the banking companies Act – 1949, followed by rapid industrial finance.

- Role played by banks was instrumental behind industrialization with the impetus given to both heavy and small scale industries.
- After the adoption of social control banks started taking steps in extending credit to agriculture and small borrowers

- On July 19, 1969: Fourteen banks are nationalised – Allahabad Bank, Bank of Maharastra, BOB, BOI, and Canara Bank of India, Dena Bank, IOB, Indian Bank, Syndicate Bank PNB, UBI, UCO, and Union Bank.
- In 1993: Guidelines for setting up private sector banks are issued and Rupee is made convertible on the trade account starting the process of convertibility. In September 1993, new bank of India is merged into PNB.
- Then every year are made changes in the banking sector for developing banking structure in India.
- Then respectively in 1973, 1978, 1980, 1986, 1987, 1991, 1992, are changed in banking structure in India.

The partition of India in 1947 adversely impacted the economies of Punjab and West Bengal, paralysing banking activities for months. India's independence marked the end of a regime of the Laissez-faire for the Indian banking.

The Government of India initiated measures to play an active role in the economic life of the nation, and the Industrial Policy Resolution adopted by the government in 1948 envisaged a mixed economy. This resulted into greater involvement of the state in different segments of the economy including banking and finance. The major steps to regulate banking included:

- The Reserve Bank of India, India's central banking authority was established in April 1935, but was nationalised on 1 January 1949 under the terms of the Reserve Bank of India (Transfer to Public Ownership) Act, 1948 (RBI, 2005b).

In 1949, the Banking Regulation Act was enacted which empowered the Reserve Bank of India (RBI) "to regulate, control, and inspect the banks in India".

- The Banking Regulation Act also provided that no new bank or branch of an existing bank could be opened without a license from the RBI, and no two banks could have common directors.

## 1.6 Nationalization in the 1960s

Despite the provisions, control and regulations of the Reserve Bank of India, banks in India except the State Bank of India (SBI), continued to be owned and operated by private persons. By the 1960s, the Indian banking industry had become an important tool to facilitate the development of the Indian economy. At the same time, it had emerged as a large employer, and a debate had ensued about the nationalization of the banking industry. Indira Gandhi, the then Prime Minister of India, expressed the intention of the Government of India in the annual conference of the All India Congress Meeting in a paper entitled "Stray thoughts on Bank Nationalization." The meeting received the paper with enthusiasm.

Thereafter, her move was swift and sudden. The Government of India issued an ordinance ['Banking Companies (Acquisition and Transfer of Undertakings) Ordinance, 1969'] and nationalised the 14 largest commercial banks with effect from the midnight of 19 July 1969. These banks contained 85 percent of bank deposits in the country. Jayaprakash Narayan, a national leader of India, described the step as a "masterstroke of political sagacity." Within two weeks of the issue of the ordinance, the Parliament passed the Banking Companies (Acquisition and Transfer of Undertaking) Bill, and it received the presidential approval on 9 August 1969.

A second dose of nationalisation of 6 more commercial banks followed in 1980. The stated reason for the nationalisation was to give the government more control of credit delivery. With the second dose of nationalisation, the Government of India controlled around 91% of the banking business of India. Later on, in the year 1993, the government merged New Bank of India with Punjab National Bank. It was the only merger between nationalised banks and resulted in the reduction of the number of nationalised banks from 20 to 19. After this, until the 1990s, the nationalised banks grew at a pace of around 4%, closer to the average growth rate of the Indian economy.

## 1.7 Liberalization in the 1990s

In the early 1990s, the then government embarked on a policy of liberalization, licensing a small number of private banks. These came to be known as New Generation tech-savvy banks, and included Global Trust Bank (the first of such new generation banks to be set up), which later amalgamated with Oriental Bank of Commerce, UTI Bank (since renamed Axis Bank), ICICI Bank and HDFC Bank. This move, along with the rapid growth in the economy of India, revitalised the banking sector in India, which has seen rapid growth with strong contribution from all the three sectors of banks, namely, government banks, private banks and foreign banks.

The next stage for the Indian banking has been set up with the proposed relaxation in the norms for foreign direct investment, where all foreign investors in banks may be given voting rights which could exceed the present cap of 10% at present. It has gone up to 74% with some restrictions.

The new policy shook the Banking sector in India completely. Bankers, till this time, were used to the 4–6–4 method (borrow at 4%; lend at 6%; go home at 4) of functioning. The new wave ushered in a modern outlook and tech-savvy methods of working for traditional banks. All this led to the retail boom in India. People demanded more from their banks and received more.

## 1.8 Present Period

All banks which are included in the Second Schedule to the Reserve Bank of India Act, 1934 are Scheduled Banks. These banks comprise Scheduled Commercial Banks and Scheduled Co-operative Banks. Scheduled Commercial Banks in India are categorised into five different groups according to their ownership and/or nature of operation. These bank groups are:

- State Bank of India and its Associates
- Nationalised Banks
- Private Sector Banks
- Foreign Banks
- Regional Rural Banks.

In the bank group-wise classification, IDBI Bank Ltd. is included in Nationalised Banks. Scheduled Co-operative Banks consist of Scheduled State Co-operative Banks and Scheduled Urban Cooperative Banks.

## 1.9 Banking Structure in India

### Chart No. 1.1 Structure of Reserve bank of India

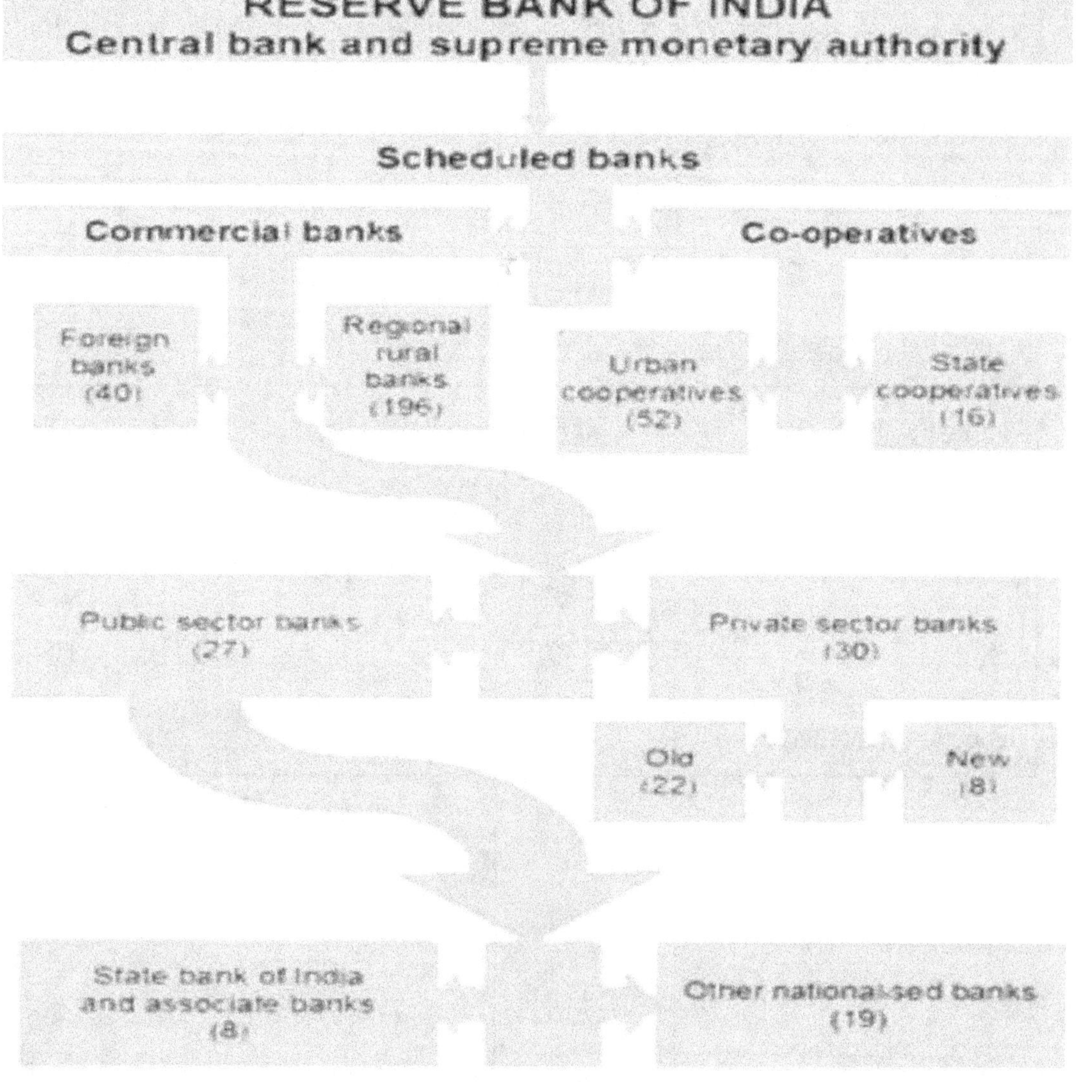


(http://en.wikipedia.org/wiki/Banking_in_India)

## 1.10 Growth of Banking in India of Scheduled Commercial Banks

Table No. 1.3 Growth of Banking in India of Scheduled Commercial Banks

| Indicators | 31 March of | | | |
|---|---|---|---|---|
| | 2005 | 2006 | 2007 | 2008 |
| Number of Commercial Banks | 284 | 218 | 178 | 169 |
| Number of Branches | 70,373 | 72,072 | 74,653 | 78,787 |
| Population per Banks (in th.) | 16 | 16 | 15 | 15 |
| Aggregate Deposits | ₹17002 Bl. (US$280 Bl.) | ₹21090 Bl. (US$350Bl.) | ₹26119Bl. (US$430 Bl.) | ₹31969Bl. (US$530 Bl.) |
| Bank Credit | ₹11004 Bl. (US$180Bl.) | ₹15071 Bl. (US$250Bl.) | ₹19312Bl. (US$320 Bl.) | ₹23619Bl. (US$390Bl.) |
| Deposit as percentage to GNP (at factor cost) | 62% | 64% | 69% | 73% |
| Per Capita Deposit | ₹16281 (US$270) | ₹19130 (US$320) | ₹23382 (US$390) | ₹28610 (US$470) |
| Per Capita Credit | ₹10752 (US$180) | ₹13869 (US$230) | ₹17541 (US$290) | ₹21218 (US$350) |
| Credit Deposit Ratio | 63% | 70% | 74% | 75% |

| Indicators | 31 March of | | | | |
|---|---|---|---|---|---|
| | 2009 | 2010 | 2011 | 2012 | 2013 |
| Number of Commercial Banks | 166 | 163 | 163 | 169 | 151 |
| Number of Branches | 82,897 | 88,203 | 94,019 | 102,377 | 109,811 |
| Population per Banks (in th.) | 15 | 14 | 13 | 13 | 12 |
| Aggregate Deposits | ₹38341 Bl. (US$640 Bl.) | ₹44928 Bl. (US$750 Bl.) | ₹52078 Bl. (US$860Bl.) | ₹59091 Bl. (US$980 Bl.) | ₹67504.54Bl. (US$1.1 Tl.) |
| Bank Credit | ₹27755 Bl. (US$460 Bl.) | ₹32448Bl. (US$540Bl.) | ₹39421Bl. (US$650Bl.) | ₹46119Bl. (US$770Bl.) | ₹52605Bl. (US$870 Bl.) |
| Deposit as percentage to GNP (at factor cost) | 77% | 78% | 78% | 78% | 79% |
| Per Capita Deposit | ₹33919 (US$560) | ₹39107 (US$650) | ₹45505 (US$760) | ₹50183 (US$830) | ₹56380 (US$940) |
| Per Capita Credit | ₹24617 (US$410) | ₹28431 (US$470) | ₹34187 (US$570) | ₹38874 (US$650) | ₹44028 (US$730) |
| Credit Deposit Ratio | 74% | 74% | 76% | 79% | 79% |

By 2010, banking in India was generally fairly mature in terms of supply, product range and reach-even though reach in rural India still remains a challenge for the private sector and foreign banks. In terms of quality of assets and capital adequacy, Indian banks are considered to have clean, strong and transparent balance sheets relative to other banks in comparable economies in its region. The Reserve Bank of India is an autonomous body, with minimal pressure from the government.

With the growth in the Indian economy expected to be strong for quite some time-especially in its services sector-the demand for banking services, especially retail banking, mortgages and investment services are expected to be strong. One may also expect M&As, takeovers, and asset sales.

In March 2006, the Reserve Bank of India allowed Warburg Pincus to increase its stake in Kotak Mahindra Bank (a private sector bank) to 10%. This is the first time an investor has been allowed to hold more than 5% in a private sector bank since the RBI announced norms in 2005 that any stake exceeding 5% in the private sector banks would need to be vetted by them.

In recent years critics have charged that the non-government owned banks are too aggressive in their loan recovery efforts in connexion with housing, vehicle and personal loans. There are press reports that the banks' loan recovery efforts have driven defaulting borrowers to suicide.

## 1.11 Roles of the Bank

A bank is thought as a reliable agency with which money is

deposited. Banks receive valuables for safe custody and undertake to return them but that is only a subsidiary function. Usually it is jeweler, needs securities and similar articles which are give to the bank as safe custody deposits. But the services rendered by a bank either as depository or as trustee, are important.

The roles of the banks can be classified under the following ways:-

1. Receiving of money on Deposits
2. Lending of money
3. Insuring of notes
4. Transferring money from place to place
5. Other functions

1. **Receiving of money on Deposit:** This is the most important function of almost all modern banks. The banks mobilize the money from the people. The banks collect the money by various types' deposits which may be in the form of fixed, saving or current deposits. The money receive on fixed deposits can be used without any risk of withdrawal before the due date an in the case of saving deposits, A bank can use a very large part of them because generally the demands of customers having such deposits are comparatively small. In case of current deposits, bank cannot use as an earning purpose because these deposits must be repaid as on demand of the depositors. By taking money on deposit, a bank provides safe – keeping for people's money. But the money is not set apart in a strong room. It is replaced or landed to the required persons or institute.

2. **Leading of Money:** This function is not only very important but is also the main source of profit to most of the banks. When a bank agrees to discount a bill or given funds in exchange for a promissory note, the transaction is known either as a discount or a loan. The enables those persons and corporations, who find their own capital in sufficient for carrying the business on a large scale, to do so with the help of the funds borrowed from a bank. A bank is an able to help not only merchant but also others. Bank also undertakes employment of surplus funds by investing in gilt -edged security.

3. **Issuing of Notes:** This function is considered to be the most paying part of a banker's business. This function is in modern times, performed generally by central banking institutions. Its importance to banks in general has dwindled in some of the important countries, in which the cheque currency has replaced bank notes to a large extend.

**4 Transferring money from place to place:** Generally, modern banks are in a position to remit money from one place or country to another by means of drafts upon their breaches or agents. They can enable merchants and others to receive money from their debtors, in other cities or countries. These facilities have helped not only the internal trade of different countries but also international commerce.

**5 Other Functions:** In addition to the main functions given above, modern banks perform miscellaneous services such as

1. The issue of various forms of credits e.g. Letters of credit, Traveler's cheques, Credit cards.

2. Under writing of capital issues
3. The acceptance of bills of exchange where by the banker lends his name to his customer in return for a commission.
4. The sage custody of valuables
5. Acting as executors and trustees for customers
6. Preparing income tax returns for their customers
7. Furnishing guarantees on behalf of customers etc.
8. Managing issue of shares and debentures
9. Dealing with any property received as security against any loan / advances.
10. Contracting, negotiating and issuing public and private loan.

## 1.12 Significant of Banking System

The purpose of this study has been to assess the role of the Indian banking system in the socioeconomic field in the post nationalization period and to evaluate its achievements and short comings. The public sector in the banking industry dominates and plays a significant role in the overall development of the economy of the country. Bank is an important institution for society and economy. Their importance can explain as follows:

1. **Helpful to society:** Bank proves equally helpful in development of industrial and economic developments of the nation small savings obtained by banks from public are used for providing loans to industries and the government.
2. **Loan Facilities:** Modern business word more belief in running the business on credit. Bank helps customer by providing loan

facilities if required. Banks proved equally helpful in financing for imports and exports

3. **Encouraging saving:** Banks pays interest on the amount deposited in it create awareness of people towards savings. Hence banks play leading role in encouraging savings. The nation is also benefited from it since people's savings are invested for nation's building.

4. **Facilitate remittances:** Bank plays important role in remittance safely and at the minimum cost. With the expansion of large banking net work it is not costly and risky to send money from to any place of the world.

5. **Safety of depositing:** Money deposited in banks and other valuable assets kept in bank are fully safe it is required no more to keep risk with anyone who realized importance of bank.

6. **Other Facilities:** It is no more required to physically handling money to avoid risk bank issues traveler cheque etc., and provides facilities to pay anything through cheques. Bank also plays role as reliable representative in colleting cheques, bill of exchange, and amount of hundies on behalf of their esteemed customers.

## 1.13 Reason of Poor Banking System

**1.** Deteriorating quality of customer service particularly in urban and metropolitan areas.

**2.** The recovery position in priority lending is not too encouraging.

**3.** The problem of maintaining industrial relations and motivating staff at all levels of the organization.

**4.**The cost of operations have been increased and placing a serious constraint on profitability.

**5.**Appalling quality of housing keeping and mounting, unmatched entries, not completion of day to day balancing.

**6.**Rapid growth of volume, creating problems of manageability.

**7.**With the larger funds at their command, banks want to deploy them in a higher volume of wholesale lending opportunities. Due to the risk or supervision element is sometimes not adequately taken into account, the quality of the traditional portfolio has deteriorated and industrial sickness has seriously constrained the economy in general and the banks in particular.

**8.**A part from agricultural lending, the quality of lending and recovery activities is not quite satisfactory.

**a.** All these point to the adequacy of control

**b.** The planning process have not stabilized and have not received due attention particularly in the context of the rapidly changing environment and transformed character of the banks from elite class banking to mass banking.

With the increasing proportion of statutory obligations on the banks, which are likely to be increased and given the present structure of deposit and lending interest rates. The banks have to raise their profitability by developing greater cost consciousness, improvement in reconverts, reduction in NPA and non performing loans, improvement in the quality of their loan assets, increasing in non-interest income and in the productivity of the staff.

## 1.14 Modification in The Banking Sector

Banking sector reforms were initiated to upgrade the operating standards, health and financial soundness of the banks. The Government of India setup the Narasimham committee (1991) to examine all aspects relating to structure, organization and functioning of the Indian banking system. The recommendations of the committee aimed at creating a competitive and efficient banking system. Another committee which is Khan Committee was instituted by the Reserve Bank in December 1997 to examine the harmonization of the role and operations so development financial institutions and banks. It submitted its report in 1998. The major recommendations were a gradual more towards universal banking, exploring the possibility of gain full merger as between banks, banks and financial institutions. Then, the Verma committee was established. This committee recommended the need for greater use of information technology even in the weak public sector banks, restructuring of weak banks but not merging them with strong banks, voluntary retirement scheme (VRS) for at least 25% of the staff. The banking sector reforms aimed at improving the policy frame work, financial hearth and institutional infrastructure there two phase of the banking reforms. The first phase of the banking reforms is complete and second generation reforms are under way.

**Part – I: 1991 – Narasimham Committee – I**

**a.** Deregulation of the interest rate structure

**b.** Progressive reduction in pre-emptive reserves

c. Liberalization of the branch expansion policy
d. Introduction of prudential norms
e. Decreasing the emphasis laid on directed credit and phasing out the confessional rate of interest to priority sector.
f. Deregulation of the entry norms for private Sector banks and foreign banks.
g. Permitting public and private sector banks to access the capital market.
h. Setting up of asset reconstruction fund.
i. Constituting the special debt recovery tribunal.
j. Freedom to appoint chief executive and officers of the banks.
k. Changes in the institutions of the board
l. Bringing NBFC, under the ambit of regulatory framework.

**Part – II: April 1998 Narasimham Committee – II**

**1. Capital Adequacy.**

a. Capital adequacy ratio to be raised from and percent to 10 percent by 2002.
b. 100 percent of fixed income portfolio marked to market by 2001.
c. 5 percent market risk weight for fixed income securities and open foreign exchange position limits.
d. Commercial risk weight (100%) to government guaranteed advances.

**2. Asset Quality**

**a.** Banks should aim to reduce gross nonperforming assets to 3% and net NPA to zero percent by 2002.

**b.** Go day overdue norm to be applied for cash based income recognition

**c.** Government guaranteed irregular accounts to be classified as NPAs and provide for.

**d.** Directed credit obligations to be reduced from 40 percent to 10 percent.

**3. Systems and Methods**

**a.** Banks to start recruitment of skilled specialized manpower form the market.

**b.** Overstaffing to be dealt with by reemployment and right sizing via VRS

**c.** Public sector banks to be given flexibility in remuneration structure.

**d.** Rapid introduction of computerization and technology.

**4. Industry Structure**

**a.** Only two categories of financial sector players to emerge: banks and non bank finance companies.

**b.** Merges to be driven by market and business considerations

**c.** Weak banks should be converted into “narrow banks”

**d.** Entry of new private sector banks and foreign banks to continue

**e.** Banks to be given greater functional autonomy and minimum government shareholding 33 percent for state bank of India, 51 percent for other public sector banks

**5. Regulation and supervision**

a. Banking regulation and supervision to be progressively de inked from monetary policy.

b. Board for financial regulation and supervision to be constituted with statutory powers.

c. Board members should be professionals.

d. Greater reemphasis on public disclosure as opposed to disclosure to regulators.

**6. Legal Amendments**

a. Board range of legal reforms to facilitate recovery of problem loans.

b. Introduction of laws governing electronic funds transfer

The first phase of the banking reforms is competing but the second phase is under the way. The second generation reforms are those that did not form part of the first generation reforms. Many of the important recommendations of Narasimham committee – II have been accepted and are under implementations the second generation banking reform concentrate on strengthening the foundation of the banking system by structure, technological up graduation and human resource development.

## 1.15 Challenges of Banking Sector

The first phase of financial reforms laid the basis for a sound banking system. Considerable process has been made in implementing the reforms and the banking system is moving towards the second phase now.

At present the Indian banking system faces several difficult challenges.

Some of them are home ground like as

1. High cost of doing business
2. Level of NPA
3. Low level of customer satisfaction

Some of challenges are external like as

1. Phenomenal growth in the volume of capital inflows
2. Integration of financial market across the globe.

In view of these domestic and international developments of efficient banking system, it is necessary to plan out a path for the development of efficient banking in the new century.

Some other challenges are given below which are being faced by the banks at present.

- Talents
- To build banking product
- To develop micro enterprises in the individual and not on the whole group.

There are several areas of concern which need to be tackle carefully

1) Branch Expansion
2) Resource Mobilization
3) Deployment of resource
4) Sick units
5) International banking scenario
6) Staff per se
7) Planning per se
8) Customer service

9) Records
10) Computerization
11) Profitability

The most direct result of changes in banking structure and its impact on the profitability of Banks, the position is aggravated when seen against the background of large wage bill, legacy of nonperforming assets and extensive branch network of public have to image market risk including environment, besides credit risk, banks have to manage market risk including interest risk and exchange risk, and also operational risk. The increase in financial flows across borders with all the attendant risks, which will only grow with liberalization under WTO and the march towards full capital account convertibility, will put further pressure on banks. Competition has become keener on account of advances in communication technology banks can reach their customers anywhere any time and customers are also to get instant access to their accounts from any corner of the globe at any time. With increasing competition among banks, customers are also becoming more discerning and demanding. To meet customer expectations, banks will have to offer a broad range of deposit, investment and credit products through diverse distribution channels including upgraded branches, ATMs telephone and internet. The key to attract and retain customers, therefore lies in efficient customer service including customized and value added products to meet various needs of individual customers as also to meet the needs of divers types of customers.

## 1.16 Steps to be taken by the banks to face these challenges:

- Become proficient in managing assets and liabilities according to risk and return.
- Invest in technology for better MIS, Management Information System and product development (including derivatives), risk management, fund management and customer services.
- Become more customers centric, offering a wide range of products through multiple delivery channels.
- Pay greater attention to profitability, including cost reduction and increasing fee based income.

The key to meeting these challenges lies in putting in place the necessary systems and skilled staff, training and equipping the workforce and making all out efforts to motivate and retain staff with expertise.

The IT revolution has had a great impact on the Indian banking system. The use of computers has led to the introduction of online banking in India. The use of computers in the banking sector in India has increased many folds after the economic liberalisation of 1991 as the country's banking sector has been exposed to the world's market. Indian banks were finding it difficult to compete with the international banks in terms of customer service, without the use of information technology.

The RBI set up a number of committees to define and co-ordinate banking technology. These have included:

**1)** In 1984 was formed the Committee on Mechanisation in the Banking Industry (1984) whose chairman was Dr. C Rangarajan,

Deputy Governor, Reserve Bank of India. The major recommendations of this committee were introducing MICR technology in all the banks in the metropolises in India. This provided for the use of standardized cheque forms and encoders. In 1988, the RBI set up the Committee on Computerisation in Banks(1988) headed by Dr. C Rangarajan. It emphasized that settlement operation must be computerized in the clearing houses of RBI in Bhubaneshwar, Guwahati,
Jaipur, Patna and Thiruvananthapuram. It further stated that there should be National Clearing of Inter-city cheques at kolkata, Mumbai, Delhi, Chennai and MICR should be made operational. It also focused on computerisation of branches and increasing connectivity among branches through computers. It also suggested modalities for implementing on-line banking. The committee submitted its reports in 1989 and computerisation began from 1993 with the settlement between IBA and bank employees' associations.

**2)** In 1994, the Committee on Technology Issues relating to Payment systems, Cheque Clearing and securities settlement in the Banking Industry (1994) was set up under Chairman W.S. Saraf. It emphasized Electronic Funds Transfer (EFT) system, with the BANKNET communications network as its carrier. It also said that MICR clearing should be set up in all branches of all those banks with more than 100 branches.

**3)** In 1995, the Committee for proposing Legislation on Electronic Funds Transfer and other Electronic Payments (1995) again emphasized EFT system.

## 1.17 Expansion of Banking Infrastructure

As per the census of 2011, 58.7% of households are availing banking services in the country. There are 102,343 branches of Scheduled Commercial Banks (SCBs) in the country, out of which 37,953 (37%) bank branches are in the rural areas and 27,219 (26%) in semi-urban areas, constituting 63% of the total numbers of branches in semi-urban and rural areas of the country. However, a significant proportion of the households, especially in rural areas, are still outside the formal fold of the banking system. To extend the reach of banking to those outside the formal banking system, Government and Reserve Bank of India (RBI) are taking various initiatives from time to time some of which are enumerated below:

- Opening of bank branches: Government had issued detailed strategy and guidelines on Financial Inclusion in October 2011, advising banks to open branches in all habitations of 5,000 or more population in under-banked districts and 10,000 or more population in other districts. Out of 3,925 such identified villages/habitations, branches have been opened in 3,402 villages/habitations (including 2,121 Ultra Small Branches) by end of April, 2013.
- Each household to have at least one bank account: Banks have been advised to ensure service area bank in rural areas and banks assigned the responsibility in specific wards in urban area to ensure that every household has at least one bank account.
- Business Correspondent model: With the objective of ensuring greater financial inclusion and increasing the outreach of the

banking sector, banks were permitted by RBI in 2006 to use the services of intermediaries in providing financial and banking services through the use of Business Facilitators (BFs) and Business Correspondents (BCs). Business correspondents are retail agents engaged by banks for providing banking services at locations other than a bank branch/ATM. BCs and the BC agents (BCAs) represent the bank concerned and enable a bank to expand its outreach and offer limited range of banking services at low cost, particularly where setting up a brick and mortar branch is not viable. BCs as agents of the banks, thus, are an integral part of the business strategy for achieving greater financial inclusion. Banks had been permitted to engage individuals/entities as BC like retired bank employees, retired teachers, retired government employees, ex-servicemen, individual owners of kirana/medical/fair price shops, individual Public Call Office (PCO) operators, agents of Small Savings Schemes of Government of India, insurance companies, etc. Further, since September 2010, RBI had permitted banks to engage "for profit" companies registered under the Indian Companies Act, 1956, excluding Non-Banking Financial Companies (NBFCs), as BCs in addition to individuals/entities permitted earlier. According to the data maintained by RBI, as in December, 2012, there were over 152,000 BCs deployed by Banks. During 2012-13, over 183.8 million transactions valued at ₹165 billion (US$2.7 billion) had been undertaken by BCs till December 2012.

- Swabhimaan Campaign: Under "Swabhimaan" - the Financial Inclusion Campaign launched in February 2011, banks had provided banking facilities by March, 2012 to over 74,000 habitations having population in excess of 2000 using various models and technologies including branchless banking through Business Correspondents Agents (BCAs). Further, in terms of Finance Minister's Budget Speech 2012-13, the "Swabhimaan" campaign has been extended to habitations with population of more than 1,000 in North and to habitations which have crossed population of 1,600 as per census 2001. About 40,000 such habitations have been identified to be covered under the extended "Swabhimaan" campaign.

- Setting up of ultra-small branches (USBs): Considering the need for close supervision and mentoring of the Business Correspondent Agents (BCAs) by the respective banks and to ensure that a range of banking services are available to the residents of such villages, Ultra Small Branches (USBs) are being set up in all villages covered through BCAs under Financial Inclusion. A USB would comprise a small area of 100 sq ft (9.3 $m^2$) - 200 sq ft (19 $m^2$) where the officer designated by the bank would be available with a laptop on pre-determined days. While the cash services would be offered by the BCAs, the bank officer would offer other services, undertake field verification and follow up on the banking transactions. The periodicity and duration of visits can be progressively enhanced depending upon business potential in the area. A total of over 50,000 USBs have been set up in the country by March 2013.
- Banking facilities in Unbanked Blocks: All the 129 unbanked blocks (91 in North East States and 38 in other States) identified

in the country in July 2009, had been provided with banking facilities by March 2012, either through Brick Mortar Branch or Business Correspondents or Mobile van. As a next step it has been advised to cover all those blocks with BCA and Ultra Small Branch which have so far been covered by mobile van only.

- USSD Based Mobile Banking: National Payments Corporation of India (NPCI) worked upon a "Common USSD Platform" for all banks and telcos who wish to offer the facility of Mobile Banking using Unstructured Supplementary Service Data (USSD) based Mobile Banking. The Department helped NPCI to get a common USSD Code *99# for all telcos. More than 20 banks have joined the National Uniform USSD Platform (NUUP) of NPCI and the product has been launched by NPCI with BSNL and MTNL. Other telcos are likely to join in the near future. USSD based Mobile Banking offers basic Banking facilities like Money Transfer, Bill Payments, Balance Enquiries, Merchant Payments etc. on a simple GSM based Mobile phone, without the need to download application on a phone as required at present in the IMPS based Mobile Banking.

## 1.18 Steps taken by Reserve Bank of India (RBI) to strengthen the Banking Infrastructure

- RBI has permitted domestic Scheduled Commercial Banks (excluding RRBs) to open branches in tier 2 to tier 6 cities (with population up to 99,999 as per census 2001) without the need to take permission from RBI in each case, subject to reporting.

- RBI has also permitted SCBs (excluding RRBs) to open branches in rural, semi-urban and urban centres in North Eastern States and Sikkim without having the need to take permission from RBI in each case, subject to reporting.
- Regional Rural Banks (RRBs) are also allowed to open branches in Tier 2 to Tier 6 centres (with population up to 99,999 as per Census 2001) without the need to take permission from RBI in each case, subject to reporting, provided they fulfill the following conditions, as per the latest inspection report:
- CRAR of at least 9%;
- Net NPA less than 5%;
- No default in CRR / SLR for the last year;
- Net profit in the last financial year;
- CBS compliant.
- Domestic SCBs have been advised that while preparing their Annual Branch Expansion Plan (ABEP), they should allocate at least 25% of the total number of branches proposed to be opened during the year in unbanked Tier 5 and Tier 6 centres i.e. (population up to 9,999) centres which do not have a brick and mortar structure of any SCB for customer based banking transactions.
- RRBs have also been advised to allocate at least 25% of the total number of branches proposed to be opened during a year in unbanked rural (Tier 5 and Tier 6) Centres).
- New private sector banks are required to ensure that at least 25% of their total branches are in semi-urban and rural centres on an ongoing basis.

This chapter deals with financial performance of the banks with a view to getting conceptual background of the bank. The researcher has evaluated various maters regarding conceptual framework of the nationalized banks. Like concept of the bank, Banking Structure, historical background of banking system pre and post independent era, improvement of the banking system (Before 1950, and After 1950), role of the bank, significance of the Banking system, reason of poor Banking system, challenges, Modification in banking system and Steps taken by Reserve Bank of India (RBI) to strengthen the banking infrastructure etc.

# CHAPTER No.-2
# NATIONALISED BANKS IN INDIA

Nationalized banks dominate the banking system in India. The history of nationalised banks in India dates back to mid-20th century, when Imperial Bank of India was nationalized (under the SBI Act of 1955) and re-christened as State Bank of India (SBI) in July 1955. Then on 19th July 1960, its seven subsidiaries were also nationalised with deposits over 200 crores. These subsidiaries of SBI were State Bank of Bikaner and Jaipur (SBBJ), State Bank of Hyderabad (SBH), State Bank of Indore (SBIR), State Bank of Mysore (SBM), State Bank of Patiala (SBP), State Bank of Saurashtra (SBS), and State Bank of Travancore (SBT). However, the major nationalization of banks happened in 1969 by the then-Prime Minister Indira Gandhi. The major objective behind nationalization was to spread banking infrastructure in rural areas and make cheap finance available to Indian farmers. The nationalised 14 major commercial banks were Allahabad Bank, Andhra Bank, Bank of Baroda, Bank of India, Bank of Maharashtra, Canara Bank, Central Bank of India, Corporation Bank, Dena Bank, Indian Bank, Indian Overseas Bank, Oriental Bank of Commerce (OBC), Punjab and Sind Bank, Punjab National Bank (PNB), Syndicate Bank, UCO Bank, Union Bank of India, United Bank of India (UBI), and Vijaya Bank. In the year 1980, the second phase of nationalization of Indian banks took place, in which 7 more banks were nationalised with deposits over

200 crores. With this, the Government of India held a control over 91% of the banking industry in India. After the nationalization of banks there was a huge jump in the deposits and advances with the banks. At present, the State Bank of India is the largest commercial bank of India and is ranked one of the top five banks worldwide. It serves 90 million customers through a network of 9,000 branches. This Chapter Mainly deals with 26 nationalized banks brief high lights which cover points such as No. of Branches, Various product offer by the bank, multiple services offered by the banks and address of its head offices. Following is given table relates to publics banks in India.

**Table No. 2.1 List of Nationalized Banks in India**

| **NATIONALISED BANKS (19)** | |
|---|---|
| 2.1 | Allahabad Bank |
| 2.2 | Andhra Bank |
| 2.3 | Bank of Baroda |
| 2.4 | Bank of India |
| 2.5 | Bank of Maharashtra |
| 2.6 | Canara Bank |
| 2.7 | Central Bank of India |
| 2.8 | Corporation Bank |
| 2.9 | Dena Bank |
| 2.10 | Indian Bank |
| 2.11 | Indian Overseas Bank |
| 2.12 | Oriental Bank of Commerce |
| 2.13 | Punjab & Sind Bank |
| 2.14 | Punjab National Bank |

| | |
|---|---|
| 2.15 | Syndicate Bank |
| 2.16 | UCO Bank |
| 2.17 | Union Bank of India |
| 2.18 | United Bank of India |
| 2.19 | Vijaya Bank |
| 2.20 | **State Bank of India (SBI)** |
| **ASSOCIATES OF SBI** | |
| 2.20.1 | State Bank of Indore (Merged with SBI) |
| 2.20.2 | State Bank of Saurashtra (Merged with SBI) |
| 2.20.3 | State Bank of Bikaner & Jaipur |
| 2.20.4 | State Bank of Hyderabad |
| 2.20.5 | State Bank of Mysore |
| 2.20.6 | State Bank of Patiala |
| 2.20.7 | State Bank of Travancore |
| **Other Public Sector Bank** | |
| 2.21 | IDBI Ltd. |

## BRIEF INTRODUCTION ABOUT NATIONALIZED BANKS:

Following is given brief details about 19 selected nationalized banks, SBI bank and its branches details and also include IDBI banks details in brief to understand its performance.

### 2.1. Allahabad Bank

Allahabad Bank is one of the premier nationalized banks in India. It is also the oldest joint stock bank of India. It was incorporated by a group of Europeans at Allahabad on April 24, 1865. It was the time Indian economy had started shifting towards organized trade and business affairs. After some years in 1920, the P&O Bank brought Allahabad Bank and its headquarters at Kolkata. The Allahabad bank got an entirely new identity when it was nationalized in 1969 along with 13 other banks in India. Since then the Allahabad Bank had a smooth journey towards progress. Today it is one of the leading banks in India with a whooping business of over Rs.1,00,000 crores.

**Branches and Business:** Allahabad has adopted CBS (Core Banking Service) since 2006 and has developed 24 hours connectivity with its 2165 branches across the length and breath of the country. In 143 years of it existence the bank has come a long way by developing a wide grip over all the corners of India. At present the Allahabad Bank has 44 Zonal Offices 6 Staff Training Colleges and 3 Staff Training centers for imparting training centers in India. Apart from general branches, the bank has also come up with specialized branches, like Industrial Finance Branches, International Branches, Finance Branches, Recovery Branches, NRI Branches Specialized Personal Banking Branches, Specialized Savings Bank Branches, Quick Collection Service Branches, Trading Finance Branches and Service Branches in many major cities of India. The businesses of the bank are thriving successfully. In the end of March 2007, the Allahabad Bank crosses a land mark of Rs.1, 00,000 crores. The bank's business also registered a 6.90%

growth during April-Sept 2007, when its business increased up to Rs.1, 08,458 crores from Rs.1, 01,458 crores in merely 5 months. On Year-on-Year basis, the business of the bank has grown at a rate of 19.87%. The bank also registered an immense growth in total deposit record when its business went up to Rs.65,896 at end of September 2007 crores from Rs.54,006 crore in September 2006.

**Product and Services**

**Deposit Products:** Diamond Jubilee Deposit Scheme, Rs. 5 Banking, Gold Deposit and Flexi-fix Deposit

**Retail Credit Products:** All Bank Housing Finance Scheme, Personal Loan Scheme for Pensioners, All Bank Property Loan, All Bank Saral Loan Scheme, All Bank Educational Loan Scheme, Overdraft Facility in Savings Bank Account, Personal Loan Scheme for Doctors/ Medical Practitioners, Loan against NSC/ KVP, All Bank Mobike Scheme, All Bank Rent Loan, AllBank Gyan Dipika Scheme, All Bank Car Finance Scheme, AllBank Pilot Training Loan Scheme, All Bank Furnishing Loan, All Bank Gold Loan Scheme, All Bank Reverse Mortgage Scheme, All Bank, Abhusan Scheme and All Bank Trade Scheme

**Other Credit Products:** Kisan Credit Card, Kisan Shakti Yojana and All Bank-Expo

**Services:** All Ayushman Bima Yojana, Cash Management Services, Depository Services, Visa Cum Debit Card Services, Real Time Gross Settlement, National Electronic Funds Transfer, Gold Card Scheme For Exporters, Charter for MSME's, Government Business, Regional MSME care centres

**Head Office:** Allahabad Bank, 2, N S Road, Kolkata – 700001,West Bengal, **Website:** www.allahabadbank.com

## 2.2. Andhra Bank

Andhra Bank is an Indian bank based in Hyderabad. The bank was established in the year 1923, and its founder was Dr. Bhogaraju Pattabhi Sitaramayya, a well known freedom fighter. The initial authorized capital of the bank was Rs. 10.00 lacs, while the paid up capital was Rs. 1.00 lac at the time of its registration.

**Financial Details:** Total Business volume of the bank in the third quarter of the 2008-09 financial year stood at Rs. 95, 822 Crores, while the Total Deposit volume during the same tenure was Rs. 53,795 Crores. As of 31st of December, 2008, Andhra Bank had a client base of more than 18.5 Million customers with 2194 Business Delivery Channels. Till the same date, the bank had 1,410 branches spread across 22 states and 2 Union Territories, out of which 1,067 branches have been enabled with Centralized Core Banking Solution (CBS). While the total number of ATMs summed up to 685, the bank had a Per Employee Productivity of Rs 6.92 Crore.

**Products and Schemes:** Apart from regular banking services and solutions, Andhra Bank has introduced some attractive services such as AB Premium Current Account and AB Privilege Corporate Salary Savings Bank Account with extra benefits to the customers. Also, the bank has launched AB Saral Housing Loan scheme featuring housing loans upto Rs. 20 Lacs. Andhra Bank has also partnered with various financial institutions like Kotak Mahindra, Reliance, Birla Sun Life Mutual Fund and Fidelity Mutual Fund, assisting them in sales of their Mutual Fund products. The bank has also signed a Memorandum of Understanding (MoU) with Maruti Suzuki Ltd. for financing 4 wheeler vehicles.

**Pioneering Efforts:** Andhra Bank is the first bank in India to have launched mobile biometric ATMs. These ATMs stop at predestinated sites, and instead of entering the personal identification number (PIN), the customers have to match their finger prints with their recorded finger prints in the bank database. This has enabled even the illiterate or uneducated customers of the bank to enjoy the ATM facility being offered by the bank.

**Social Activities:** As an initiative to empower the society, the bank has established 10 Rural Training Institutes, which have provided training to 76,300 candidates for getting successfully self employed. The institutes offer free training, lodging, boarding facilities coupled with to and fro travel expenditure to the candidates undergoing the training programmes.

**Head Office:** Andhra Bank, 5-9-11, Saifabad, Hyderabad City, AndhraPradesh-500004 **Website:** http://www.andhrabank.in.

## 2. 3. Bank of Baroda

Bank of Baroda is one of the most prominent banks in India, having its total assets as Rs. 1,43,146 Crores as on 31st of March 2007. The bank was founded by Maharaja Sayajirao Gaekwad III (also known as Shrimant Gopalrao Gaekwad), the then Maharaja of Baroda on 20th of July 1908 with a paid capital of Rs. 10 Lacs. From its introduction in a small building of Baroda, the bank has come a long way to achieve its current position as one of the most important banks in India. On 19th of July 1969, Bank of Baroda was nationalized by the Government of India along with 13 other commercial banks.

**Financial Details:** As of March 2007, the bank had total deposits worth Rs. 1,24,915 Crores while it had a total number of 2956 branches located worldwide as on April 2009, out of which 626 were located in Metro cities, 524 in Urban areas, 642 in Semi-Urban locations, 1092 in Rural areas and 72 were located outside India. The bank has 10 Zonal Offices and 43 Regional Offices which help it control its operations nationally.

**International Presence:** Along with a huge network of its branches spread across India, Bank of Baroda has its overseas branches located in 14 other countries, which include Bahamas,

Bahrain, Belgium, China, Fiji Islands, Hong Kong, Mauritius, Republic of South Africa, Seychelles, Singapore, Sultanate of Oman, United Arab Emirates, United Kingdom and United States of America. Apart from it, the bank has established its subsidiaries in 7 countries viz. Botswana, Ghana, Guyana, Kenya, Tanzania, Trinidad & Tobago and Uganda, and its representative offices in 3 countries which are Australia, Malaysia and Thailand.

**Other Details:** Bank of Baroda had a total workforce of 38063 employees offering their services to the institution as of September 2006. Out of these, 13525 were Officers, 16497 were Clerks while 8041 were Sub-Staff members. The bank offers a wide array of customized and specialized services to meet the diverse needs of its customers, and these services have been categorized into Personal Banking, Business Banking, Corporate Banking, International Banking, Treasury Banking and Rural Banking services.

**Head Office: 1)** Bank of Baroda, Suraj Plaza-1, Sayaji Ganj,, Baroda-390005 **2)** Bank Of Baroda, Baroda Corporate Centre,, Plot No - C-26, G - Block, Bandra - Kurla Complex, Bandra (East), Mumbai-400051 **Website:** www.bankofbaroda.com.

**2.4. Bank of India**

Bank of India was founded on September 7, 1906 by a group of eminent businessmen from Mumbai. In July 1969 Bank of India was nationalized along with 13 other banks. Beginning with a paid-up capital of Rs.50 lakh and 50 employees, the Bank has made a rapid growth over the years. It has evolved into a mighty institution with a strong national presence and sizable international operations. In business volume, Bank of India occupies a premier position among the nationalized banks. Presently, Bank of India has 2609 branches in India spread over all states/ union territories including 93 specialized branches. These branches are controlled through 48 Zonal Offices. Bank of India has several firsts to its credit. The Bank has been the first among the nationalised banks to establish a fully computerised branch and ATM facility at the Mahalaxmi Branch at Mumbai way back in 1989. It pioneered the introduction of the Health Code System in 1982, for evaluating/ rating its credit portfolio. Bank of India was the first Indian Bank to open a branch outside the country, at London, in 1946, and also the first to open a branch in Europe, Paris in 1974. The Bank has sizable presence abroad, with a network of 23 branches (including three representative office ) at key banking and financial centres viz. London, New York, Paris, Tokyo, Hong-Kong, and Singapore.

## 2.5. Bank of Maharashtra

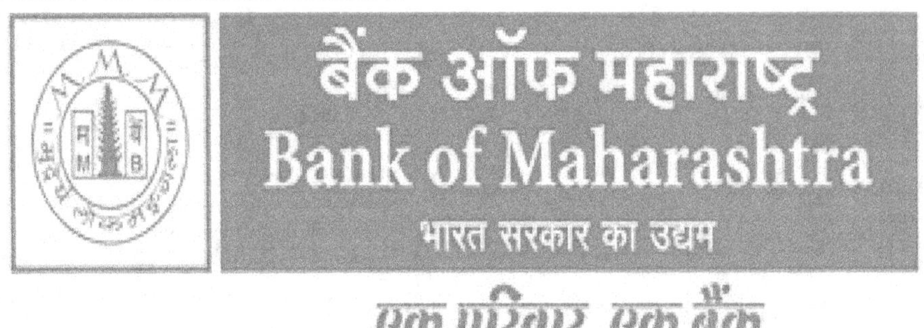


Bank of Maharashtra is an Indian bank based in the city of Pune. The bank was established in the year 1935 with an initial authorized capital worth Rs. 10.00 Lacs, although it became operational in the early phase of the next year. The bank got nationalized by the Government of India in the year 1969. With a total number of 1421 branches located all over India as of April 2009, the bank claims to have the largest number of branches within the state of Maharashtra, among all the Public Sector banks. Commonly known as a common man's bank, Bank of Maharashtra adopts a philosophy of "Technology with personal touch", and follows its motto stating "One Family, One Bank, Bank of Maharashtra".

**Facilities:** All the branches of Bank of Maharashtra have been fully computerized, with Depository services and Demat facilities being offered at 131 branches as of April 2009. The bank aims at increasing its ATM network from 345 to 500 soon, apart from planning to install Biometric ATMs at some selected branches. Apart from it, introduction of Phone Banking, Internet Banking and Mobile Banking is also on the cards.

**Other Highlights:** Apart from providing regular banking services to the customers, Bank of Maharashtra has established two Joint Ventures to fulfill its other commitments towards the general public and society. These Joint Ventures are M-SETI and Mahabank Info Centre. Mahabank Self-Employment Training Institute (M-SETI) is an effort initiated by Mahabank Agricultural Research & Rural Development Fund (MARDEF), a trust run by Bank of Maharashtra receiving help from National Bank for Rurl Development (NABARD). The institute runs various self-employment oriented training courses for the rural unemployed youth from the districts of Pune, Kolhapur, Satara, Sangli, Nashik, Ahmednagar, Jalgaon, Dhule and Nandurbar. Mahabank Info Centre is a yet another initiative by Bank of Maharashtra aimed at providing various retail baking related information to the customers, and enabling smoother operations for them.

**Head Office:** Bank of Maharashtra, Lokmangal, 1501, Shivajinagar, Pune (Maharashtra) - 411 005.

**Website:** www.bankofmaharashtra.in

## 2.6. Canara Bank

Canara Bank is one of the most prominent commercial banks of India. The bank was established in the year 1906 at Mangalore, Karnataka by a well known personality Mr. Ammembal Subba Rao Pai. Initially, it was founded with the name Canara Bank Hindu Permanent Fund, but later on the name was changed to Canara Bank Limited. Mr. Ammembal Subba Rao Pai had envisioned the bank to not only offer financial services but also fulfill social causes such as removal of superstitions and ignorance, promotion of habit of saving, providing assistance to the people in need and develop a sense of humanity among the people.

**Key Attributes:** Apart from setting other benchmarks in the field of providing comprehensive banking services to the consumers, Canara Bank has a number of achievements to its credit, which include being the first bank in India to have launched Inter-City ATM network, being the first bank to have been awarded ISO Certification for one of its branches, providing credit card for farmers for the first time in India along with offering Agricultural Consultancy Services.

**Vital Details:** Canara Bank has established a strong presence in the country, with 2710 branches across the nation as of September 2008. The bank boasts of having the maximum number of ATM installations among all the nationalized banks summing up to more than 2000 of them at 698 centres. Also, 1351 branches of the bank provide Internet and Mobile Banking (IMB) services, while 'Anywhere Banking' services are being provided at 2027 of its branches. All the branches of Canara Bank are enabled with Real

Time Gross Settlement (RTGS) and National Electronic Fund Transfer (NEFT) transaction facilities, insuring smooth and swift money transfer from any corner of the nation to another corner.

**Products and Services:** Canara Bank offers a host of banking and value added services to its customers, which include Personal Banking Services, Corporate Banking Services, NRI Banking Services and Priority & SME Credit Services.

**Head Office:** Canara Ban, Head Office, 112, J C Road, BANGALORE - 560 002**Website:** http://www.canarabank.com

## 2.7. Central Bank of India

Central Bank of India is one of the oldest commercial banks of India, and reportedly is the first truly Indian bank which was totally owned and established by Indian without any foreign help. Sir Sorabji Pockhanawala was the founder of the bank, who had always dreamt of establishing a thoroughly Indian bank, who was so happy and excited about the project that he reportedly termed the Central Bank of India as "property of the nation and the country's asset". The first Chairman of the bank was Sir Pherozesha Mehta, a yet another Indian enthusiast. In the year 1969 the bank was nationalized by the Government of India.

**Key Attributes:** Central Bank of India claims to be the first bank to be conferred with the National Award for Excellence in Micro and Small Enterprises (MSE) Lending for the year 2007-08. The bank entered a partnership with Kotak Mahindra Assets Management Company in December 2008, under which all the Kotak Mutual Fund products will be made available through Central Bank of India branches.

**Products and Services:** Central Bank of India offers a host of banking services to its customers including Regular Banking Services such as Deposits and Loans, International Banking Services, and other services including Centralcard Electronic Cards, Debit Cards, No-Frills Savings Deposit Account under the name Cent Bachat Khata, and Finance options for domestic and international tours under the name Cent Safar.

**Presence in India:** Central Bank of India has a strong presence in the country with over 3000 branches and more than 250 extension counters nationwide as of April 2009. The headquarters of the bank are located in Mumbai, the financial capital of India, along with 16 other zonal offices established in different cities of the nation, including Agra, Ahmedabad, Bhopal, Chandigarh, Chennai, Guwahati, Hyderabad, Kolkata, Lucknow, Mumbai Metro Zonal Office, Muzaffarpur, Nagpur, New Delhi, Patna, Pune and Raipur.

**Head Office:** Central Bank of India, Chander Mukhi, Narman Point, Mumbai – 400 021,

**Website:** http://www.centralbankofindia.co.in

## 2.8. Corporation Bank

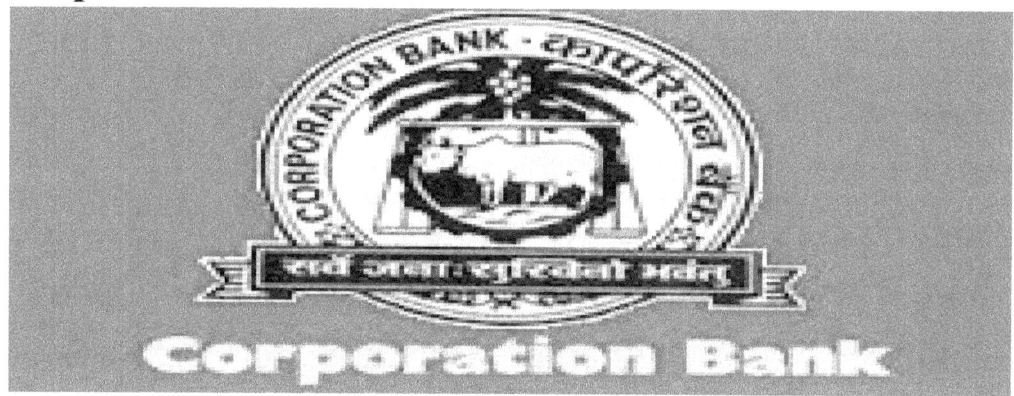


Corporation Bank is an Indian bank based in Mangalore, Karnataka. The bank was founded in the year 1906 at a town named Udupi in Karnataka with an investment of just Rs. 5000. A group of enthusiasts including Khan Bahadur Haji Abdulla Haji Kasim Saheb Bahadur were the founders of the bank. Interestingly, Udupi was not much far from Mangalore, and the banking needs of the people were being solely controlled by some local rich individuals. Hence, to find a way out of the existing monopoly of the money lenders, Corporation Bank was established with the initial name 'The Canara Banking Corporation (Udupi) Ltd'.

**Key Attributes:** Corporation Bank has an array of awards and recognitions to its credit, including National Award for Assistance to Exporters from the President of India for the year 1976-77, Shiromani Award for Banking from Union Minister of Commerce in the year 1992, Best Bank Award for Excellence in Banking Technology from Institute for Development and Research in Banking Technology (IDRBT) in the year 2001, and Best Bank Award for Innovative Usage and Application on INFINET (Indian Financial Network) from the same institution in the year

2002. Apart from it, Corporation Bank has been the path breaker among the Indian banks in many ways, as it was the first bank in the country to launch Cash Management Services, Gold Banking, m-Commerce and 100% Core Banking Services (CBS) compliance.

**Products and Services:** Corporation Bank offers a wide range of banking products and services to its customers, including Personal Banking Services, Internet Banking Services, Value Added Banking Services, Corporate Banking Services and Credit Card & Debit Card Services. The bank allocates due attention towards its corporate and international business customers, bringing some customized services such as Gold Card Scheme for Exporters. Also, the bank has introduced some specialized services to cater to the specific needs of Micro and Small Enterprises (MSE) customers, enabling them leverage its potential to their maximum benefit.

**Head Office:** Corporation Bank , Mangaladevi Temple Road, Pandeshwar, Mangalore-575 001, Karnataka, India.

**Website:** http://www.corpbank.com

## 2.9. Dena Bank

Dena Bank is an Indian commercial bank based in Mumbai. The bank was founded by the Devkaran Nanjee family on the 26th of May, 1938. At the time of establishment, its name was Devkaran Nanjee Banking Company Ltd. Further, the banking company was incorporated as a Public Ltd. Company in December 1939, changing its name to Dena Bank Ltd. The bank was nationalized by the Government of India along with 13 other commercial banks in the year 1969.

**Key Attributes:** Dena Bank was one of the six Public Sector Banks which had been chosen by the World Bank in the year 1995 for granting a loan of Rs. 72.3 Crores under Financial Sector Development project. Also, it is one of the few banks which have been given a loan by the World Bank for technological advancement and training. Dena Bank has maintained a strong technological infrastructure with state-of-the-art IT innovations and solutions implemented at its branches and back-end. 100% branches of the bank have been fully computerized, and the bank has established its own network called "DENANET" to ensure seamless connectivity and smooth workflow all the way through its banking process. DENANET is comprised of VSATs, leased lines, dial-up lines and ISDN backups, and is completely integrated with the Indian Financial Network (INFINET) of the Reserve Bank of India (RBI).

**Regular Banking Services:** Dena Bank offers a host of Regular Banking Services to its customers, including Personal Banking Services comprising of Deposit, Loan and Investment Services, Priority and Small & Medium Enterprises (SME) services,

International Banking Services, Corporate Banking Services and a host of other Value Added Services.

**Network Based Services:** Leveraging the potential of its own advanced high-speed Information Network DENANET, Dena Bank offers a host of network based services to its customers in addition to the Regular Banking Services. These services include Data Transfer, Remote Support, Real Time Gross Settlement (RTGS), Dena Bill Pay, Dena m-banking, Any Branch Banking, Multi-City Cheque Facility, Internet Banking and Dena e-Tax Pay.

**Head Office:** Dena Bank, Dena Corporate Centre, C-10, G Block, Bandra-Kurla Complex Bandra [E]. Mumbai- 400 051 Website: http://www.denabank.com

## 2.10. Indian Bank

Indian Bank is one of the indigenous banks of India that emerged as a result of the Swadeshi Movement during the British Raj. The bank was established on 15th of August, 1907. One of the prime figures associated with the establishment of the bank was V. Krishnaswamy Iyer, a lawyer from Madras (Now Chennai). The bank soon spread its wings outside India too, and opened its branch in Colombo, Sri Lanka in the year 1932 and Rangoon, Burma in 1940. The bank was further nationalized by the Government of India in the year 1969.

**Global Presence:** The modest beginning made by the Indian

Bank has come a long way since then, with 1642 branches located nationwide within India and Overseas branches in Singapore and Colombo as of April 2009. The bank also has 40 Overseas Correspondent banks in 70 countries, giving a strong presence internationally. A 22,000 strong workforce of dedicated employees takes pride in serving the Indian Bank.

**Banking Activities:** Indian Bank offers a wide variety of Banking Products and Services to its customers, including various Deposit Schemes, Loan Options, Financial Services, Stock Investment Services and a number of specialized services such as Remittance, Collection, Day Banking Branches, Cash Management and Electronic Funds Transfer. As of April 2009, the bank has Core Banking Solution (CBS) implemented in its 1642 branches and 66 extension counters. The bank has 755 connected Automatic Teller Machines (ATMs) installed in 225 locations nationwide.

**Subsidiary Companies:** Apart from its Regular Banking Services, the Indian Bank has also been offering various other services through its 3 subsidiary companies, which are Indbank Merchant Banking Services Ltd., IndBank Housing Ltd. and IndFund Management Ltd.

**Rural Banking:** Indian Bank has been a leader in bringing new initiatives for development of rural banking and extending help to the farmers of India. The bank has received award from Honorable Union Minister of Finance for Excellence in Agricultural Lending. Apart from it, the bank also received the Best Performer Award for Micro-Finance activities in Tamil Nadu and Union Territory of Puducherry from National Bank for

Agriculture and Rural Development (NABARD).

**Head Office:** Indian Bank, PB No.1384, 66, Rajaji Salai, Chennai 600 001, Tamil Nadu, Website: http://www.indianbank.in

## 2.11. Indian Overseas Bank

Established in 1937, Indian Overseas Bank (IOB) is a leading bank based in Chennai, India. IOB had the distinction of simultaneously commencing operations in three branches at Karaikudi, Chennai, and Yangon (Myanmar). Since IOB aimed to encourage overseas banking and foreign exchange operations, it soon opened its branches in Penang and Singapore. Today, Indian Overseas Bank boasts of a vast domain in banking sector with over 1400 domestic branches and 6 branches overseas.

IOB was the first bank to venture into consumer credit, as it introduced the popular Personal Loan scheme. In 1964, the Bank started computerization in the areas of inter-branch reconciliation and provident fund accounts. Indian Overseas Bank was one of the 14 major banks which were nationalized in 1969. After nationalization, the Bank emphasized on opening its branches in rural parts of India. In 1979, IOB opened a Foreign Currency Banking Unit in the free trade zone in Colombo. In the year 2000, Indian Overseas Band undertook an initial public offering (IPO) that brought the government's share in the bank's equity down to 75%. The equity shares of IOB are listed in the Madras Stock Exchange (Regional), Bombay Stock Exchange, and National Stock Exchange of India Ltd., Mumbai. Since its inception, IOB has absorbed various banks including the latest — Bharat Overseas Bank — in 2007. The Bank's IT department has developed software, which is used by its 1200 branches to provide online banking to customers. Indian Overseas Bank also has a network of about 500 ATMs throughout India. Its International VISA Debit Card is accepted at all ATMs belonging to the Cash Tree and NFS networks. IOB also offers Internet Banking; it's one of the banks that the Govt. of India has approved for online payment of taxes. Indian Overseas Bank offers investment options like Mutual Funds and Shares. It provides a wide range of consumer and commercial banking services, including Savings Account, Current Account, Depositary Services, VISA Cards, Credit Cards, Debit Cards, Online Banking, Any Branch Banking, Home Loans, NRI Account, Agricultural Loans, Payment of Bills / Taxes, Provident Fund Scheme, Forex Collection Services, Retail Loans, etc.

**Head Office:** Indian Overseas Bank, 763, Anna Salai, Chennai – 600002, **URL:** www.iob.com

**2.12. Oriental Bank of Commerce (OBC)**

Established on 19th Feb' 1943 in Lahore, Oriental Bank of Commerce (OBC) is one of the public sector banks in India. Its modest beginning is creditable to its founder Late Rai Bahadur Lala Sohan Lal, the first Chairman of the OBC. Within four years of coming into existence, the country partitioned, the Bank shifted its Registered Office from Lahore to Amritsar. The Oriental Bank of Commerce was nationalized on 15th April 1980, and paved its way to count amongst the strongest banks in India. OBC has a network of 530 branches and 505 ATM's spread throughout India, out of which 490 branches offer centralized banking solutions. With High Capital Adequacy Ratio, Oriental Bank of Commerce is known be a consistent profit-making bank. It offers various services and products, like current/ savings account, general loans, educational loans, agricultural loans, etc, for the benefit of customers. For its effective services, the National Institute of Bank Management (NIBM) rated OBC Bank as "Customer Friendly" Bank.

**OBC India Grameen Project:** OBC's Grameen Project aims to reduce poverty & to identify the reasons which are responsible for the failure or success. OBC is implementing a Grameen Project in Dehradun District (UP) and Hanumangarh District (Rajasthan). This Scheme has a unique feature of disbursing small loans, ranging from Rs. 75 onwards. The OBC has various Agriculture Loan Schemes for farmers, such as, Composite Credit Scheme for Agricultural Leading, Overdraft Facility to Farmers, Advance against Warehouse Receipts to Farmers & Purchase of Land for Agriculture Purposes, Agriculture Clinic & Agriculture Business

Centers.

**Comprehensive Village Development Programme:** On 13 April 1997 at the occasion of Baisakhi, OBC launched another unique scheme, 'The Comprehensive Village Development Programme' in three villages of Punjab. After the success of this scheme in these villages, the Bank extended the programme to more villages. Today, it covers 10 villages in Punjab, 4 in Haryana and 1 in Rajasthan. This programme focuses on providing a comprehensive and integrated package, which offers finance to the villagers.

**Special Services For Women:** Oriental Bank of Commerce has also implemented 14 point action plan for strengthening the credit delivery to women. Under this scheme bank provide various loans to women, such as, Oriented Mahila Vikas Yojana, Scheme for Professional & self Employed Women, Scheme for Beauty Parlor/ Boutiques/ Saloons/Tailoring, Scheme for Financing Working Women, etc.

**Head Office:** Oriental Bank of Commerce, Harsha Bhawan, E-Block, Connaught Place, New Delhi – 110001, URL: www.obcindia.com

## 2.13. Punjab & Sind Bank(PSB)

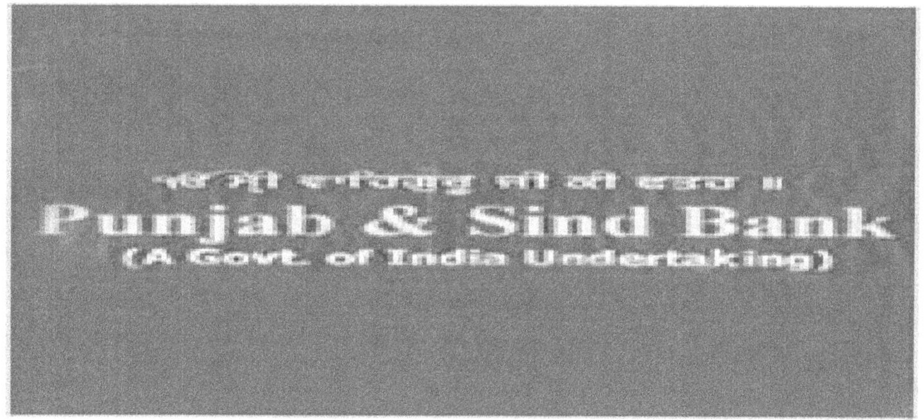

Punjab & Sind Bank, established in 1908, is headquartered at New Delhi. Having more than 800 branches across the country, the bank has around 10,000 employees dedicated to the banking services and customer care. The bank offers usual banking services along with innovative banking methods including Internet and phone banking, international banking, merchant banking, hire, purchase, leasing and credit cards.

**Objective:** The bank was founded by luminaries like Bhai Vir Singh, Sir Sunder Singh Majitha and Sardar Tarlochan Singh in the holy city of Amritsar on the principle of social commitment to help the weaker section of the society in their economic endeavours to raise their standard of life.

**Achievements and Activities:** Punjab & Sind Bank is the first bank in Northern India to obtain ISO 9002 certification for its selected branches. Its Housing Finance Branch caters to the credit need of the house aspirants.

The bank has entered into agreements for Non Life insurance business with M/s Bajaj Allianz General Insurance Company and Life Insurance business arrangements with M/s Aviva Life Insurance Company India Pvt. Ltd. Its customers can now avail insurance related services under one roof.

**Nationalisation:** Punjab & Sind Bank was nationalized in 1980 along with six other banks by the Government of India.

**Products & Services:**

**Deposits:** Savings Account, Recurring Deposit, Fixed Deposits, Current Accounts

**Loans:** Priority Sector Loans, Housing Loan, Home Enhancement Loans, Personal Loan, Education Loan, Car Loans, Business Loans

**Other Services:** NRI Services, Punjab & Sind Bank-ICICI Bank Credit Card, Gold Card Schemes, RBI Citizens' Charter including cash and deposits Locker Facilities, RTGS, NEFT, PSB e-funds Transfer, Tax Payment, E-bill Payments, PSB- Aviva Allianz Insurance

**Head Quarter:** Punjab & Sind Bank, 21, Rajendra Place, New Delhi - 110008

**Email:** ho@psb.co.in. **Website:** http://www.psbindia.com/

## 2.14. Punjab National Bank(PNB)

Punjab National Bank (PNB) is the second largest government-owned commercial bank in India. Having more than 3.5 crore customer, Punjab National Bank has one of the largest branch networks in India. The bank's assets for financial year 2007 were about US$60 billion.

**Products and Services**:

**Savings Fund Account -** Total Freedom Salary Account, PNB Prudent Sweep, PNB Vidyarthi SF Account, PNB Mitra SF

**Account Current Account -** PNB Vaibhav, PNB Gaurav, PNB Smart Roamer

**Fixed Deposit Schemes -** Spectrum Fixed Deposit Scheme, Anupam Account, Mahabachat Schemes, Multi Benefit Deposit

**Scheme Credit Schemes -** Flexible Housing Loan, Car Finanace, Personal Loan, Credit Cards

**Social Banking -** Mahila Udyam Nidhi Scheme, Krishi Card, PNB Farmers Welfare Trust

**Corporate Banking -** Gold Card scheme for exporters, EXIM finance

**Business Sector -** PNB Karigar credit card, PNB Kushal Udhami, PNB Pragati Udhami, PNB Vikas Udhami. Apart from these, the PNB also offers locker facilities, senior citizens schemes, PPF schemes and various E-services.

**Awards and Distinctions:** Ranked among top 50 companies by the leading financial daily, Economic Times.

- Ranked as 323rd biggest bank in the world by Bankers Almanac (January 2006), London.
- Earned 9th place among India's Most Trusted top 50 service brands in Economic Times- A.C Nielson Survey.
- Included in the top 1000 banks in the world according to The Banker, London.
- Golden Peacock Award for Excellence in Corporate Governance - 2005 by Institute of Directors.
- FICCI's Rural Development Award for Excellence in Rural Development – 2005

**PNB Overseas Offices:** PNB has a banking subsidiary in the United Kingdom, as well as branches in Hong Kong and Kabul. It has representative offices in Almaty, Shanghai, and Dubai.

**Coming into Being:** The bank was established in 1895 at Lahore. PNB's founders included several leaders of the Swadeshi movement like Dyal Singh Majithia, Lala HarKishen Lal, Lala Lalchand, Kali Prosanna Roy, EC Jessawala, Prabhu Dayal, Bakshi Jaishi Ram, and Lala Dholan Dass. Lala Lajpat Rai was actively associated with the banks's management in its early years. It holds the distinction of being the first Indian bank to have been started solely with Indian capital. In 1969, it was nationalized by the Government of India along with 13 other banks.

**Head Office:** Punjab National Bank, 7, Bhikhaiji Cama Place, New Delhi - 110066 Phone: 91-11-2371 6185, Fax: 91-11-26196176, Website: www.pnbindia.com

## 2.15. Syndicate Bank

Established in the year 1925, Syndicate Bank had its first office in the coastal region of Karnataka, Udupi. It was then named as 'Canara Industrial & Banking Syndicate Ltd'. The bank was initiated by a trio - Sri Upendra Ananth Pai, a businessman, Sri Vaman Kudva, an engineer and Dr.T M A Pai, a physician, with a capital of Rs. 8000. During that time, the crisis in the handloom industry crippled the local weavers completely. The main aim of Syndicate Bank was to provide financial assistance to them, by mobilizing small savings from the community. Three years later, in 1928, the bank came up with Pigmy Deposit Scheme, in which it collected as little as 2 annas per day, at the doorsteps of the depositors through its agents. The scheme existing till date, earns the bank a sum of Rs. 2 crore daily. In the same year, Syndicate bank opened its first branch at Brahmavar in Dakshina Kannada District. It became a member of the Clearing House for the first time at Bombay, in 1937. Almost a decade later, Syndicate Bank opened 29 branches opened in a single day in rural areas. Its 100th branch opened at Ilkal in Karnataka in 1957. The bank with its socio-economic aim was making extensive growth and advancement and entered Foreign Exchange business by opening Foreign Exchange Department at Bombay. In 1964, the bank changed its name to 'Syndicate Bank Limited' and the head office was also shifted from Udupi to Manipal. The bank had then set up an Economic Research Department, being one of the first few Banks to emphasize on research in Banking, even before nationalization. In 1971, it opened the first specialized branch in Foreign Exchange, in Delhi. Five years later, it opened its first overseas branch opened at London. In 1984, Syndicate Bank opened its 1000th branch in Hauz Khas, Delhi. In the same year, it undertook the management of Musandam Exchange Co. in Muscat. Five years thence, in 1989, Syndicate Bank opened its 1500th branch at Kanakumbi. In 1999, it raised a capital of Rs. 125 Crore from its more than 4 lakh shareholders. Next year, in 2000, the bank established its first specialized Capital Market Services, at Mumbai. In 2003, Syndicate Bank entered into a MOU with Bajaj Allianz, for distribution of Life Insurance products. In 2004, Syndicate Bank amalgamated with United India Insurance Co. Ltd. for distribution of Non-Life Insurance products. In 2004, Syndicate Bank also started utility bill payment services through Internet banking introduced. In 2005, the bank commenced the online reservation of railway tickets through Indian Railway Catering & Tourism Corporation Ltd for its customers. It was during this time that it entered into a MOU with SFAC for promoting of investments in Agri-business products. The 2000th branch was opened at Tondiarpet, Chennai, in 2006. In the same year, the bank commenced the first BPO outfit of a Nationalized Bank, SyndBank Services Limited. This was a wholly owned subsidiary of Syndicate Bank. With the age of progressive banking, Syndicate Bank has created a name for itself in the last 80 years. Rooted in rural India, the Bank has a clear picture of the grass root realities and a vision of future India. Changing with the changing times, the Bank has well equipped itself with all the facilities of the new age, without, however, altering its distinctive socio-economic and cultural culture. Syndicate Bank's unique principle of mutual development, of both the Bank and the people, has won it a long list of clientele, which includes both the rural and the semi-urban class.

**Products & Services:** Deposits, Loans, Internet Banking, Insurance, Cash Management Services, ATM Services, Recovery

Channel, NRI Services, Electronic Funds Transfer (EFT) System, Synd Demat (Depository Participant Services), Syndicate Gift Cheques

**Head Office :** Syndicate Bank, Head Office, Post Box No.1, Manipal – 576104, (Udupi Dist.) Karnataka , India, Phones (EPABX): 0820-2571181 to 2571196
Website: http://syndicatebank.in/

## 2.16. UCO Bank (United Commercial Bank Ltd)

UCO Bank is a commercial bank established in 1943. The idea to establish the bank was first conceived by G.D. Birla, the famous industrialist, after the historic 'Quit India Movement' in 1942. The idea was culminated on the 6th of January 1943, when The United Commercial Bank Ltd. was born with its Registered and Head Office at Kolkata. A commercial bank and a Government of India Undertaking, it comprises of government representatives as well as renowned professionals like accountants, management experts, economists, businessmen, and so on, in its Board of Directors. United Commercial Bank has stretched out to of all segments of the economy - be it agriculture, industry, trade and commerce, services or infrastructure. Along with 13 other major commercial banks of India, United Commercial Bank was nationalized on 19th July, 1969, by the Government of India. Thereafter the Bank expanded rapidly. To keep pace with the developing scenario and expansion of business, the Bank undertook an exercise in organizational restructuring in the year 1972. Under the act of Indian Parliament, in 1985, its name changed from United Commercial Bank to the present name, UCO Bank. As of 2005, the bank has 2000 Service Units spread all over India. A distinctive feature of UCO bank is its introduction of 'NO HOLIDAY' branches. These bank branches work on all the 365 days of a year. With the age of global banking, UCO bank has also changed to be adept with the newest technology, boasting of specialized computerized branches in both India and overseas.

**Branches & ATM Services:** Headquartered in Kolkata, UCO Bank has about 35 Regional Offices spread all over India. Overseas, it has two branches in Singapore and Hong Kong. UCO bank has a total of 414 ATMs across the states of Andhra Pradesh, Assam, Bihar, Chattisgarh, Chandigarh, Goa Gujarat, Haryana, Himachal Pradesh, Jharkhand, Karnataka, Kerala, Madhya Pradesh, Maharashtra, Meghalaya, Nagaland, New Delhi, Orissa, Pondicherry, Punjab, Rajasthan, Sikkim, Tamil Nadu, Tripura, Uttar Pradesh and West Bengal.

**Products & Services:** NRI Banking, Foreign Currency Loans, Finance/Services to Exporters, Finance/Services to Importers, Remittances, Forex & Treasury Services, Resident Foreign Currency (Domestic) Deposits, Correspondent Banking Services and General Banking Services

**Head Office:** UCO Bank, Head Office, 10 B.T.M Sarani, Kolkata – 700001, **Website:** www.ucobank.com

## 2.17. Union Bank of India

Union Bank of India was inaugurated by the Father of the Nation, Mahatama Gandhi, on November 11, 1919. Started as a limited company in Mumbai, it was one of the few Financial Commercial banks in India. Until 1947, UBI had only 4 branches - 3 in Mumbai and 1 in Saurashtra, all concentrated in key trade centres. Catering to all the sectors of the society, be it agriculture, industry, trade and commerce, services or infrastructure, the bank has also played a major role in rendering services to the financial needs of every section. Apart from this, the bank also extended financial support to educational, housing and trade sector. Union Bank of India undertook the task of establishment of village knowledge centers and self-employment training centers. It was in 1975, that the Union Bank of India was nationalized. It was, then, that it merged with the Belgaum Bank, a private sector bank. Another merger was on cards in 1985, this time with the Miraj State Bank. Union Bank is a Public Sector Unit with 55.43% Share Capital held by the Government of India. The Bank came out with its Initial Public Offer (IPO) in August 20, 2002 and Follow on Public Offer in February 2006. Presently 44.57 % of Share Capital is presently held by institutions, individuals and others.

**Tech-Savvy:** With the age of global banking, Union Bank of India also changed its style, boasting of urbanized and computerized core banking systems. A front runner among public sector banks in modern-day banking, it has all the facilities that a modern bank should have - internet banking and centrally computerized branches. UBI was one of the pioneer public sector banks, which launched Core Banking Solution in 2002. As of September 2005, more than 670 branches/extension counters of Bank are networked under Core Banking Solution. The Bank has launched multiple Electronic Delivery Channels and has installed nearly 423 networked ATMs.

**Products & Services:** Deposits, Accounts, Loans, Cards, Insurance, Cash, Management Service, Mutual Funds, Demat, ATMs, E Banking Or Online Banking, Remittance Service, Bill Payment Service, Tax Payment Service, ATM Banking, Tele Banking, Online Demat Trading, Cash Management Services, Mutual Funds, Railway Tickets Booking, 8% Tax Saving Bonds, Public Provident Fund (PPF), Direct Tax Collection, Central Excise and Service Tax Collection Services, and Special Savings Schemes for Senior Citizens

**Head Office:** 239 Vidhan Bhavan Marg, Central Office, Nariman Point, Mumbai-21. **Phone -** (022) 22892000

**Website:** www.unionbankofindia.co.in

## 2.18. United Bank of India

Originally established as United Bank of India Ltd., the bank was a result of merger of four Bengali banks - Comilla Banking Corporation Ltd., Bengal Central Bank Ltd., Comilla Union Bank Ltd. and Hooghly Bank Ltd. in 1950. Almost two decade later, in 1969, United Bank of India was one among the major banks that were nationalized. Thereafter, the bank expanded in a major way, covering all the states of India. It also was an active participant in the growth and developmental activities, mainly in the rural and semi-urban regions. Acknowledging the efforts made by United Bank of India, it was honoured as a Lead Bank in several districts of India. Presently, it the Lead Bank in 30 districts in the States of West Bengal, Assam, Manipur and Tripura. The Bank also holds the position of being the Convener of the State Level Bankers' Committees (SLBC) for the States of West Bengal and Tripura. The bank is known to spread its banking services especially in the Eastern and North-Eastern parts of India. United Bank of India supported the 4 Regional Rural Banks (RRB) at West Bengal, Assam, Manipur and Tripura. Thanks to United Bank of India, even places with little or no reach such as the Sunderbans in West Bengal, today, have an access to banking services. UBI had established two floating mobile branches on motor launches. These moved from one island to another on different days of the week, providing people with all the facilities. However, the floating branches paved way to the full-fledged bank branches at these centres. The largest lender to the tea industry, UBI is also recognized as the 'Tea Bank', for its longstanding involvement with the financing of tea gardens.

**Branches & ATM Services:** Presently the Bank has a three-tier organizational set-up consisting of the Head Office, 28 Regional Offices. Out of its total 1450 branches, 500 of them have been automated either fully or partially. Its branches in all the metropolitan cities of India are equipped with Electronic Fund Transfer System. UBI has ATMs all over the country and having Cash Tree arrangement with 11 other Banks.

**Products & Services:** Deposit Scheme, Credit Scheme, NRI Services, United Mobile Services, FOREIGN Exchange, Insurance Policies, RTGS, Tax- Collection, E-Payment, Nomination Facility, Lockers, Credit Cards, ATM Cum Debit Cards, and Remittance Service in tie up with Western Union Money Transfer

**Third Party Banking Products:** Mutual Funds, Life Insurance in tie up with Tata AIG Life Insurance Company, Non- Life Insurance policies in tie-up with Bajaj Allianz Insurance Company Ltd, Credit Card in tie-up with SBI cards, Foreign Remittance Services in tie-up with Western Union, Demat Depository Services in association with Central Depository Services (India) Ltd. (CSDL)

**Head Office:** United Bank of India, 11, Hemanta Basu Sarani, Kolkata - 700 001, West Bengal, India, Phone: 248-7470, Website: www.unitedbankofindia.com

## 2.19. Vijaya Bank

Vijaya Bank was flagged off on 23rd October 1931. Late Shri A.B.Shetty, along with other enterprising farmers in Mangalore, Karnataka, founded the bank to inculcate banking habits in the farming community of Dakshina Kannada district in Karnataka State. In 1958, it was promoted and became a scheduled bank. From 1963 to 68, the Vijaya bank grew both in terms of size and stature - 9 small banks had merged with it, thus contributing to its growth and advancement. On April 15, 1980, the bank was nationalized. Vijaya Bank boasts of being one of the few banks which has undertaken the principal membership of VISA International and MasterCard International. Vijay Bank has been constantly focusing on technological upgradation. As on October 2005, all the 913 branches have been computerized, covering 97% of the bank's total business.

**Branches & ATM Services:** As of March 2009, Vijaya bank has a network of 1101 branches, 43 Extension Counters and 364 ATMs, spanning across all 28 states and 4 union territories in the country, with the highest number of branches in its home state, Karnataka. At present, 736 branches, 38 extension counters and 11 service branches of Vijaya Bank, covering 93.3% of its total business, are functioning on CBS. At the same time, 747 branches are enabled with RTGS and NEFT.

**Products & Services**:

**Deposit Schemes:** Savings Bank, V Platinum Savings Bank Account, Vijaya Saral Savings, Current Account, VStar Savings Scheme and Term Deposit

**Loans & Advances:** Retail Lending Schemes, Loans Against Securities, Non Fund Based Facilities, Advances to Agriculture, SSIs and Others, Government Sponsored Schemes and Special Schemes for Women

**NRI Services:** Deposits, Loans, Remittances, FOREX Branches, FCNR(B) Branches, and Helpline for NRIs

**Remittance Collection and Facilities:** FOREX Remittances, Inland Remittances, Electronic Remittance Services, Inward / Outward Collection Instruments

**Credit Cards:** Domestic Cards, Global cards and Debit cards

**Forex:** FOREX market Information, Card Rates and Treasury

**Other Services:** Merchant Banking, Vijaya Raksha, V-Arogya Bima Policy, Credit Cards, Mutual Funds, Leasing, Hiring and Purchases

**Head Office:** Vijaya Bank, 41/2, Head Office Building, Trinity Circle, Mahatma Gandhi Road, Bangalore G.P.O., Bangalore –

560001, **Phone:** 080-25550693, 25584385,
**Website:** http://www.vijayabank.com/

## 20. State Bank of India (SBI)

The evolution of State Bank of India can be traced back to the first decade of the 19th century. It began with the establishment of the Bank of Calcutta in Calcutta, on 2 June 1806. The bank was redesigned as the Bank of Bengal, three years later, on 2 January 1809. It was the first ever joint-stock bank of the British India, established under the sponsorship of the Government of Bengal. Subsequently, the Bank of Bombay (established on 15 April 1840) and the Bank of Madras (established on 1 July 1843) followed the Bank of Bengal. These three banks dominated the modern banking scenario in India, until when they were amalgamated to form the Imperial Bank of India, on 27 January 1921. An important turning point in the history of State Bank of India is the launch of the first Five Year Plan of independent India, in 1951. The Plan aimed at serving the Indian economy in general and the rural sector of the country, in particular. Until the Plan, the commercial banks of the country, including the Imperial Bank of India, confined their services to the urban sector. Moreover, they were not equipped to respond to the growing needs of the economic revival taking shape in the rural areas of the country. Therefore, in order to serve the economy as a whole and rural sector in particular, the All India Rural Credit Survey Committee recommended the formation of a state-partnered and state-sponsored bank. The All India Rural Credit Survey Committee proposed the takeover of the Imperial Bank of India, and integrating with it, the former state-owned or state-associate banks. Subsequently, an Act was passed in the Parliament of India in May 1955. As a result, the State Bank of India (SBI) was established on 1 July 1955. This resulted in making the State Bank of India more powerful, because as much as a quarter of the resources of the Indian banking system were controlled directly by the State. Later on, the State Bank of India (Subsidiary Banks) Act was passed in 1959. The Act enabled the State Bank of India to make the eight former State-associated banks as its subsidiaries. The State Bank of India emerged as a pacesetter, with its operations carried out by the 480 offices comprising branches, sub offices and three Local Head Offices, inherited from the Imperial Bank. Instead of serving as mere repositories of the community's savings and lending to creditworthy parties, the State Bank of India catered to the needs of the customers, by banking purposefully. The bank served the heterogeneous financial needs of the planned economic development.

**Branches:** The corporate center of SBI is located in Mumbai. In order to cater to different functions, there are several other establishments in and outside Mumbai, apart from the corporate center. The bank boasts of having as many as 14 local head offices and 57 Zonal Offices, located at major cities throughout India. It is recorded that SBI has about 10000 branches, well networked to cater to its customers throughout India.

**ATM Services:** SBI provides easy access to money to its customers through more than 8500 ATMs in India. The Bank also facilitates the free transaction of money at the ATMs of State Bank Group, which includes the ATMs of State Bank of India as well as the Associate Banks – State Bank of Bikaner & Jaipur, State Bank of Hyderabad, State Bank of Indore, etc. You may also transact money through SBI Commercial and International Bank Ltd by using the State Bank ATM-cum-Debit (Cash Plus) card.

**Products and Services**

**Personal Banking:** SBI Term Deposits SBI Loan For Pensioners, SBI Recurring Deposits Loan Against Mortgage Of Property, SBI Housing Loan Loan Against Shares & Debentures, SBI Car Loan Rent Plus Scheme, SBI Educational Loan and Medi-Plus Scheme

**Other Services:** Agriculture/Rural Banking, NRI Services, ATM Services, Demat Services, Corporate Banking, Internet Banking, Mobile Banking, International Banking, Safe Deposit Locker, RBIEFT, E-Pay, E-Rail, SBI Vishwa Yatra Foreign Travel Card, Broking Services, Gift Cheques

**Head Office**: State Bank of India, Corporate Centre, Madam Cama Road, Mumbai 400 021, India,

**Website:** www.statebankofindia.com

**Subsidiaries:** The State Bank Group includes a network of eight banking subsidiaries and several non-banking subsidiaries. Through the establishments, it offers various services including merchant banking services, fund management, factoring services, primary dealership in government securities, credit cards and insurance.

**The SBI's Subsidiaries are:**

20.1 State Bank of Indore (Merged with SBI)
20.2 State Bank of Saurashtra (Merged with SBI)
20.3 State Bank of Bikaner & Jaipur
20.4 State Bank of Hyderabad
20.5 State Bank of Mysore
20.6 State Bank of Patiala
20.7 State Bank of Travancore (SBT)

### 2.20.1 State Bank of Indore (Merged with SBI)

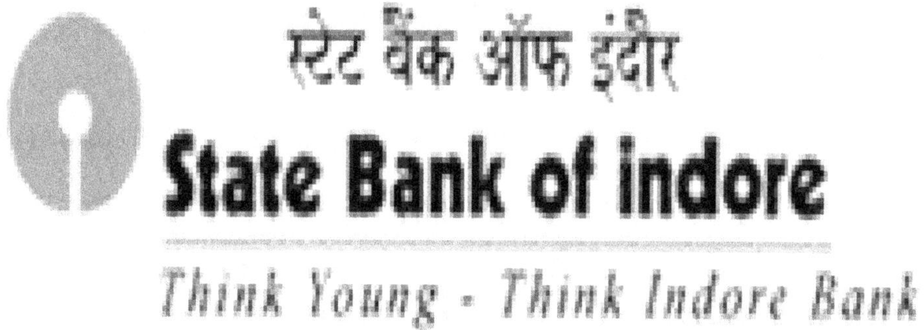


One of the nationalized banks in India, State Bank of Indore was formerly named as Bank of Indore Ltd. It was established under a special charter of His Highness Maharaja Tukojirao Holker-III, the then ruler of Malwa region. The Bank is also known as Indore Bank in Malwa region. It became a subsidiary of

State Bank of India on 1 January 1960, under the State Bank of India Subsidiary Banks Act, 1959. Bank of Indore Ltd. and came to be known as State Bank of Indore, after its association with SBI. In the following year (1962), State Bank of Indore took over the business of The Bank of Dewas Ltd. In 1965, State Bank of Indore took over The Dewas Senior Bank Ltd. as well. State Bank of Indore was upgraded to class 'A' category bank in 1971. Over the years, the Bank has been making significant growth in terms of its business. The business turnover of the Bank crossed Rs.47000 Crore at the end of December 2008. It has emerged as the premier bank of Madhya Pradesh due to its steady progress. The Bank aims to be the premier financial institution of Indore and wants to secure its position as a prominent part of the State Bank group. Apart from general banking operations, State Bank of Indore has undertaken multi-faceted banking activities too. It has also succeeded to great extent in reaching the rural sectors, especially agricultural segment in the country. In the process, the Bank has provided many useful services to its customers, such as credit and loans to the farmers. Schemes such as Kisan Gold Card Scheme and the Kisan Credit Card Scheme are part of the efforts taken by State Bank of Indore to reach its customers in the rural areas of the country.

**Products and Services:** Deposit Schemes, NRI Services, ATM Services, Cross Selling, Personal Segment, Small Industry Segment, Business Segment, International Banking, C & I Segment and Internet Banking

**Head Office:** State Bank of Indore, 5 Yashwant Niwas, Indore,

Madhya Pradesh – 452003 India. **Phone:** +91 731 2542444. **Website:** www.indorebank.org

### 2.20.2 State Bank of Saurashtra (Merged with SBI)

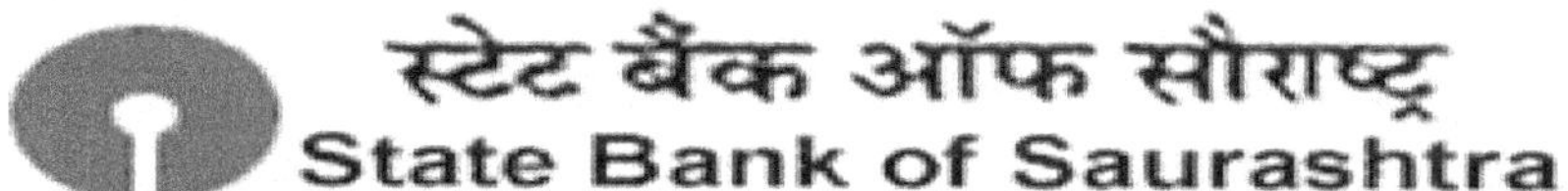


Merged Into State Bank of India in 2008

State Bank of Saurashtra (SBS) is one of the Associate Banks of State Bank of India. The history of the establishment of SBS can be traced back to pre-independence period. Prior to 1948, the region of Saurashtra (a part of the present day Gujarat), consisted many small, medium and large princely states. The larger states of Saurashtra included Bhavnagar, Rajkot and Porbandar, while Palitana and Vadia were its smaller states. These states established their own Darbar (palace). Out of the Darbars, the oldest one was Bhavnagar Darbar Bank, founded in 1902. The Darbar banks were established to cater to the needs of the governments of their respective princely states. Local savings were deposited in the banks. The banks of the princely states were amalgamated, when the state of Saurashtra was established in 1948. The Bhavnagar Darbar Bank came to be known as the State Bank of Saurashtra in 1950, under Saurashtra State Bank (Amalgamation) Ordinance, 1950. On 1 July 1950, the other four Darbar Banks, including Rajkot State Bank, Porbandar State Bank, Palitana Darbar Bank and Vadia State Bank, became the branches of State Bank of

Saurashtra.

**Branches:** After the formation of a separate state of Gujarat in 1960, SBS started its main area of operation from Saurashtra, which then became a part of Gujarat. It was in the same year, when State Bank of India took over State Bank of Saurashtra, under the State Bank of India (Subsidiary Banks) Act, 1959. By this time, SBS had 24 branches. SBS became one of the seven Associate Banks of SBI, with which it was merged with it on 13 August 2008. At the time of the merger, SBS had a network of 423 branches spread over 15 states and the Union Territory of Daman and Diu.

**Products and Services:** Personal Loans, Deposit Schemes, NRI Schemes, Debit and Credit Cards, Life Insurance, Mutual Funds, Deposit Schemes for Senior Citizens and Government Business

**Head Office:** State Bank of Saurashtra, Nilambaug Chowk, Bhavnagar-364 001(Gujarat) India. **Phone:** +91 0278 2431809, 2510949 **Telefax:** +91 278 2431809

### 2.20.3 State Bank of Bikaner & Jaipur (SBBJ)

A subsidiary of State Bank of India, State Bank of Bikaner and Jaipur (SBBJ) is one of the reputed banks of Rajasthan. SBBJ was established in 1963, when the erstwhile State Bank of Jaipur

(founded in 1943) and State Bank of Bikaner (founded in 1944) were amalgamated. Headquartered in Rajasthan, the Bank is nationalized, with its branches located at all the important centers in India. SBBJ has 860 branches out of which, 849 are business branches, eight are service branches, 2 are asset recovery branches and the rest 1 is treasury branch. A transparent corporate governance policies are followed by SBBJ. The Bank is heading for a smooth migration to Basel II. The Bank migrated all its branches to Core Banking Solution (CBS) during 2005-2006. The Bank boasts of having as many as 453 ATMs throughout India, all of them being the part of over 10000 ATMs of State Bank Group. Apart from the ATMs facility, SBBJ also provides the option of internet banking, which is extended to all its branches for retail customers. However, the select branches of the Bank provide internet banking facility for corporate customers only. In order to improve the efficiency of operations and to satisfy the customers in a better way, SBBJ has started Business Process Reengineering (BPR) initiatives. It is committed to offer value added services to its customers and aims at maintaining full customer satisfaction. It is recorded that the Bank's business has crossed the mark of Rs 59,427 Crore, with a net profit of Rs. 315.00 Crore at the end of March 2008. The Bank offers a plethora of services to its customers. Given below is the list of services offered by State Bank of Bikaner & Jaipur.

**Product and Services:** Personal Banking, NRI Services, International Banking, Corporate Banking, Agricultural Products, Service to SMEs, Govt. Business, E-mitra, Demat Services,

Internet Banking, ATM Services, Real Time Gross Settlement, Cross Selling Activities and National Electronic And Fund Transfer

**Head Office:** Tilak Marg, Jaipur – 302005, **Phone:** 0141-5101613, **Website:** www.sbbjbank.com

### 2.20.4 State Bank of Hyderabad (SBH)

A subsidiary of State Bank of India, State Bank of Hyderabad was established as Hyderabad State Bank on 8 August 1941. The Bank started its operations with the distinction of being the central bank of the princely state of Hyderabad, covering the present-day Telangana region of Andhra Pradesh, Hyderabad-Karnataka of Karnataka and Marathwada of Maharashtra, when it was established. Apart from functioning as a commercial bank, it managed Osmania Sikka (the currency of Hyderabad in those days) and managed public debt as well. The first branch of the Bank was established at Gunfoundry, Hyderabad on 5 April 1942. Hyderabad State Bank conducted the takeover of the assets and liabilities of the Hyderabad Mercantile Bank Ltd. in 1953. It was in the same year, when the Bank started its Government and Treasury business as an agent of the Reserve Bank of India. In 1956, the RBI took over the Bank. Since then, Hyderabad State Bank came to be known as State Bank of Hyderabad (SBH), which was the subsidiary of RBI during the period. On 1 October 1959, SBH became a subsidiary of the State Bank of India.

**ATM Services:** State Bank of Hyderabad offers easy access to money to its customers, through the ATM cum debit cards issued by it. The ATM cum debit card issued by the Bank can be used at more than 12500 ATMs of Andhra Bank, Bank of India, Corporation Bank, Dena Bank, HDFC Bank, Indian Bank, IndusInd Bank, Punjab National Bank, UCO Bank, Union Bank of India , UTI Bank, Canara Bank and Bank of Rajasthan, which are members of bilateral sharing arrangement. Apart from withdrawing money from your Savings and Current accounts, you can view the current balance and the mini statement of the last five transactions on your SBH account, by using the ATM cum debit card.

**Other services provided by State Bank of Hyderabad are :** Demat/ Depository Services, NRI Services, Electronic Fund Transfer System, Internet Banking, RTGS, NEFT & GRPT, Safe Deposit Lockers, International Banking and SBI Life

**Head Office:** State Bank of Hyderabad, Hybank Towers, Gunfoundary, Hyderabad, Andhra Pradesh - 500001, India. **Phone:** +91 40 23387713, **Website:** www.sbhyd.com

### 2.20.5 State Bank of Mysore (SBM)

State Bank of Mysore was originally established as Bank of Mysore Ltd. in 1913, under the sponsorship of the erstwhile Government of Mysore. Engineer-Statesman Late Dr. M. Visves varaya headed the banking committee during the time, to establish the Bank. In March 1960, the Bank became a subsidiary of State Bank of India, which holds 92.33% of its shares. In the present time, State Bank of Mysore caters to its customers through its wide network of branches, spread in different parts of India.

**Branches and ATM Services:** The Bank has as many as 671 branches, with 20 extension counters all over India and six specialized SSI branches. The Bank has 4 industrial finance branches, 3 corporate accounts branches, 4 specialized personal banking branches, 10 agricultural development branches, 3 treasury branches, 1 asset recovery branch and 7 service branches, which provide wide range of services to the customers. The customers of State Bank of Mysore are now provided easy access to money through more than 7500 State Bank Group ATMs and the ATMs of UTI Bank, HDFC Bank, Indian Bank, Andhra Bank, Punjab National Bank, Corporation Bank and Dena Bank, Union Bank of India, Bank of India, UCO Bank, Canara Bank, IndusInd Bank & Bank of Rajasthan. State Bank of Mysore boasts of being the first ever Karnataka-based Bank to have fully networked branches. The Bank is included in Core Banking Solution from 31 December 2005. Within one year, the Bank converted all its branches to Core Banking, in order to make it more convenient for its customers, who can now bank with State Bank of Mysore, anytime, anywhere in India. The net worth of State Bank of Mysore, recorded in on 31 March 2008, is Rs.13778.10 Millions and the Bank. The capital adequacy ratio of the Bank, as recorded at the end of March 2008, is 11.73%.

**Products and Services:** Deposits, Personal Banking Schemes, C & I Banking Schemes, Agri Banking Schemes, SME Banking Schemes, ATM Services, NRI Services, Internet Banking, Real Time Gross Settlement (RTGS) Transactions and National Electronic Fund Transfer (NEFT)

**Head Office:** State Bank of Mysore, K.G. Road, Bangalore - 560009, India, **Phone:** 91 80 22353901 to 22353909 **Fax:** 91 80 22283684, **Website:** www.statebankofmysore.co.in

### 2.20.6 State Bank of Patiala (SBP)

An Associate Bank of the State Bank of India, State Bank of Patiala (SBP) was established in 1917 by Late His Highness Bhupinder Singh, the Maharaja of erstwhile Patiala state. SBP started its operations from one branch called 'Chowk Fort', in

Patiala. During the time of the establishment, the state owned Bank was known as Patiala State Bank. It was set up for the purpose of promoting the growth of agriculture, trade and industry. The operations of Patiala State Bank witnessed a drastic change, when Patiala and east Punjab States Union (PEPSU) was formed in 1948. During that time, the Bank was reorganized and the Reserve Bank of India (RBI) controlled it. Patiala State Bank was renamed State Bank of Patiala on 1 April 1960, when it became a wholly owned undertaking of the Government of Punjab. On that day, SBP became a subsidiary of the State Bank of India (SBI). Since it was renamed, SBP has grown significantly in terms of its size and the volume of business. It is now one of the prominent Banks of India. Another milestone in the history of SBP was the computerization of all its branches on 24 January 2003. With this development, the Bank became India's first fully computerized Public Sector Bank.

**Branches and ATM Services:** The business of State Bank of Patiala has grown manifold since its establishment. Recent records say that State Bank of Patiala is networked by its 830 service outlets. There are as many as 750 branches of SBP, spread across the major cities of India, out of which, the majority of branches are located in its home State, Haryana, Himachal Pradesh, Rajasthan, Jammu & Kashmir, Delhi and Chandigarh. The Bank provides easy access to money to its customers through its ATMs spread over 16 states of India.

**Products and Services:** E-Products (ATM card and International Card), Personal Banking, Agriculture and Rural Banking, NRI

Services, SME & Corporate Banking, Govt. Business, Internet Banking

**Head Office:** State Bank of Patiala, Head Office, The Mall, Patilala - 147 001, Punjab, India. **Website:** www.sbp.co.in. **Phone:** 0175-2304943, 2215078

### 2.20.7 State Bank of Travancore (SBT)

The State Bank of Travancore (SBT) came into existence as Travancore Bank Ltd. in 1945. It was sponsored by the former Princely State of Travancore, Kerala. Apart from conducting general banking business, the Bank undertook government treasury work and foreign exchange business. Travancore Bank Ltd. was made as a subsidiary of the State Bank of India in 1960 and a member of the State Bank Group, under the SBI subsidiary Banks Act 1959, under the special statute of the Parliament of India. SBT is now one of the most prominent nationalized banks of India. State Bank of Travancore continues to provide dedicated services to its customers, since 60 years of its establishment. The Bank boasts of using world class technology through the implementation of 100% Core Banking Solution (CBS). The 24 hours working exchange bureau of the Bank is located in Calicut, while its 8am-8pm branches are established in Kesavadasapuram (Trivandrum), Thrissur, Kaloor (Ernakulam) and Alwarpet

(Chennai). According to the recent records, the total business of SBT, recorded is Rs. 66644 Crores and its NRI business of Rs.8755 Crores. Apart from commercial banking, SBT has also shown its active participation in social development, by offering credit to the priority sectors and the special schemes announced by the Government. SBT has lent as much as 40% of net bank credit to the priority sectors. The Bank plays a developmental role, by meeting the need-based requirements of the small scale industry, agriculture and small business. The branches of SBT located in the rural and semi-urban areas of the country have been catering to the needs of farmers.

**Branches And ATM Services:** State Bank of Travancore marks its national presence in India, with a network of its 712 branches spread over 16 states of the country, out of which 580 branches are located in Kerala. The Bank boasts of providing easy access to money to its customers through its 389 ATMs throughout the country, with the largest ATM network in its home state. It is also a member of the largest ATM network in the country. In conjunction with the State Bank Group, SBT has introduced debit cards, enabled with Maestro and Cirrus.

**Products & Services of SBT**:

**Personal Banking:** Deposit schemes, Janapriya account, Personal finances, Public Provident Fund, Reverse Mortgage Loan and Special Housing Loan Product

**Business Banking:** SME financing, MSME Care Centre, Financing Trade & Services, Gold card for exporters and Debt restructuring for SME

**Social and Rural Banking:** Welfare Measures, Agriculture Finance, and Micro Finance

**Other Services:** NRI Services , Insurance/MF/Credit Card, Demat Services, Custodial Services, International Debit Card, Pilgrim Service Center, E-payment of Taxes and Duties over Internet, Online Booking of Railway tickets and Online Bill Payments, Multi-City cheques for Business Customers , Real Time Internet Banking Transaction and Transfer of Funds to Other Banks in India via NEFT & RTGS

**Head Office**: State Bank of Travancore,
Poojapura, Thiruvananthapuram - 695 012, Kerala, India.
**Phone:** 0484–2351919.**Website:** www.statebankoftravancore.com

## 2.21. IDBI Bank (Industrial Development Bank of India Limited)

The Industrial Development Bank of India Limited, now more popularly known as IDBI Bank, was established as a wholly-owned subsidiary of Reserve Bank of India. The foundation of the bank was laid down under an Act of Parliament, in July 1964. The main aim behind the setting up of IDBI was to provide credit and other facilities for the Indian industry, which was still in the initial stages of growth and development. In February 1976, the ownership of IDBI was transferred to Government of India. After the transfer of its ownership, IDBI became the main institution, through which the institutes engaged in financing, promoting and developing industry were to be coordinated. In January 1992, IDBI accessed domestic retail debt market for the first time, with innovative Deep Discount Bonds, and registered path-breaking success. The following year, it set up the IDBI Capital Market Services Ltd., as its wholly-owned subsidiary, to offer a broad range of financial services, including Bond Trading, Equity Broking, Client Asset Management and Depository Services. In September 1994, in response to RBI's policy of opening up domestic banking sector to private participation, IDBI set up IDBI Bank Ltd., in association with SIDBI. In July 1995, public issue of the bank was taken out, after which the Government's shareholding came down (though it still retains majority of the shareholding in the bank). In September 2003, IDBI took over Tata Home Finance Ltd, renamed 'IDBI Home finance Limited', thus diversifying its business domain and entering the arena of retail finance sector. The year 2005 witnessed the merger of IDBI Bank with the Industrial Development Bank of India Ltd. The new entity continued to its development finance role, while providing an array of wholesale and retail banking products (and does so till date). The following year, IDBI Bank acquired United Western Bank (which, at that time, had 230 branches spread over 47 districts, in 9 states). In the financial year of 2008, IDBI Bank had a net income of Rs 9415.9 crores and total assets of Rs 120,601 crores.

**The Present:** Today, IDBI Bank is counted amongst the leading public sector banks of India, apart from claiming the distinction of being the 4th largest bank, in overall ratings. It is presently regarded as the tenth largest development bank in the world, mainly in terms of reach. This is because of its wide network of 509 branches, 900 ATMs and 319 centers. Apart from being involved in banking services, IDBI has set up institutions like The National Stock Exchange of India (NSE), The National Securities Depository Services Ltd. (NSDL) and the Stock Holding Corporation of India (SHCIL).

**Products & Services:**

**Personal Banking:** Deposits, Loans, Payments - Tax Payments, Stamp Duty Payments, Easy Fill, Bill Payment, Card to Card Money Transfer, Pay Mate, Online Payments, Mutual Fund, Demat Account, IPO, Insurance - Family Care, Wealth insurance, Cards - Debit Card, Credit Card, Cash Card, Gift Card, International Debit-cum-ATM Card, World Currency Card, Institutional Banking, Lockers, India Post, NRI Services, Phone Banking, SMS Banking, Account Alerts and Internet Banking

**Corporate Banking:** Project Finance, Infrastructure Finance, Syndication, Underwriting & Advisory Services, Carbon Credits Business, Working Capital, Cash Management Services, Trade Finance, Tax Payments, Derivatives, Technology Upgradation Fund Scheme (TUFS), Film Financing Scheme, Direct Discounting Bills and Rehabilitation Finance

**Others:** SME Finance and Agri-business Products

**Head Office:**IDBI Tower,WTC Complex, Cuffe Parade, Colaba,Mumbai–400005,**Tel:** 91-22-22189111

**Fax:** 91-22-22181294 /5179 **Website:** www.idbi.com

# CHAPTER NO. 3
# DATA ANALYSIS OF SELECTED NATIONALIZED BANKS

## Research Methodology:

For this study purpose I have selected **19 Nationalized Banks** of India (SBI with Its branches and IDBI are excluded from the study)

**3.1. Time of Study:** as per data available last three to four years data is taken i.e. 2009-2010 to 2012-13

**3.2. Types of Data:** Mainly the study is depended on Secondary Data, Descriptive and Analytical Base

**3.3. Parameter for Data:** mainly following parameter is considered for the study

1) Deposits 2) Assets 3) Income 4) Expenses 5) Credit Deposit Ratio 6) Capital Return on assets and Adequacy Ratio 7) Net NPA to Net Advance Ratio

**3.4. Data Analysis:** For Data analysis Statistic tools are use here. To know the variation in year wise performance ANOVA test is used here for the study. And ratio analysis is also used where as applicable. Appropriate chart is also prepared to understand the performance of data. Analysis of variance (ANOVA) enables us to infer whether populations from which here more than two samples are having the same mean value. By testing significant of difference between more than two samples means. To test the equality of variances F test is used. By comparing the observed value with table value of F and analyzing the significant of difference (if any) the Hypothesis tested. Here in my study I want to know performance year's wise means only one factor is used hence one way ANOVA test is used.

### 3.5) Total Assets Performance of Selected Nationalized Banks for Last Four Years

**Table No.3.1 Total Assets Performance of Nationalized Banks**

| S. N. | NATIONALISED BANKS | Total Assets (Rs. in Crore) | | | | | |
|---|---|---|---|---|---|---|---|
| | | **2010** | **2011** | **2012** | **2013** | **Total** | **Avg.** |
| 1 | **Allahabad Bank** | 121699 | 1,51,286 | 1,82,935 | 2,04,373 | 6,60,293 | 1,65,073 |
| 2 | **Andhra Bank** | 90342 | 1,08,901 | 1,24,545 | 1,46,299 | 4,70,087 | 1,17,522 |
| 3 | **Bank of Baroda** | 278317 | 3,58,397 | 4,47,321 | 5,47,135 | 16,31,171 | 4,07,793 |
| 4 | **Bank of India** | 274966 | 3,51,173 | 3,84,535 | 4,52,603 | 14,63,277 | 3,65,819 |
| 5 | **Bank of Maharashtra** | 71056 | 76,442 | 91,137 | 1,16,953 | 3,55,588 | 88,897 |
| 6 | **Canara Bank** | 264741 | 3,35,945 | 3,74,160 | 4,12,343 | 13,87,189 | 3,46,797 |
| 7 | **Central Bank of India** | 182672 | 2,09,757 | 2,29,800 | 2,68,130 | 8,90,358 | 2,22,590 |
| 8 | **Corporation Bank** | 111667 | 1,43,509 | 1,63,560 | 1,93,442 | 6,12,179 | 1,53,045 |
| 9 | **Dena Bank** | 57587 | 70,838 | 87,388 | 1,13,440 | 3,29,253 | 82,313 |
| 10 | **Indian Bank** | 101389 | 1,21,718 | 1,41,419 | 1,62,823 | 5,27,349 | 1,31,837 |
| 11 | **Indian Overseas Bank** | 131092 | 1,78,784 | 2,19,637 | 2,44,656 | 7,74,169 | 1,93,542 |

| | | | | | | | |
|---|---|---|---|---|---|---|---|
| 12 | **Oriental Bank of Commerce** | 137431 | 1,61,343 | 1,77,535 | 2,00,697 | 6,77,006 | 1,69,252 |
| 13 | **Punjab & Sind Bank** | 56665 | 68,550 | 72,905 | 80,478 | 2,78,598 | 69,650 |
| 14 | **Punjab National Bank** | 296633 | 3,78,325 | 4,58,192 | 4,78,877 | 16,12,027 | 4,03,007 |
| 15 | **Syndicate Bank** | 139051 | 1,56,539 | 1,82,468 | 2,15,122 | 6,93,180 | 1,73,295 |
| 16 | **UCO Bank** | 137319 | 1,63,398 | 1,80,498 | 1,98,651 | 6,79,868 | 1,69,967 |
| 17 | **Union Bank of India** | 195162 | 2,35,984 | 2,62,211 | 3,11,861 | 10,05,219 | 2,51,305 |
| 18 | **United Bank of India** | 77005 | 90,041 | 1,02,010 | 1,14,615 | 3,83,671 | 95,918 |
| 19 | **Vijaya Bank** | 70207 | 82,013 | 95,764 | 1,10,982 | 3,58,966 | 89,742 |
| | **Total** | 2795001 | 3442945 | 3978023 | 4573480 | 14789449 | 3697362 |
| | **Avg.** | 147105 | 181208 | 209370 | 240709 | 778392 | 194598 |
| **% increase (with the base of 2010 year on Avg. total bases)** | | 100.00% | 123.18% | 142.32% | 163.63% | | |

(Various Bulletins of IBA)

The above shows Total Assets performance of 19 Nationalized Banks of the years 2010-11 to 20112-13. The amount is shows in Crores of rupees. The totals of 19 banks for four years are Rs. 14789449 with the average of Rs. 194598 the same things are represented through below Colum chart. The statically work for Hypothesis testing through ANOVA test is calculated below to understand its performance and consistency.

**Chart No. 3.1 Total Assets Performance of Nationalized Banks**

**Hypothesis Testing:** The researcher wanted to find out that if there is any significant difference regarding the total Assets Performance among all 19 Banks of Nationalized during 2009-10 to 2012-13.

**Null Hypothesis:** There would significant difference regarding the performance of Total Assets among all 19 Banks of Nationalized during 2009-10 to 2012-13.

**Alternative Hypothesis:** There would no significant difference regarding the performance of Total Assets among all 19 Banks of Nationalized during 2009-10 to 2012-13.

**Calculations:** N=76, K=4, T= 14789449, CF =2877997534285, $\sum_i\sum_j\sum X_{ij}2$ = 38880041059214, T.S.S = 1010043524929, $\sum T_i2$ =878696503837, S.S. Between (SSC): 878696503837,
S.S. Within (SSE): 131347021092

**Table No. 3.1.1 ANOVA of Total Assets of Nationalized Banks**

| Variation | d. f. | SS | MSS | F |
|---|---|---|---|---|
| **Between** | h-1 =19-1 =18 | 878696503837 | 48816472435 | 21.18 |
| **Within** | N-h=76-19=57 | 131347021092 | 2304333703 | |
| **Total** | N-1=76-1=75 | 1010043524929 | | |

**Fcal > Ftab = 21.18>1.70= Rejected**

The above ANOVA Table represents the calculated value of F-is 21.18 which is more than the table value of, 1.70, at 5% level of significant. So Null Hypothesis is rejected. It indicates that there is significant difference regarding the performance of Total Assets among all 19 Banks of Nationalized during 2009-10 to 2012-13.

### 3.6) Gross Non-Performing Assets (NPA) of Selected Nationalized Banks for Last Four Years

**Table No. 3.2 Gross Non-Performing Assets (NPA) of Nationalized Bank**

| S. N. | NATIONALISED BANKS | Gross NPA (Rs. in Crore) | | | | | |
|---|---|---|---|---|---|---|---|
| | | 2010 | 2011 | 2012 | 2013 | Total | Avg. |
| 1 | **Allahabad Bank** | 1,222 | 1,648 | 2,059 | 5,137 | 10,066 | 2,516 |

| | | | | | | | |
|---|---|---|---|---|---|---|---|
| 2 | **Andhra Bank** | 488 | 996 | 1,798 | 3,714 | 6,996 | 1,749 |
| 3 | **Bank of Baroda** | 2,401 | 3,153 | 4,465 | 7,983 | 18,001 | 4,500 |
| 4 | **Bank of India** | 4,883 | 4,812 | 5,894 | 8,765 | 24,353 | 6,088 |
| 5 | **Bank of Maharashtra** | 1,210 | 1,174 | 1,297 | 1,138 | 4,818 | 1,205 |
| 6 | **Canara Bank** | 2,590 | 3,137 | 4,032 | 6,260 | 16,019 | 4,005 |
| 7 | **Central Bank of India** | 2,458 | 2,394 | 7,273 | 8,456 | 20,582 | 5,145 |
| 8 | **Corporation Bank** | 651 | 790 | 1,274 | 2,048 | 4,764 | 1,191 |
| 9 | **Dena Bank** | 642 | 842 | 957 | 1,452 | 3,893 | 973 |
| 10 | **Indian Bank** | 510 | 740 | 1,851 | 3,565 | 6,667 | 1,667 |
| 11 | **Indian Overseas Bank** | 3,611 | 3,090 | 3,920 | 6,608 | 17,229 | 4,307 |
| 12 | **Oriental Bank of Commerce** | 1,469 | 1,921 | 3,580 | 4,184 | 11,154 | 2,788 |
| 13 | **Punjab & Sind Bank** | 206 | 424 | 763 | 1,537 | 2,931 | 733 |
| 14 | **Punjab National Bank** | 3,214 | 4,379 | 8,720 | 13,466 | 29,779 | 7,445 |
| 15 | **Syndicate Bank** | 2,007 | 2,599 | 3,183 | 2,979 | 10,767 | 2,692 |
| 16 | **UCO Bank** | 1,666 | 3,150 | 4,086 | 7,130 | 16,033 | 4,008 |

| | | | | | | | |
|---|---|---|---|---|---|---|---|
| 17 | **Union Bank of India** | 2,671 | 3,623 | 5,450 | 6,314 | 18,057 | 4,514 |
| 18 | **United Bank of India** | 1,372 | 1,356 | 2,176 | 2,964 | 7,868 | 1,967 |
| 19 | **Vijaya Bank** | 994 | 1,259 | 1,718 | 1,533 | 5,505 | 1,376 |
| | **Total** | 34,265 | 41,486 | 64,497 | 95,233 | 2,35,481 | 58,870 |
| | **Avg.** | 1,803 | 2,183 | 3,395 | 5,012 | 12,394 | 3,098 |
| **% increase (with the base of 2010 year on Avg. total bases )** | | 100.00% | 121.07% | 188.29% | 277.98% | | |

(Various Bulletins of IBA)

The above shows Gross Non Performing Assets (NPA) performance of 19 Nationalized Banks of the years 2010-11 to 20112-13. The amount is shows in Crores of rupees. The totals of 19 banks for four years are Rs. 235481 with the average of Rs. 3098 the same things are represented through below Colum chart. The statically work for Hypothesis testing through ANOVA test is calculated below to understand its performance and consistency.

**Chart No. 3.2 Gross Non Performing Assets (NPA) of Nationalized Bank**

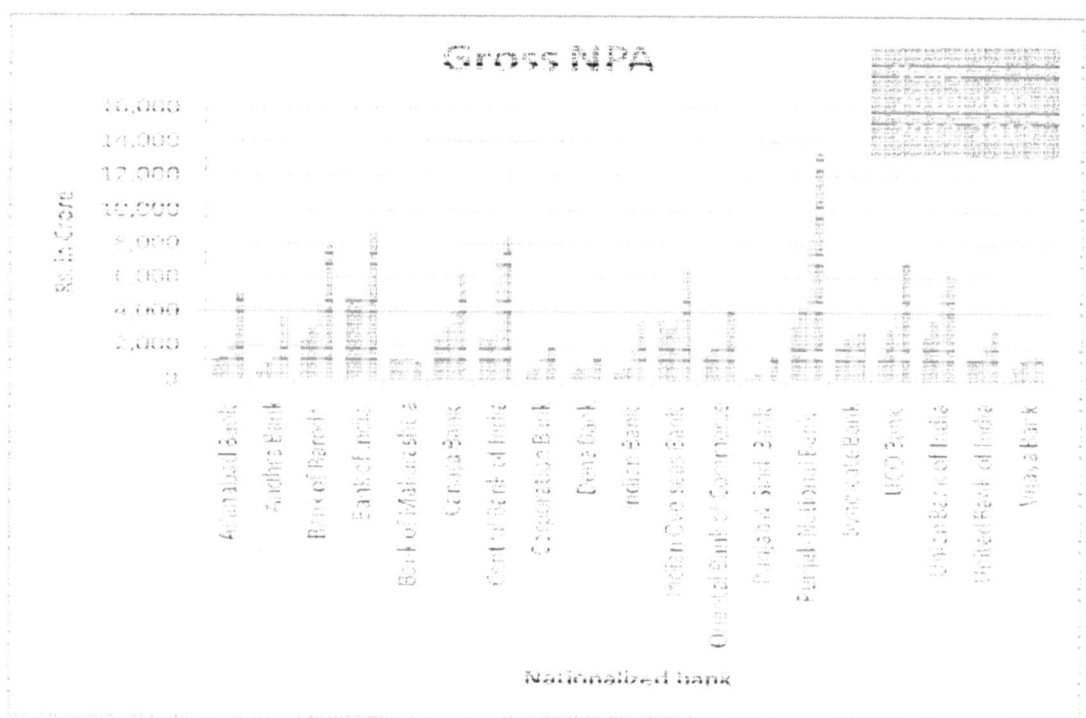


**Hypothesis Testing:** The researcher wanted to find out that if there is any significant difference regarding Gross NPA of Performance among all 19 Banks of Nationalized during 2009-10 to 2012-13.

**Null Hypothesis:** There would no significant difference regarding the performance of Gross NPA among all 19 Banks of Nationalized during 2009-10 to 2012-13.

**Alternative Hypothesis:** There would significant difference regarding the performance of Gross NPA among all 19 Banks of Nationalized during 2009-10 to 2012-13.

**Calculations:** N=76, K=4, T= 235418, CF =729624676, $\sum_i\sum_j\sum X_{ij}2$=31185758706,T.S.S = 456134030, $\sum T_i 2$ =3960993860, S.S. Between (SSC): 260623789, S.S. Within(SSE) : 195510241

**Table No. 3.2.1 ANOVA of Gross NPA of Nationalized Banks**

| Variation | d. f. | SS | MSS | F |
|---|---|---|---|---|
| **Between** | h-1=19-1 =18 | 260623789 | 14479099 | 4.221 |
| **Within** | N-h=76-19 =57 | 95510241 | 3430004.226 | |
| **Total** | N-1=76-1 =75 | 456134030 | | |

**Fcal > Ftab = 4.221>1.70= Rejected**

The above ANOVA Table represents the calculated value of F-is 4.221which is more than the table value of,1.70, at 5% level of significance. So Null Hypothesis is rejected. It indicates that there is significant difference regarding the performance of Gross NPA among all 19 Banks of Nationalized during 2009-10 to 2012-13.

## 3.7) Net Non Performing Assets (NPA) of Selected Nationalized Bank for last four Years

**Table No.3.3 Net Non Performing Assets (NPA) of Nationalized Bank**

| S. N. | NATIONALISED BANKS | Net NPA (Rs. in Crore) | | | | | |
|---|---|---|---|---|---|---|---|
| | | **2010** | **2011** | **2012** | **2013** | **Total** | **Avg.** |
| 1 | **Allahabad Bank** | 470 | 736 | 1,092 | 4,127 | 6,425 | 1,606 |
| 2 | **Andhra Bank** | 96 | 274 | 756 | 2,409 | 3,534 | 884 |
| 3 | **Bank of Baroda** | 602 | 791 | 1,544 | 4,192 | 7,129 | 1,782 |
| 4 | **Bank of India** | 2,207 | 1,945 | 3,656 | 5,947 | 13,756 | 3,439 |
| 5 | **Bank of Maharashtra** | 662 | 619 | 470 | 393 | 2,143 | 536 |
| 6 | **Canara Bank** | 1,800 | 2,330 | 3,386 | 5,278 | 12,794 | 3,199 |

| | | | | | | | |
|---|---|---|---|---|---|---|---|
| 7 | **Central Bank of India** | 727 | 847 | 4,557 | 4,988 | 11,118 | 2,780 |
| 8 | **Corporation Bank** | 197 | 398 | 869 | 1,411 | 2,875 | 719 |
| 9 | **Dena Bank** | 428 | 549 | 572 | 917 | 2,465 | 616 |
| 10 | **Indian Bank** | 145 | 397 | 1,197 | 2,384 | 4,123 | 1,031 |
| 11 | **Indian Overseas Bank** | 1,995 | 1,328 | 1,907 | 4,027 | 9,258 | 2,315 |
| 12 | **Oriental Bank of Commerce** | 724 | 938 | 2,459 | 2,903 | 7,024 | 1,756 |
| 13 | **Punjab & Sind Bank** | 117 | 238 | 548 | 1,110 | 2,013 | 503 |
| 14 | **Punjab National Bank** | 982 | 2,039 | 4,454 | 7,237 | 14,711 | 3,678 |
| 15 | **Syndicate Bank** | 963 | 1,031 | 1,185 | 1,125 | 4,304 | 1,076 |
| 16 | **UCO Bank** | 966 | 1,825 | 2,264 | 4,069 | 9,124 | 2,281 |
| 17 | **Union Bank of India** | 965 | 1,803 | 3,025 | 3,353 | 9,147 | 2,287 |
| 18 | **United Bank of India** | 779 | 757 | 1,076 | 1,970 | 4,582 | 1,145 |
| 19 | **Vijaya Bank** | 582 | 741 | 998 | 910 | 3,231 | 808 |
| | **Total** | 15,407 | 19,586 | 36,014 | 58,750 | 1,29,758 | 32,439 |
| | **Avg.** | 811 | 1,031 | 1,895 | 3,092 | 6,829 | 1,707 |

| **% increase (with the base of 2010 year on Avg. total bases )** | 100% | 127.12% | 233.66% | 381.25% | | |
|---|---|---|---|---|---|---|

(Various Bulletins of IBA)

The above shows Net Non Performing Assets (NPA) performance of 19 Nationalized Banks of the years 2010-11 to 20112-13. The amount is shows in Crores of rupees. The totals of 19 banks for four years are Rs. 129758 with the average of Rs. 1707 the same things are represented through below Colum chart. The statically work for Hypothesis testing through ANOVA test is calculated below to understand its performance and consistency.

**Chart No. 3.3 Net Non Performing Assets (NPA) of Nationalized Bank**

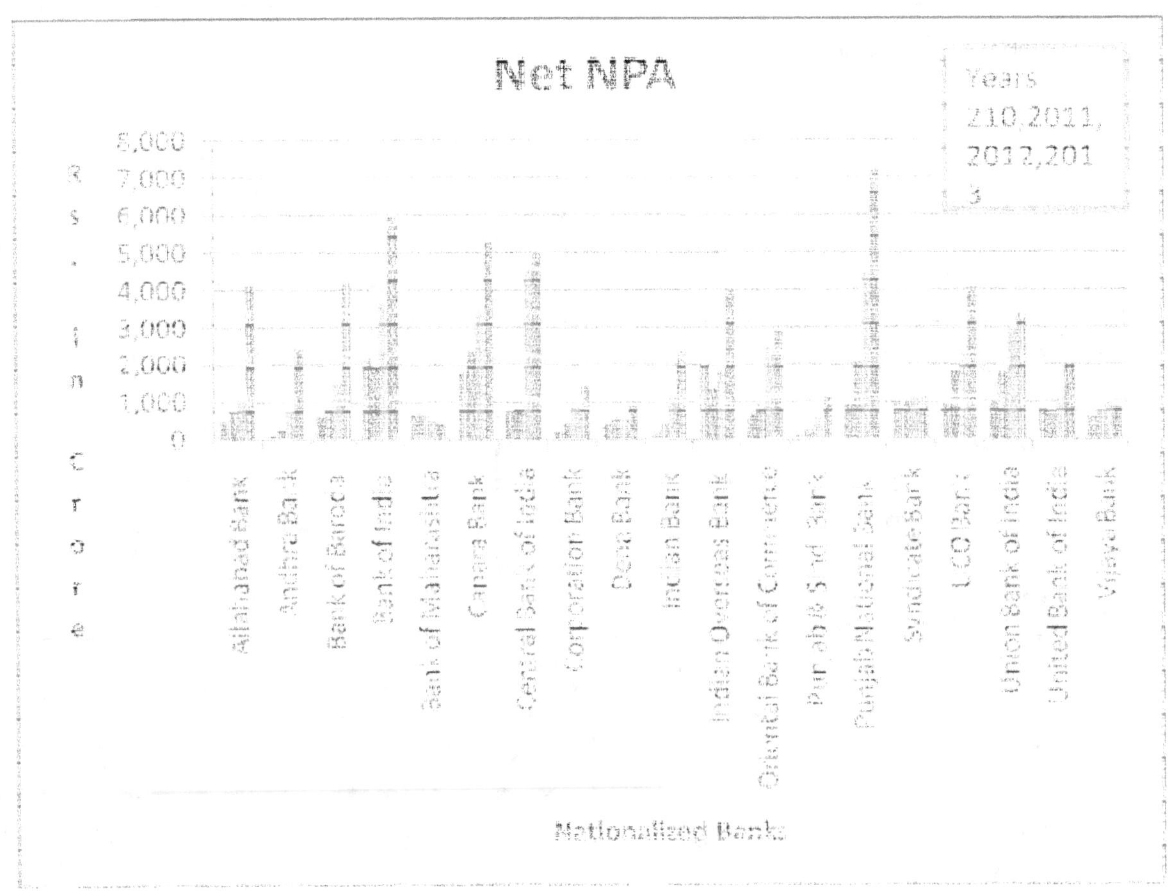

**Hypothesis Testing:** The researcher wanted to find out that if there is any significant difference regarding Gross NPA of Performance among all 19 Banks of Nationalized during 2009-10 to 2012-13.

**Null Hypothesis:** There would no significant difference regarding the performance of Net NPA among all 19 Banks of Nationalized during 2009-10 to 2012-13.

**Alternative Hypothesis:** There would significant difference regarding the performance of Net NPA among all 19 Banks of Nationalized during 2009-10 to 2012-13.

**Calculations:** N=76, K=4, T=129758, CF =221541156.9, $\sum_i \sum_j \sum X_{ij}2$ = 396277573, T.S.S = 174736416, $\sum T_i 2$ =1189465018, S.S. Between (SSC): 75825097.72 , S.S. Within(SSE) : 98911319

**Table No. 3.3.1 ANOVA of Net NPA of Nationalized Banks**

| Variation | d. f. | SS | MSS | |
|---|---|---|---|---|
| **Between** | h-1 = 19-1 =18 | 75825097.72 | 4212505 | 2.42 |
| **Within** | N-h=76-19=57 | 98911319 | 1735286 | |
| **Total** | N-1=76-1=75 | 74736416 | | |

**Fcal > Ftab = 2.42>1.70= Rejected**

The above one way ANOVA Table represents the calculated value of F-is 2.42 which is more than the table value of, 1.70, at 5% level of significance. So Null Hypothesis is rejected. It indicates that there is significant difference regarding the performance of Net NPA among all 19 Banks of Nationalized during 2009-10 to 2012-13.

## 3.8) Interest Income of Selected Nationalized Bank for last four Years

## Table No.3.4 Interest Income of Nationalized Bank

| S.N. | NATIONALISED BANKS | Interest Income (Rs. in Crore) | | | | | |
|---|---|---|---|---|---|---|---|
| | | 2010 | 2011 | 2012 | 2013 | Total | Avg. |
| 1 | Allahabad Bank | 8369 | 11,015 | 15,523 | 17,436 | 52,343 | 13,086 |
| 2 | Andhra Bank | 6373 | 8,291 | 11,339 | 12,910 | 38,913 | 9,728 |
| 3 | Bank of Baroda | 16698 | 21,886 | 29,674 | 35,197 | 1,03,455 | 25,864 |
| 4 | Bank of India | 17878 | 21,752 | 28,481 | 31,909 | 1,00,019 | 25,005 |
| 5 | Bank of Maharashtra | 4736 | 5,563 | 7,214 | 9,613 | 27,126 | 6,782 |
| 6 | Canara Bank | 18752 | 22,940 | 30,851 | 34,078 | 1,06,621 | 26,655 |
| 7 | Central Bank of India | 12064 | 15,221 | 19,149 | 21,861 | 68,295 | 17,074 |
| 8 | Corporation Bank | 6988 | 9,135 | 13,018 | 15,334 | 44,475 | 11,119 |
| 9 | Dena Bank | 4010 | 5,034 | 6,794 | 8,899 | 24,737 | 6,184 |
| 10 | Indian Bank | 7714 | 9,361 | 12,231 | 13,893 | 43,199 | 10,800 |
| 11 | Indian Overseas Bank | 10246 | 12,101 | 17,897 | 20,677 | 60,921 | 15,230 |
| 12 | Oriental Bank of Commerce | 10257 | 12,088 | 15,815 | 17,705 | 55,865 | 13,966 |
| 13 | Punjab & Sind Bank | 3934 | 4,933 | 6,475 | 7,340 | 22,681 | 5,670 |

| | | | | | | | |
|---|---|---|---|---|---|---|---|
| 14 | **Punjab National Bank** | 21422 | 26,986 | 36,476 | 41,893 | 1,26,778 | 31,695 |
| 15 | **Syndicate Bank** | 10047 | 11,451 | 15,268 | 17,121 | 53,887 | 13,472 |
| 16 | **UCO Bank** | 9526 | 11,371 | 14,632 | 16,752 | 52,281 | 13,070 |
| 17 | **Union Bank of India** | 13303 | 16,453 | 21,028 | 25,125 | 75,908 | 18,977 |
| 18 | **United Bank of India** | 5249 | 6,341 | 7,961 | 9,251 | 28,803 | 7,201 |
| 19 | **Vijaya Bank** | 5201 | 5,844 | 7,988 | 9,052 | 28,085 | 7,021 |
| | **Total** | **192768** | **237765** | **317815** | **366044** | **1114392** | **278598** |
| | **Avg.** | **10146** | **12514** | **16727** | **19265** | **58652** | **14663** |
| **% increase (with the base of 2010 year on Avg. total Bases )** | | **100.00%** | **123.33%** | **164.86%** | **189.87%** | | |

(Various Bulletins of IBA)

The above Table shows Interest Income performance of 19 Nationalized Banks of the years 2010-11 to 20112-13. The amount is shows in Crores of rupees. The totals of 19 banks for four years are Rs. 1114392 with the average of Rs. 14663 the same things are represented through below Colum chart. The statically work for Hypothesis testing through ANOVA test is calculated below to understand its performance and consistency.

## Chart No.3.4 Interest Income of Nationalized Bank

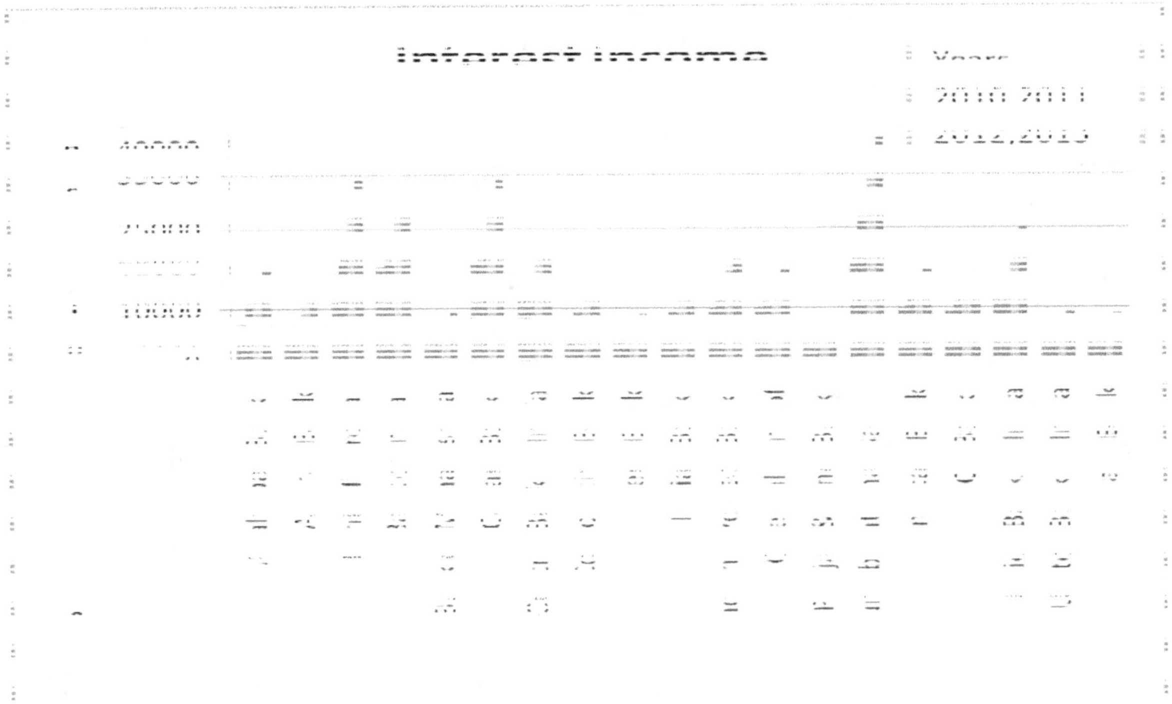

**Hypothesis Testing:** The researcher wanted to find out that if there is any significant difference regarding Interest Income of Performance among all 19 Banks of Nationalized during 2009-10 to 2012-13.

**Null Hypothesis:** There would no significant difference regarding the performance of Interest Income among all 19 Banks of Nationalized during 2009-10 to 2012-13.

**Alternative Hypothesis:** There would significant difference regarding the performance of Interest Income among all 19 Banks of Nationalized during 2009-10 to 2012-13.

**Calculations:** N=76, K=4, T=1114392, CF =16340387519, $\sum_i\sum_j\sum X_{ij}2$ = 21884514777, T.S.S = 5544127258, $\sum T_i2$ =82621730480, S.S. Between (SSC): 4315045101

S.S. Within (SSE): 1229082157

**Table No. 3.4.1 ANOVA of Interest Income of Nationalized Banks**

| Variation | d. f. | SS | MSS | F |
|---|---|---|---|---|
| Between | h-1=19-1 =18 | 4315045101 | 239724728 | 11.11 |
| Within | N-h=76-19=57 | 1229082157 | 21562845 | |
| Total | N-1=76-1=75 | 5544127258 | | |

**Fcal > Ftab = 11.11>1.70= Rejected**

The above ANOVA Table represents the calculated value of F-is 11.11 which is more than the table value of, 1.70, at 5% level of significance. So Null Hypothesis is rejected. It indicates that there is significant difference regarding the performance of Interest Income among all 19 Banks of Nationalized during 2009-10 to 2012-13.

### 3.9) Other Income of Selected Nationalized Bank for last four Years

**Table No. 3.5 Other Income of Nationalized Bank**

| S. N. | NATIONALISED BANKS | Other Income (Rs. in Crore) | | | | | |
|---|---|---|---|---|---|---|---|
| | | 2010 | 2011 | 2012 | 2013 | Total | Avg. |
| 1 | Allahabad Bank | 1,516 | 1,370 | 1,299 | 1,477 | 5,662 | 1,415 |
| 2 | Andhra Bank | 965 | 897 | 860 | 1,047 | 3,769 | 942 |
| 3 | Bank of Baroda | 2,806 | 2,809 | 3,422 | 3,631 | 12,669 | 3,167 |
| 4 | Bank of India | 2,617 | 2,642 | 3,321 | 3,766 | 12,346 | 3,086 |
| 5 | Bank of Maharashtra | 591 | 531 | 641 | 912 | 2,675 | 669 |
| 6 | Canara Bank | 2,858 | 2,811 | 2,928 | 3,153 | 11,750 | 2,937 |
| 7 | Central Bank of | 1,735 | 1,265 | 1,395 | 1,667 | 6,063 | 1,516 |

| | | | | | | | |
|---|---|---|---|---|---|---|---|
| | India | | | | | | |
| 8 | Corporation Bank | 1,493 | 1,256 | 1,493 | 1,608 | 5,850 | 1,462 |
| 9 | Dena Bank | 589 | 534 | 582 | 655 | 2,360 | 590 |
| 10 | Indian Bank | 1,316 | 1,182 | 1,180 | 1,287 | 4,965 | 1,241 |
| 11 | Indian Overseas Bank | 1,143 | 1,225 | 1,681 | 1,973 | 6,022 | 1,506 |
| 12 | Oriental Bank of Commerce | 1,200 | 960 | 1,240 | 1,655 | 5,055 | 1,264 |
| 13 | Punjab & Sind Bank | 412 | 437 | 417 | 417 | 1,684 | 421 |
| 14 | Punjab National Bank | 3,610 | 3,613 | 4,203 | 4,216 | 15,641 | 3,910 |
| 15 | Syndicate Bank | 1,167 | 915 | 1,076 | 1,174 | 4,333 | 1,083 |
| 16 | UCO Bank | 966 | 925 | 966 | 952 | 3,809 | 952 |
| 17 | Union Bank of India | 1,975 | 2,039 | 2,448 | 2,552 | 9,014 | 2,253 |
| 18 | United Bank of India | 559 | 637 | 733 | 1,067 | 2,995 | 749 |
| 19 | Vijaya Bank | 679 | 533 | 528 | 607 | 2,348 | 587 |
| | **Total** | **28,198** | **26,582** | **30,412** | **33,816** | **1,19,008** | **29,752** |
| | **Avg.** | **1,484** | **1,399** | **1,601** | **1,780** | **6,264** | **1,566** |

| % increase (with the base of 2010 year on Avg. total Bases ) | 100.00% | 94.27% | 107.00% | 119.94% | | |
|---|---|---|---|---|---|---|

(Various Bulletins of IBA)

The above Table shows Other Income performance of 19 Nationalized Banks of the years 2010-11 to 20112-13. The amount is shows in Crores of rupees. The totals of 19 banks for four years are Rs. 119008 with the average of Rs.1566 the same things are represented through below Colum chart. The statically work for Hypothesis testing through ANOVA test is calculated below to understand its performance and consistency.

**Chart No.3.5 Other Income of Nationalized Bank**

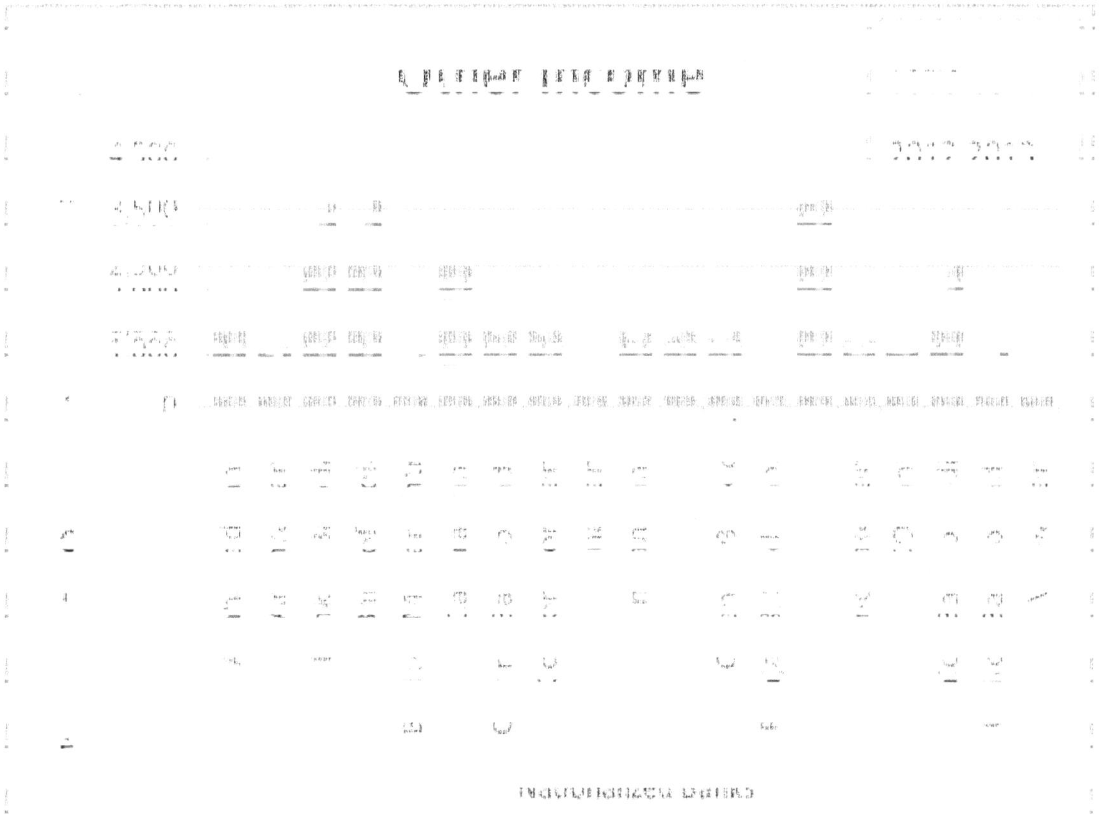

**Hypothesis Testing:** The researcher wanted to find out that if there is any significant difference regarding Other Income of Performance among all 19 Banks of Nationalized during 2009-10 to 2012-13.

**Null Hypothesis:** There would no significant difference regarding the performance of Other Income among all 19 Banks of Nationalized during 2009-10 to 2012-13.

**Alternative Hypothesis:** There would significant difference regarding the performance of Other Income among all 19 Banks of Nationalized during 2009-10 to 2012-13.

**Calculations:** N=76, K=4, T=119008, CF =1863538634, $\sum_i \sum_j \sum X_{ij} 2$ = 264416538, T.S.S = 78062674, $\sum T_i 2$ =1643899649, S.S. Between (SSC): 74621049, S.S. Within (SSE): 3441625

**Table No. 3.5.1 ANOVA of Other Income of Nationalized Banks**

| Variation | d. f. | SS | MSS | F |
|---|---|---|---|---|
| **Between** | h-1=19-1 =18 | 74621049 | 4145614 | 68.65 |
| **Within** | N-h=76-19=57 | 3441625 | 60379.39 | |
| **Total** | N-1=76-1=75 | 78062674 | | |

**Fcal > Ftab = 68.65>1.70= Rejected**

The above ANOVA Table represents the calculated value of F-is 68.65 which is more than the table value of, 1.70, at 5% level of significance. So Null Hypothesis is rejected. It indicates that there is significant difference regarding the performance of Other Income among all 19 Banks of Nationalized during 2009-10 to 2012-13.

## 3.10)Total Income of Selected Nationalized Bank for last four Years

### Table No. 3.6.Total Income of Nationalized Bank.

| S. N. | NATIONALISED BANKS | Total Income (Rs. in Crore) | | | | | |
|---|---|---|---|---|---|---|---|
| | | 2010 | 2011 | 2012 | 2013 | Total | Avg. |
| 1 | Allahabad Bank | 9,885 | 12,385 | 16,822 | 18,913 | 58,005 | 14,501 |
| 2 | Andhra Bank | 7,337 | 9,188 | 12,199 | 13,957 | 42,681 | 10,670 |
| 3 | Bank of Baroda | 19,505 | 24,695 | 33,096 | 38,827 | 1,16,123 | 29,031 |
| 4 | Bank of India | 20,495 | 24,393 | 31,802 | 35,675 | 1,12,365 | 28,091 |
| 5 | Bank of Maharashtra | 5,327 | 6,094 | 7,855 | 10,525 | 29,801 | 7,450 |
| 6 | Canara Bank | 21,610 | 25,752 | 33,778 | 37,231 | 1,18,371 | 29,593 |
| 7 | Central Bank of India | 13,800 | 16,486 | 20,545 | 23,528 | 74,358 | 18,589 |
| 8 | Corporation Bank | 8,481 | 10,391 | 14,510 | 16,942 | 50,325 | 12,581 |
| 9 | Dena Bank | 4,599 | 5,567 | 7,376 | 9,555 | 27,098 | 6,774 |
| 10 | Indian Bank | 9,031 | 10,543 | 13,411 | 15,179 | 48,164 | 12,041 |
| 11 | Indian Overseas Bank | 11,389 | 13,327 | 19,578 | 22,650 | 66,943 | 16,736 |
| 12 | Oriental Bank of Commerce | 11,457 | 13,048 | 17,055 | 19,359 | 60,920 | 15,230 |

| | | | | | | | |
|---|---|---|---|---|---|---|---|
| 13 | **Punjab & Sind Bank** | 4,346 | 5,370 | 6,892 | 7,757 | 24,365 | 6,091 |
| 14 | **Punjab National Bank** | 25,032 | 30,599 | 40,679 | 46,109 | 1,42,419 | 35,605 |
| 15 | **Syndicate Bank** | 11,215 | 12,366 | 16,344 | 18,295 | 58,220 | 14,555 |
| 16 | **UCO Bank** | 10,492 | 12,296 | 15,598 | 17,704 | 56,090 | 14,023 |
| 17 | **Union Bank of India** | 15,277 | 18,491 | 23,477 | 27,677 | 84,922 | 21,231 |
| 18 | **United Bank of India** | 5,808 | 6,979 | 8,694 | 10,318 | 31,798 | 7,950 |
| 19 | **Vijaya Bank** | 5,880 | 6,377 | 8,516 | 9,659 | 30,432 | 7,608 |
| | **Total** | **2,20,965** | **2,64,347** | **3,48,227** | **3,99,861** | **12,33,400** | **3,08,350** |
| | **Avg.** | **11,630** | **13,913** | **18,328** | **21,045** | **64,916** | **16,229** |
| **% increase (with the base of 2010 year on Avg. total bases)** | | **100.00%** | **119.63%** | **157.59%** | **180.95%** | | |

(Various Bulletins of IBA)

The above Table shows Total Income performance of 19 Nationalized Banks of the years 2010-11 to 20112-13. The amount is shows in Crores of rupees. The totals of 19 banks for four years are Rs. 1233400 with the average of Rs.16229 the same things are represented through below Colum chart. The statically work for Hypothesis testing through ANOVA test is calculated below to understand its performance and consistency.

**Chart No.3.6 Total Income of Nationalized Bank**

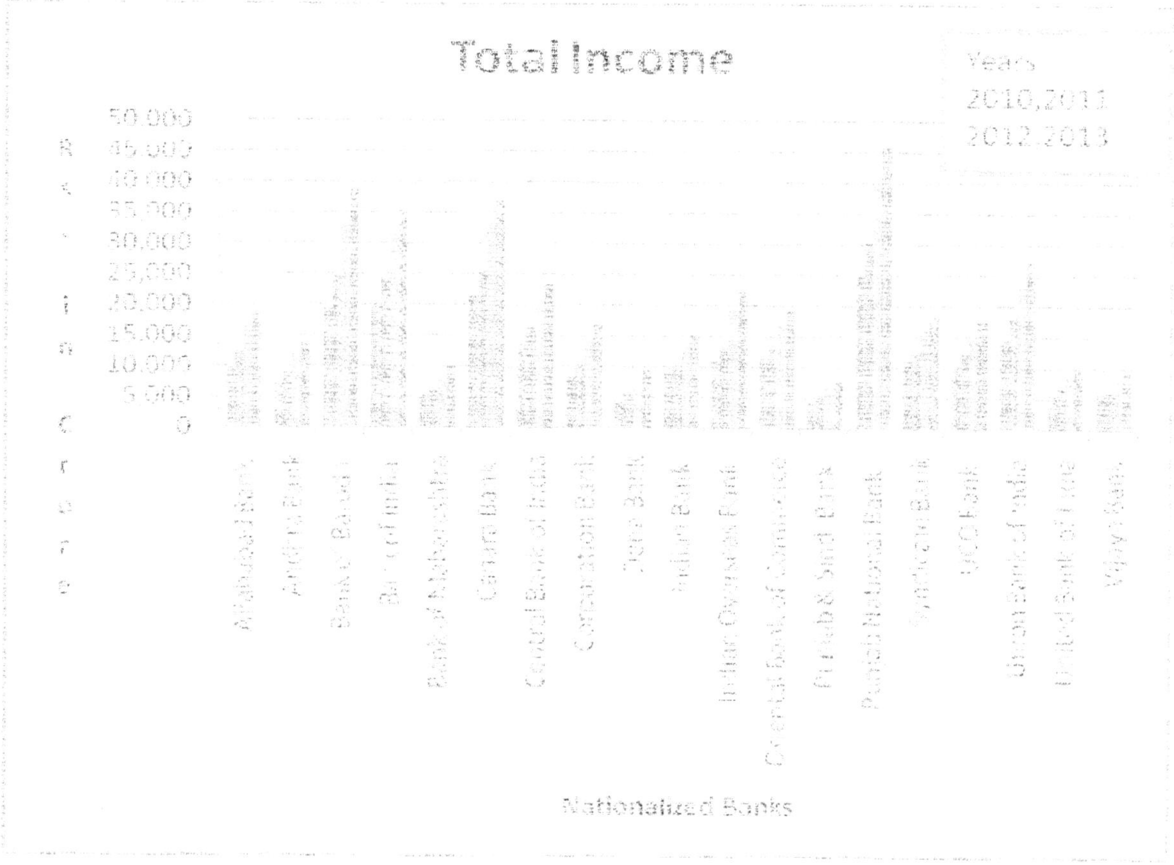

**Hypothesis Testing:** The researcher wanted to find out that if there is any significant difference regarding Total Income of Performance among all 19 Banks of Nationalized during 2009-10 to 2012-13.

**Null Hypothesis:** There would no significant difference regarding the performance of Total Income among all 19 Banks of Nationalized during 2009-10 to 2012-13.

**Alternative Hypothesis:** There would significant difference regarding the performance of Total Income among all 19 Banks of Nationalized during 2009-10 to 2012-13.

**Calculations:** N=76, K=4, T=1233400, CF =20016781120, $\sum_i\sum_j\sum X_{ij}2$= 26843856115, T.S.S = 6827074995, $\sum T_i2$ =102066348475, S.S. Between (SSC): 5499805999

S.S. Within (SSE): 1327268996

**Table No. 3.6.1 ANOVA of Total Income of Nationalized Banks**

| Variation | d. f. | SS | MSS | F |
|---|---|---|---|---|
| **Between** | h-1 = 19-1 =18 | 5499805999 | 305544778 | 13.12 |
| **Within** | N-h=76-19=57 | 1327268996 | 23285421 | |
| **Total** | N-1=76-1=75 | 6827074995 | | |

**Fcal > Ftab = 13.12>1.70= Rejected**

The above ANOVA Table represents the calculated value of F-is 13.12 which is more than the table value of, 1.70, at 5% level of significance. So Null Hypothesis is rejected. It indicates that there is significant difference regarding the performance of Total Income among all 19 Banks of Nationalized during 2009-10 to 2012-13.

## 3.11) Interest Expended of Selected Nationalized Bank for last four Years

**Table No.3.7 Interest Expended of Nationalized Bank**

| S. N. | NATIONALISED BANKS | Interest Expended (Rs. in Crore) | | | | | |
|---|---|---|---|---|---|---|---|
| | | 2010 | 2011 | 2012 | 2013 | TOTAL | AVG. |
| 1 | Allahabad Bank | 5719 | 6,992 | 10,361 | 12,569 | 35,641 | 8,910 |
| 2 | Andhra Bank | 4178 | 5,070 | 7,579 | 9,153 | 25,981 | 6,495 |
| 3 | Bank of Baroda | 10759 | 13,084 | 19,357 | 23,881 | 67,081 | 16,770 |
| 4 | Bank of India | 12122 | 13,941 | 20,167 | 22,885 | 69,115 | 17,279 |

| | | | | | | | |
|---|---|---|---|---|---|---|---|
| 5 | **Bank of Maharashtra** | 3439 | 3,595 | 4,697 | 6,580 | 18,311 | 4,578 |
| 6 | **Canara Bank** | 13071 | 15,241 | 23,161 | 26,199 | 77,672 | 19,418 |
| 7 | **Central Bank of India** | 9519 | 9,895 | 13,981 | 16,123 | 49,518 | 12,380 |
| 8 | **Corporation Bank** | 5084 | 6,196 | 9,871 | 11,908 | 33,059 | 8,265 |
| 9 | **Dena Bank** | 2910 | 3,270 | 4,693 | 6,516 | 17,390 | 4,347 |
| 10 | **Indian Bank** | 4553 | 5,325 | 7,813 | 9,368 | 27,060 | 6,765 |
| 11 | **Indian Overseas Bank** | 7078 | 7,893 | 12,881 | 15,425 | 43,277 | 10,819 |
| 12 | **Oriental Bank of Commerce** | 7350 | 7,910 | 11,599 | 13,004 | 39,863 | 9,966 |
| 13 | **Punjab & Sind Bank** | 2750 | 3,372 | 4,973 | 5,699 | 16,795 | 4,199 |
| 14 | **Punjab National Bank** | 12944 | 15,179 | 23,062 | 27,037 | 78,222 | 19,555 |
| 15 | **Syndicate Bank** | 7307 | 7,068 | 10,183 | 11,667 | 36,225 | 9,056 |
| 16 | **UCO Bank** | 7202 | 7,526 | 10,730 | 12,170 | 37,629 | 9,407 |
| 17 | **Union Bank of India** | 9110 | 10,236 | 14,235 | 17,582 | 51,164 | 12,791 |
| 18 | **United Bank of** | 3858 | 4,172 | 5,482 | 6,764 | 20,276 | 5,069 |

| | India | | | | | | |
|---|---|---|---|---|---|---|---|
| 19 | Vijaya Bank | 3752 | 3,897 | 6,085 | 7,174 | 20,907 | 5,227 |
| | **Total** | **132706** | **149863** | **220911** | **261704** | **765185** | **1,91,296** |
| | **Avg.** | **6985** | **7888** | **11627** | **13774** | **40,273** | **10068** |
| **% increase (with the base of 2010 year on Avg. total Bases )** | | **100.00%** | **112.92%** | **166.45%** | **197.19%** | | |

(Various Bulletins of IBA)

The above Table shows Interest Expended performance of 19 Nationalized Banks of the years 2010-11 to 20112-13. The amount is shows in Crores of rupees. The totals of 19 banks for four years are Rs.765185 with the average of Rs.10068 the same things are represented through below Colum chart. The statically work for Hypothesis testing through ANOVA test is calculated below to understand its performance and consistency.

## Chart No.3.7 Interest Expended of Nationalized Bank

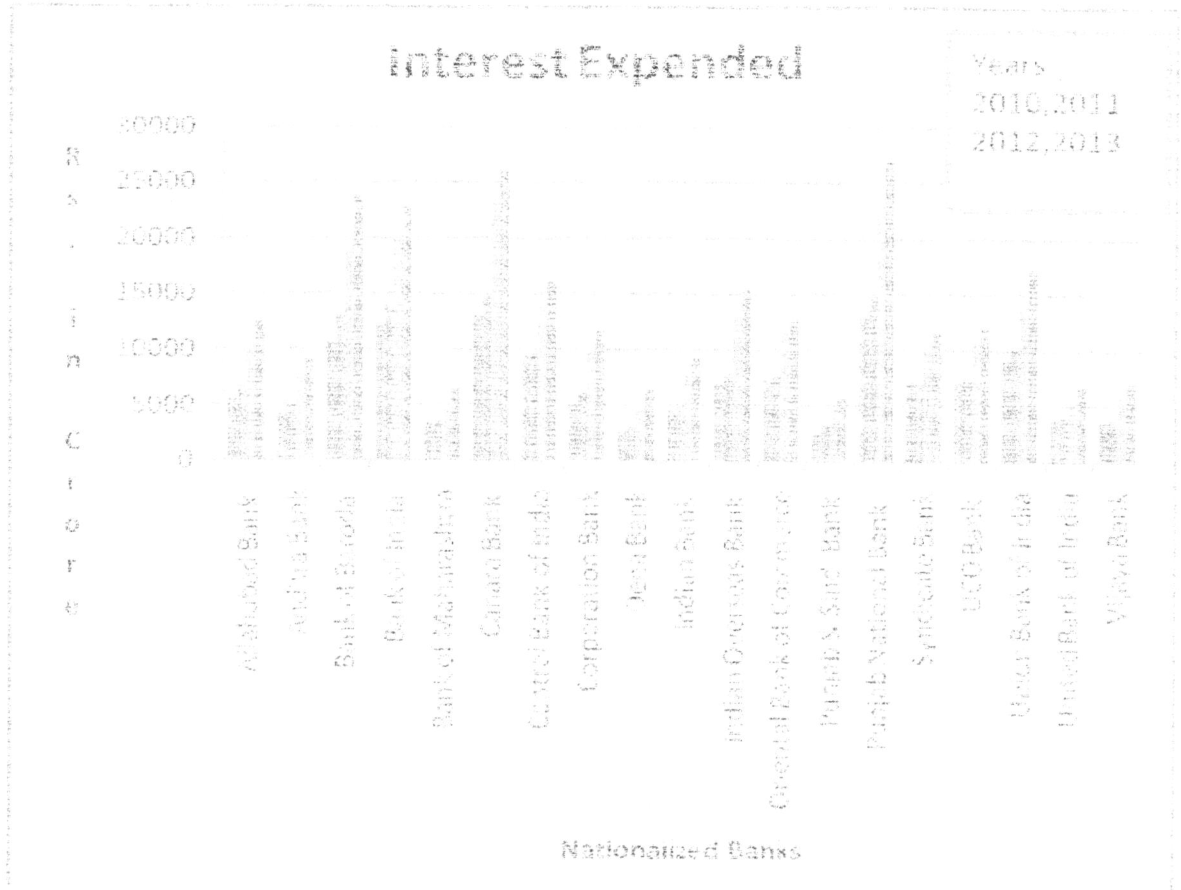


**Hypothesis Testing:** The researcher wanted to find out that if there is any significant difference regarding Interest Expended of Performance among all 19 Banks of Nationalized during 2009-10 to 2012-13.

**Null Hypothesis:** There would no significant difference regarding the performance of Interest Expended among all 19 Banks of Nationalized during 2009-10 to 2012-13.

**Alternative Hypothesis:** There would significant difference regarding the performance of Interest Expended among all 19 Banks of Nationalized during 2009-10 to 2012-13.

**Calculations:** N=76, K=4, T=765185, CF =7704049437, $\sum_i \sum_j \sum X_{ij}2$ = 10293758848, T.S.S = 2589709411, $\sum T_i 2$ =38226661213, S.S. Between (SSC): 1852615871

S.S. Within (SSE): 737093540

**Table No. 3.7.1 ANOVA of Interest Expended of Nationalized Banks**

| Variation | d. f. | SS | MSS | F |
|---|---|---|---|---|
| **Between** | h-1=19-1 =18 | 1852615871 | 102923104 | 7.95 |
| **Within** | N-h=76-19=57 | 737093540 | 12931466 | |
| **Total** | N-1=76-1=75 | 2589709411 | | |

**Fcal > Ftab = 7.95>1.70= Rejected**

The above ANOVA Table represents the calculated value of F-is 7.95 which is more than the table value of, 1.70, at 5% level of significance. So Null Hypothesis is rejected. It indicates that there is significant difference regarding the performance of Interest Expended among all 19 Banks of Nationalized during 2009-10 to 2012-13.

## 3.12) Operating Expenses of Selected Nationalized Bank for last four Years

**Table No. 3.8. Operating Expenses of Nationalized Bank**

| S. N. | NATIONALISED BANKS | Operating Expenses(Rs. in Crore) | | | | | |
|---|---|---|---|---|---|---|---|
| | | 2010 | 2011 | 2012 | 2013 | Total | Avg. |
| 1 | Allahabad Bank | 1,618 | 2,338 | 2,691 | 2,958 | 9,606 | 2,401 |
| 2 | Andhra Bank | 1,350 | 1,705 | 1,804 | 2,037 | 6,896 | 1,724 |
| 3 | Bank of Baroda | 3,811 | 4,630 | 5,109 | 5,872 | 19,421 | 4,855 |
| 4 | Bank of India | 3,668 | 5,068 | 4,941 | 5,332 | 19,008 | 4,752 |

| | | | | | | | |
|---|---|---|---|---|---|---|---|
| 5 | **Bank of Maharashtra** | 1,073 | 1,644 | 1,643 | 1,797 | 6,156 | 1,539 |
| 6 | **Canara Bank** | 3,478 | 4,419 | 4,674 | 5,142 | 17,713 | 4,428 |
| 7 | **Central Bank of India** | 2,222 | 3,999 | 3,749 | 4,232 | 14,202 | 3,551 |
| 8 | **Corporation Bank** | 1,260 | 1,642 | 1,784 | 1,997 | 6,682 | 1,670 |
| 9 | **Dena Bank** | 848 | 1,073 | 1,155 | 1,300 | 4,376 | 1,094 |
| 10 | **Indian Bank** | 1,730 | 1,926 | 2,187 | 2,751 | 8,594 | 2,149 |
| 11 | **Indian Overseas Bank** | 2,466 | 2,572 | 3,163 | 3,408 | 11,610 | 2,902 |
| 12 | **Oriental Bank of Commerce** | 1,686 | 1,892 | 2,315 | 2,665 | 8,559 | 2,140 |
| 13 | **Punjab & Sind Bank** | 718 | 984 | 1,159 | 1,119 | 3,980 | 995 |
| 14 | **Punjab National Bank** | 4,762 | 6,364 | 7,003 | 8,165 | 26,294 | 6,573 |
| 15 | **Syndicate Bank** | 2,034 | 2,548 | 2,814 | 3,179 | 10,575 | 2,644 |
| 16 | **UCO Bank** | 1,584 | 2,075 | 2,056 | 2,177 | 7,893 | 1,973 |
| 17 | **Union Bank of India** | 2,508 | 3,950 | 3,988 | 4,512 | 14,958 | 3,739 |

| 18 | United Bank of India | 1,074 | 1,299 | 1,383 | 1,504 | 5,261 | 1,315 |
|---|---|---|---|---|---|---|---|
| 19 | Vijaya Bank | 1,072 | 1,433 | 1,201 | 1,363 | 5,069 | 1,267 |
| | **Total** | **38,961** | **51,565** | **54,818** | **61,509** | **2,06,853** | **51,713** |
| | **Avg.** | **2051** | **2714** | **2885** | **3237** | **10,887** | **2,722** |
| **% increase (with the base of 2010 year on Avg. total Bases )** | | **100.00%** | **132.32%** | **140.66%** | **157.82%** | | |

(Various Bulletins of IBA)

The above Table shows Operating Expenses performance of 19 Nationalized Banks of the years 2010-11 to 20112-13. The amount is shows in Crores of rupees. The totals of 19 banks for four years are Rs.206853 with the average of Rs.2722 the same things are represented through below Colum chart. The statically work for Hypothesis testing through ANOVA test is calculated below to understand its performance and consistency.

**Chart No.3.8 Operating Expenses of Nationalized Bank**

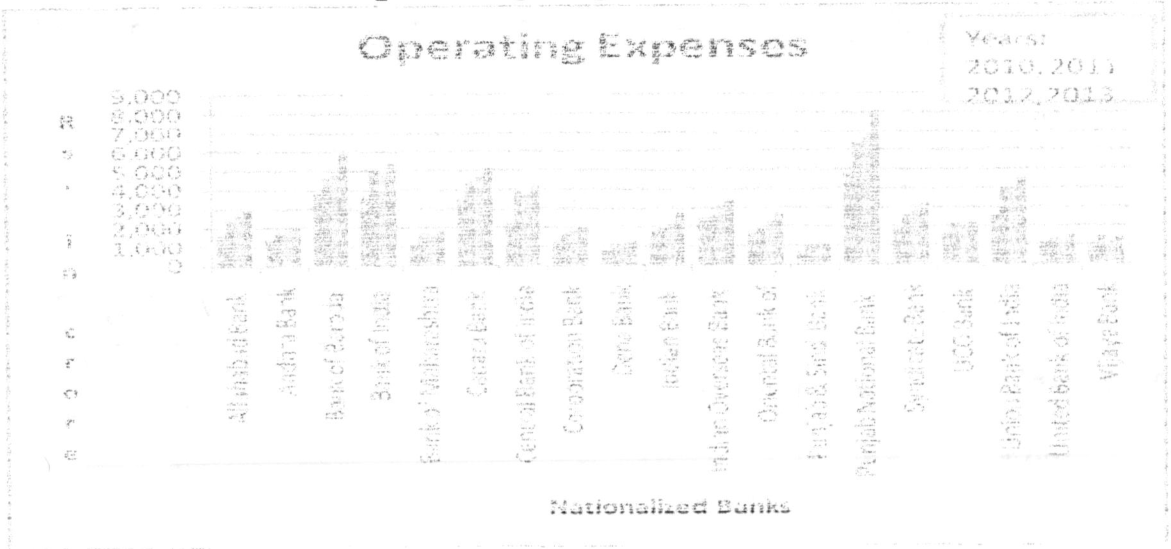

**Hypothesis Testing:** The researcher wanted to find out that if there is any significant difference regarding Operating Expenses of Performance among all 19 Banks of Nationalized during 2009-10 to 2012-13.

**Null Hypothesis:** There would no significant difference regarding the performance of Operating Expenses among all 19 Banks of Nationalized during 2009-10 to 2012-13.

**Alternative Hypothesis:** There would significant difference regarding the performance of Operating Expenses among all 19 Banks of Nationalized during 2009-10 to 2012-13.

**Calculations:** N=76, K=4, T=206853, CF=563000286.2,
$\sum_i \sum_j \sum X_{ij}2$=754993745,T.S.S=191993459,$\sum T_i 2$ =2935813209,
S.S. Between (SSC): 170953016, S.S. Within (SSE): 21040443

**Table No. 3.8.1 ANOVA of Operating Expenses of Nationalized Banks**

| Variation | d. f. | SS | MSS | F |
|---|---|---|---|---|
| **Between** | h-1=19-1 =18 | 170953016 | 9497390 | 25.72 |
| **Within** | N-h=76-19=57 | 21040443 | 369130.6 | |
| **Total** | N-1=76-1=75 | 191993459 | | |

**Fcal > Ftab = 25.72>1.70= Rejected**

The above ANOVA Table represents the calculated value of F-is 25.72 which is more than the table value of, 1.70, at 5% level of significance. So Null Hypothesis is rejected. It indicates that there is significant difference regarding the performance of Operating Expenses among all 19 Banks of Nationalized during 2009-10 to 2012-13.

## 3.13) Total Expenditure of Selected Nationalized Bank for last four Years

### Table No.3.9 Total Expenditure of Nationalized bank

| S. N. | NATIONALISED BANKS | Total Expenditure (Rs. in Crore) | | | | | |
|---|---|---|---|---|---|---|---|
| | | 2010 | 2011 | 2012 | 2013 | Total | Avg. |
| 1 | Allahabad Bank | 7,337 | 9,331 | 13,052 | 15,527 | 45,246 | 11,312 |
| 2 | Andhra Bank | 5,528 | 6,775 | 9,384 | 11,190 | 32,876 | 8,219 |
| 3 | Bank of Baroda | 14,569 | 17,713 | 24,466 | 29,754 | 86,502 | 21,626 |
| 4 | Bank of India | 15,790 | 19,009 | 25,108 | 28,216 | 88,123 | 22,031 |
| 5 | Bank of Maharashtra | 4,512 | 5,239 | 6,339 | 8,377 | 24,467 | 6,117 |
| 6 | Canara Bank | 16,549 | 19,660 | 27,835 | 31,341 | 95,385 | 23,846 |
| 7 | Central Bank of India | 11,741 | 13,894 | 17,730 | 20,355 | 63,721 | 15,930 |
| 8 | Corporation Bank | 6,344 | 7,837 | 11,654 | 13,905 | 39,741 | 9,935 |
| 9 | Dena Bank | 3,758 | 4,344 | 5,848 | 7,816 | 21,766 | 5,441 |
| 10 | Indian Bank | 6,283 | 7,251 | 10,000 | 12,119 | 35,654 | 8,914 |
| 11 | Indian Overseas Bank | 9,544 | 10,466 | 16,044 | 18,833 | 54,887 | 13,722 |
| 12 | Oriental Bank of Commerce | 9,036 | 9,803 | 13,915 | 15,669 | 48,422 | 12,105 |

| | | | | | | | |
|---|---|---|---|---|---|---|---|
| 13 | **Punjab & Sind Bank** | 3,468 | 4,356 | 6,132 | 6,818 | 20,775 | 5,194 |
| 14 | **Punjab National Bank** | 17,706 | 21,543 | 30,064 | 35,202 | 1,04,516 | 26,129 |
| 15 | **Syndicate Bank** | 9,341 | 9,616 | 12,997 | 14,845 | 46,800 | 11,700 |
| 16 | **UCO Bank** | 8,787 | 9,601 | 12,787 | 14,347 | 45,521 | 11,380 |
| 17 | **Union Bank of India** | 11,618 | 14,186 | 18,223 | 22,094 | 66,121 | 16,530 |
| 18 | **United Bank of India** | 4,932 | 5,472 | 6,865 | 8,268 | 25,537 | 6,384 |
| 19 | **Vijaya Bank** | 4,823 | 5,331 | 7,286 | 8,537 | 25,976 | 6,494 |
| | **Total** | **1,71,667** | **2,01,428** | **2,75,729** | **3,23,214** | **9,72,037** | **2,43,009** |
| | **Avg.** | **9,035** | **10,601** | **14,512** | **17,011** | **51,160** | **12,790** |
| **% increase (with the base of 2010 year on Avg. Total Bases)** | | **100.00%** | **117.33%** | **160.61%** | **188.27%** | | |

(Various Bulletins of IBA)

The above Table shows Total Expenditure performance of 19 Nationalized Banks of the years 2010-11 to 20112-13. The amount is shows in Crores of rupees. The totals of 19 banks for four years are Rs. 972037 with the average of Rs.12790 the same things are represented through below Colum chart. The statically work for Hypothesis testing through ANOVA test is calculated below to understand its performance and consistency.

**Chart No. 3.9 Total Expenditure of Nationalized bank**

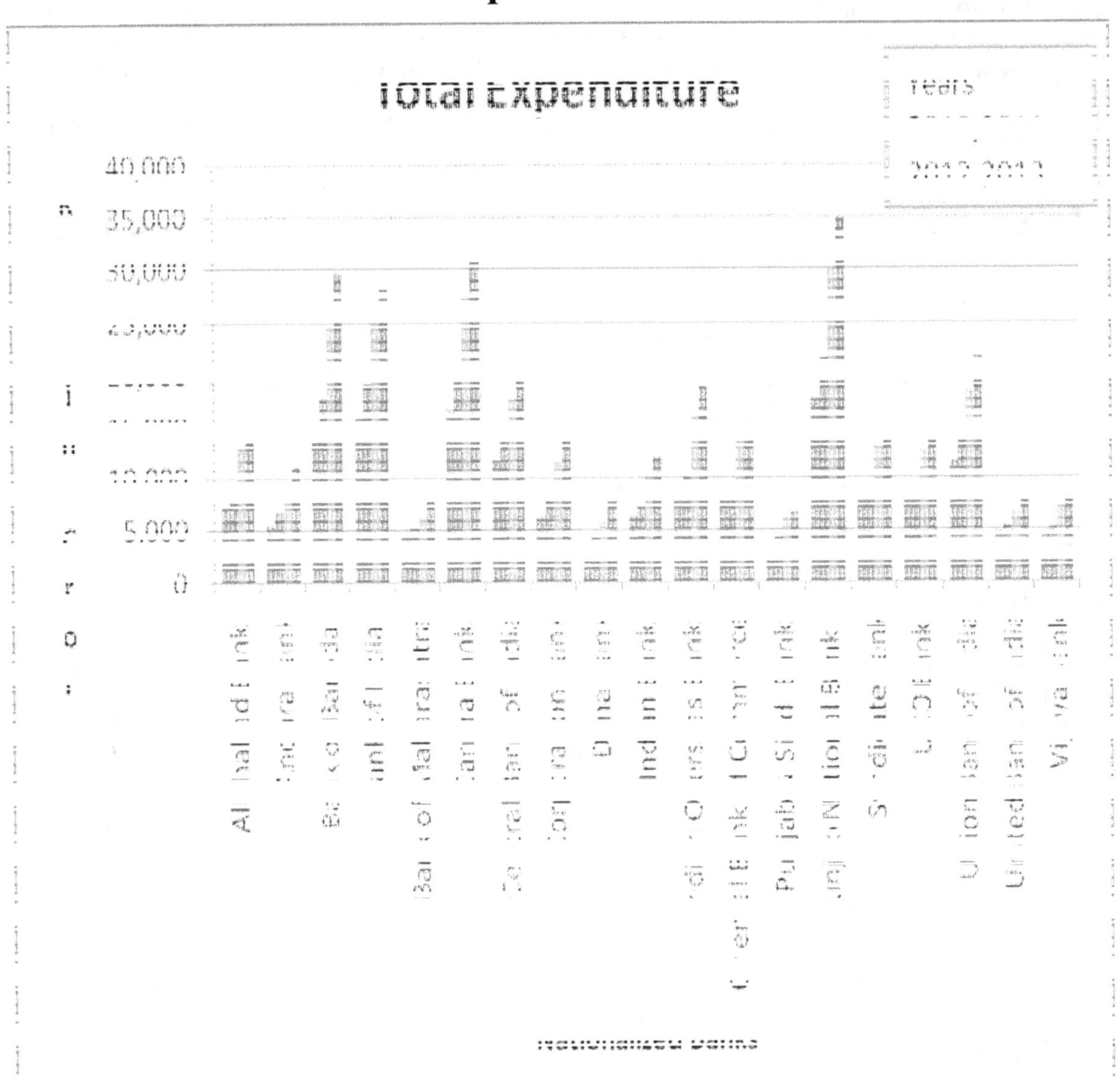


**Hypothesis Testing:** The researcher wanted to find out that if there is any significant difference regarding Total Expenditure Performance among all 19 Banks of Nationalized during 2009-10 to 2012-13.

**Null Hypothesis:** There would no significant difference regarding the performance of Total Expenditure among all 19 Banks of Nationalized during 2009-10 to 2012-13.

**Alternative Hypothesis:** There would significant difference regarding the performance of Total Expenditure among all 19 Banks of Nationalized during 2009-10 to 2012-13.

**Calculations:** N=76, K=4, T=972037, CF =12432326202, $\sum_i \sum_j \sum X_{ij}2$ = 16499383821, T.S.S = 4067057619, $\sum T_i 2$ =62131775890, S.S. Between (SSC): 3100617770

S.S. Within (SSE): 966439849

**Table No.3.9.1 ANOVA of Total Expenditure of Nationalized Banks**

| Variation | d. f. | SS | MSS | F |
|---|---|---|---|---|
| **Between** | h-1=19-1 =18 | 3100617770 | 172256543 | 10.15 |
| **Within** | N-h=6-19=57 | 966439849 | 16955085 | |
| **Total** | N-1=76-1=75 | 4067057619 | | |

**Fcal > Ftab = 10.15>1.70= Rejected**

The above ANOVA Table represents the calculated value of F-is 10.15 which is more than the table value of, 1.70, at 5% level of significance. So Null Hypothesis is rejected. It indicates that there is significant difference regarding the performance of Total Expenditure among all 19 Banks of Nationalized during 2009-10 to 2012-13.

### 3.14) Operating Profit of Selected Nationalized Bank for last Three Years

**Table No.3.10 Operating Profit**

| S. N. | NATIONALISED BANKS | Operating Profit (Rs. in Crore) | | | | |
|---|---|---|---|---|---|---|
| | | 2011 | 2012 | 2013 | Total | Avg. |
| 1 | **Allahabad Bank** | 3,055 | 3,770 | 3,385 | 10,210 | 3,403 |
| 2 | **Andhra Bank** | 2,413 | 2,815 | 2,767 | 7,995 | 2,665 |

| 3 | Bank of Baroda | 6,982 | 8,630 | 9,074 | 24,686 | 8,229 |
|---|---|---|---|---|---|---|
| 4 | Bank of India | 5,384 | 6,694 | 7,459 | 19,537 | 6,512 |
| 5 | Bank of Maharashtra | 855 | 1,515 | 2,149 | 4,519 | 1,506 |
| 6 | Canara Bank | 6,091 | 5,943 | 5,890 | 17,925 | 5,975 |
| 7 | Central Bank of India | 2,591 | 2,815 | 3,173 | 8,579 | 2,860 |
| 8 | Corporation Bank | 2,554 | 2,856 | 3,037 | 8,447 | 2,816 |
| 9 | Dena Bank | 1,224 | 1,528 | 1,739 | 4,491 | 1,497 |
| 10 | Indian Bank | 3,292 | 3,411 | 3,060 | 9,763 | 3,254 |
| 11 | Indian Overseas Bank | 2,861 | 3,534 | 3,817 | 10,212 | 3,404 |
| 12 | Oriental Bank of Commerce | 3,245 | 3,141 | 3,691 | 10,076 | 3,359 |
| 13 | Punjab & Sind Bank | 1,013 | 760 | 939 | 2,712 | 904 |
| 14 | Punjab National Bank | 9,056 | 10,614 | 10,907 | 30,577 | 10,192 |
| 15 | Syndicate Bank | 2,750 | 3,347 | 3,450 | 9,546 | 3,182 |
| 16 | UCO Bank | 2,695 | 2,811 | 3,357 | 8,863 | 2,954 |
| 17 | Union Bank of | 4,305 | 5,254 | 5,583 | 15,141 | 5,047 |

| | | | | | | |
|---|---|---|---|---|---|---|
| | **India** | | | | | |
| **18** | **United Bank of India** | 1,507 | 1,829 | 2,050 | 5,386 | 1,795 |
| **19** | **Vijaya Bank** | 1,047 | 1,230 | 1,122 | 3,399 | 1,133 |
| | **TOTAL** | **62,919** | **72,498** | **76,647** | **2,12,064** | **70,688** |
| | **Avg.** | **3,312** | **3,816** | **4,034** | **11,161** | **3,720** |
| **% increase (with the base of 2011 year on Avg. total Bases )** | | **100.00%** | **115.21%** | **121.79%** | | |

(Various Bulletins of IBA)

The above Table shows Operating Profit performance of 19 Nationalized Banks of the years 2011-12 to 20112-13. The amount is shows in Crores of rupees. The totals of 19 banks for Three years are Rs. 212064 with the average of Rs.3720 the same things are represented through below Colum chart. The statically work for Hypothesis testing through ANOVA test is calculated below to understand its performance and consistency.

## Chart No.3.10 Operating Profit

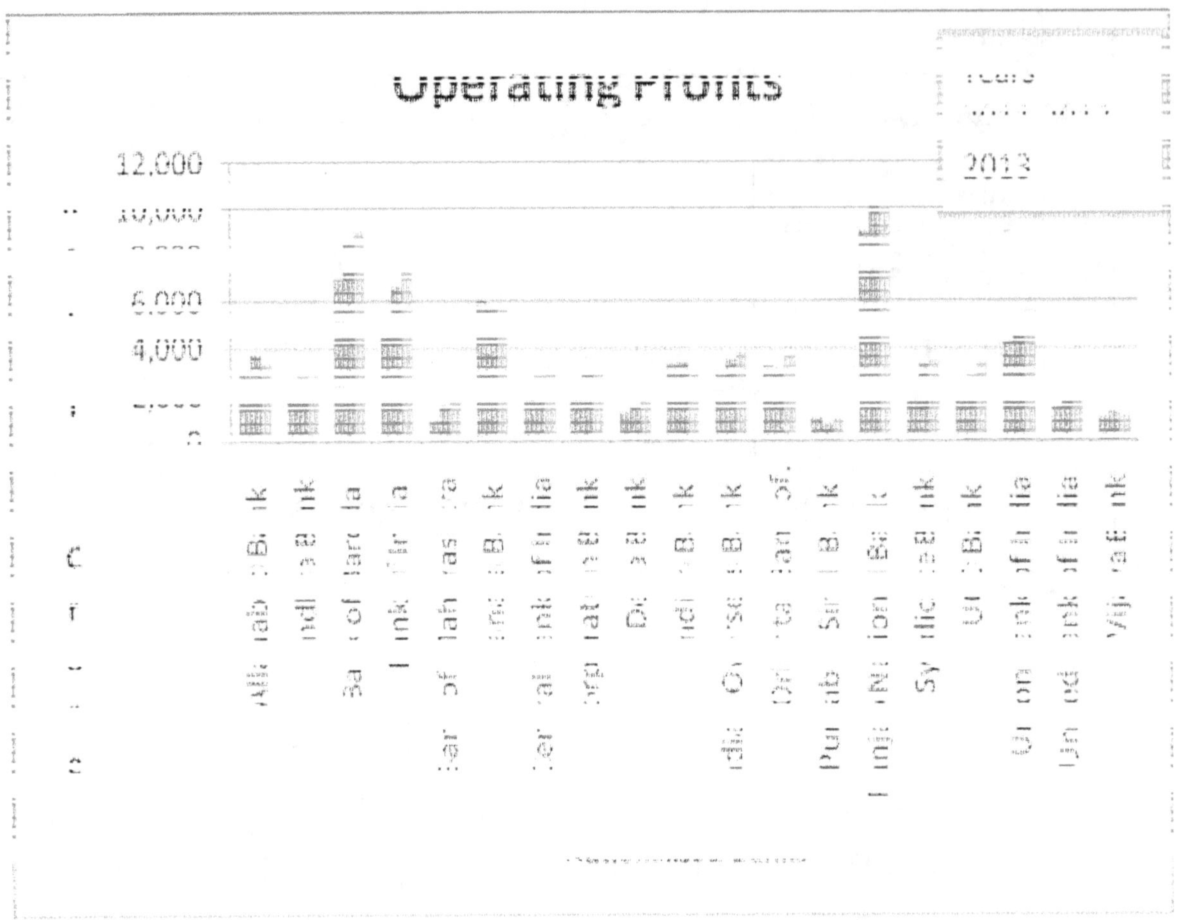


**Hypothesis Testing:** The researcher wanted to find out that if there is any significant difference regarding Total Operating Profit among all 19 Banks of Nationalized during 2010-11 to 2012-13.

**Null Hypothesis:** There would no significant difference regarding the performance of Operating Profit among all 19 Banks of Nationalized during 2010-11 to 2012-13.

**Alternative Hypothesis:** There would significant difference regarding the performance of Operating Profit among all 19 Banks of Nationalized during 2010-11 to 2012-13.

**Calculation:** N=57, K=3, T=212064, CF =788968279, $\sum_i\sum_j\sum X_{ij}2$ = 1126925692, T.S.S = 337957414, $\sum T_i2$ =3349030142, S.S. Between (SSC): 327375102,S.S. Within (SSE): 10582312

**Table No. 3.10.1 ANOVA of Operating Profit of Nationalized Banks**

| Variation | d. f. | SS | MSS | F |
|---|---|---|---|---|
| **Between** | h-1= 9-1 =18 | 327375102 | 18187505.67 | 65.30 |
| **Within** | N-h=57-19=38 | 10582312 | 278481.88 | |
| **Total** | N-1=57-1=56 | 337957414 | | |

**Fcal > Ftab = 65.30>1.70= Rejected**

The above ANOVA Table represents the calculated value of F-is 65.30 which is more than the table value of, 1.79, at 5% level of significance. So Null Hypothesis is rejected. It indicates that there is significant difference regarding the performance of Operating Profit among all 19 Banks of Nationalized during 2010-11 to 2012-13.

**3.15) Provisions and Contingencies of Selected Nationalized Bank for last four Years**

**Table No. 3.11 Provisions and Contingencies**

| S. N. | NATIONALISED BANKS | Provisions & Contingencies (Rs. in Crore) | | | | | |
|---|---|---|---|---|---|---|---|
| | | **2010** | **2011** | **2012** | **2013** | **Total** | **Avg.** |
| 1 | **Allahabad Bank** | 1,342 | 1,631 | 1,903 | 2,200 | 7,077 | 1,769 |
| 2 | **Andhra Bank** | 764 | 1,146 | 1,470 | 1,478 | 4,858 | 1,215 |
| 3 | **Bank of Baroda** | 1,877 | 2,740 | 3,574 | 4,518 | 12,709 | 3,177 |
| 4 | **Bank of India** | 2,964 | 2,896 | 4,016 | 4,709 | 14,585 | 3,646 |
| 5 | **Bank of Maharashtra** | 375 | 525 | 1,084 | 1,389 | 3,373 | 843 |
| 6 | **Canara Bank** | 2,039 | 2,066 | 2,660 | 3,018 | 9,783 | 2,446 |
| 7 | **Central Bank of** | 1,000 | 1,339 | 2,282 | 2,158 | 6,779 | 1,695 |

| | | | | | | | |
|---|---|---|---|---|---|---|---|
| | **India** | | | | | | |
| **8** | **Corporation Bank** | 966 | 1,141 | 1,350 | 1,602 | 5,059 | 1,265 |
| **9** | **Dena Bank** | 329 | 612 | 725 | 928 | 2,595 | 649 |
| **10** | **Indian Bank** | 1,192 | 1,578 | 1,716 | 1,480 | 5,966 | 1,492 |
| **11** | **Indian Overseas Bank** | 1,138 | 1,788 | 2,484 | 3,250 | 8,660 | 2,165 |
| **12** | **Oriental Bank of Commerce** | 1,287 | 1,742 | 1,999 | 2,363 | 7,391 | 1,848 |
| **13** | **Punjab & Sind Bank** | 369 | 487 | 309 | 600 | 1,764 | 441 |
| **14** | **Punjab National Bank** | 3,421 | 4,622 | 5,730 | 6,160 | 19,933 | 4,983 |
| **15** | **Syndicate Bank** | 1,060 | 1,702 | 2,033 | 1,445 | 6,241 | 1,560 |
| **16** | **UCO Bank** | 693 | 1,788 | 1,703 | 2,739 | 6,924 | 1,731 |
| **17** | **Union Bank of India** | 1,584 | 2,223 | 3,467 | 3,425 | 10,699 | 2,675 |
| **18** | **United Bank of India** | 553 | 983 | 1,196 | 1,658 | 4,391 | 1,098 |
| **19** | **Vijaya Bank** | 550 | 523 | 649 | 536 | 2,258 | 565 |
| | **TOTAL** | **23,506** | **31,532** | **40,352** | **45,657** | **1,41,045** | **35,261** |

| | | | | | | |
|---|---|---|---|---|---|---|
| **Avg.** | **1,237** | **1,660** | **2,124** | **2,403** | **7,423** | **1,856** |
| **% increase (with the base of 2010 year on Avg. total Bases )** | **100.00%** | **134.19%** | **171.70%** | **194.26%** | | |

(Various Bulletins of IBA)

The above Table shows Provision & Contingencies performance of 19 Nationalized Banks of the years 2010-11 to 20112-13. The amount is shows in Crores of rupees. The totals of 19 banks for four years are Rs. 141045 with the average of Rs.1856 the same things are represented through below Colum chart. The statically work for Hypothesis testing through ANOVA test is calculated below to understand its performance and consistency.

**Chart No.3.11 Provisions and Contingencies**

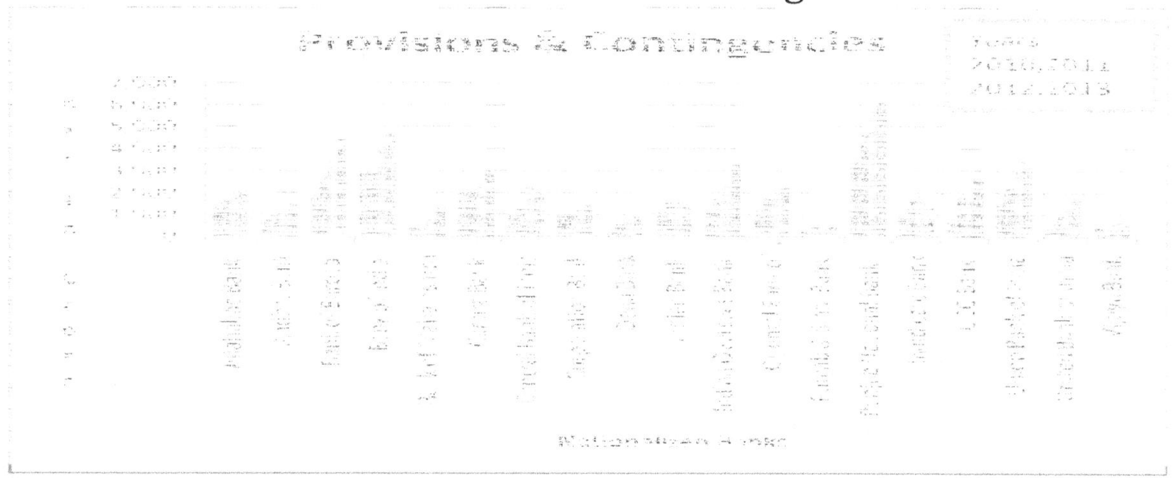

**Hypothesis Testing:** The researcher wanted to find out that if there is any significant difference regarding Provisions & Contingencies Performance among all 19 Banks of Nationalized during 2009-10 to 2012-13.

**Null Hypothesis:** There would no significant difference regarding the performance of Provisions & Contingencies among all 19 Banks of Nationalized during 2009-10 to 2012-13.

**Alternative Hypothesis:** There would significant difference regarding the performance of Provisions & Contingencies among all 19 Banks of Nationalized during 2009-10 to 2012-13.

**Calculation:** N=76, K=4, T=141045, CF =261760368.7, $\sum_i\sum_j\sum X_{ij}2$ = 379618747, T.S.S = 117858379, $\sum T_i2$ =1424669751, S.S. Between (SSC): 94407069, S.S. Within (SSE): 23451309

**Table No.3.11.1 ANOVA of Provisions & Contingencies of Nationalized Banks**

| Variation | d. f. | SS | MSS | F |
|---|---|---|---|---|
| **Between** | h-1=19-1 =18 | 94407069 | 5244837 | 12.74 |
| **Within** | N-h=76-19=57 | 23451309 | 411426.5 | |
| **Total** | N-1=76-1=75 | 117858379 | | |

**Fcal > Ftab = 12.74>1.70= Rejected**

The above ANOVA Table represents the calculated value of F-is 12.74 which is more than the table value of, 1.70, at 5% level of significance. So Null Hypothesis is rejected. It indicates that there is significant difference regarding the performance of Total Provisions & Contingencies among all 19 Banks of Nationalized during 2009-10 to 2012-13.

## 3.16) Net Profit of Selected Nationalized Bank for last four Years

**Table No.3.12 Net Profit**

| S. N. | NATIONALISED BANKS | Net Profit(Rs. in Crore) | | | | | |
|---|---|---|---|---|---|---|---|
| | | 2010 | 2011 | 2012 | 2013 | Total | Avg. |

| 1 | **Allahabad Bank** | 1,206 | 1,423 | 1,867 | 1,185 | 5,681 | 1,420 |
|---|---|---|---|---|---|---|---|
| 2 | **Andhra Bank** | 1,046 | 1,267 | 1,345 | 1,289 | 4,947 | 1,237 |
| 3 | **Bank of Baroda** | 3,058 | 4,242 | 5,007 | 4,481 | 16,787 | 4,197 |
| 4 | **Bank of India** | 1,741 | 2,489 | 2,678 | 2,749 | 9,657 | 2,414 |
| 5 | **Bank of Maharashtra** | 440 | 330 | 431 | 760 | 1,960 | 490 |
| 6 | **Canara Bank** | 3,021 | 4,026 | 3,283 | 2,872 | 13,202 | 3,301 |
| 7 | **Central Bank of India** | 1,058 | 1,252 | 533 | 1,015 | 3,859 | 965 |
| 8 | **Corporation Bank** | 1,170 | 1,413 | 1,506 | 1,435 | 5,524 | 1,381 |
| 9 | **Dena Bank** | 511 | 612 | 803 | 810 | 2,737 | 684 |
| 10 | **Indian Bank** | 1,555 | 1,714 | 1,747 | 1,581 | 6,597 | 1,649 |
| 11 | **Indian Overseas Bank** | 707 | 1,073 | 1,050 | 567 | 3,397 | 849 |
| 12 | **Oriental Bank of Commerce** | 1,135 | 1,503 | 1,142 | 1,328 | 5,107 | 1,277 |
| 13 | **Punjab & Sind Bank** | 509 | 526 | 451 | 339 | 1,825 | 456 |
| 14 | **Punjab National Bank** | 3,905 | 4,433 | 4,884 | 4,748 | 17,971 | 4,493 |

| 15 | Syndicate Bank | 813 | 1,048 | 1,313 | 2,004 | 5,179 | 1,295 |
|---|---|---|---|---|---|---|---|
| 16 | UCO Bank | 1,012 | 907 | 1,109 | 618 | 3,646 | 911 |
| 17 | Union Bank of India | 2,075 | 2,082 | 1,787 | 2,158 | 8,102 | 2,025 |
| 18 | United Bank of India | 322 | 524 | 633 | 392 | 1,871 | 468 |
| 19 | Vijaya Bank | 507 | 524 | 581 | 586 | 2,198 | 549 |
| | **TOTAL** | **25,793** | **31,388** | **32,149** | **30,917** | **1,20,247** | **30,062** |
| | **Avg.** | **1,358** | **1,652** | **1,692** | **1,627** | **6,329** | **1,582** |
| **% increase (with the base of 2010 year on Avg. total Bases )** | | **100.00%** | **121.64** | **124.59** | **119.80** | | |

(Various Bulletins of IBA)

The above Table shows Net Profit performance of 19 Nationalized Banks of the years 2010-11 to 20112-13. The amount is shows in Crores of rupees. The totals of 19 banks for four years are Rs. 120247 with the average of Rs.1582 the same things are represented through below Colum chart. The statically work for Hypothesis testing through ANOVA test is calculated below to understand its performance and consistency.

**Chart No. 3.12 Net Profit**

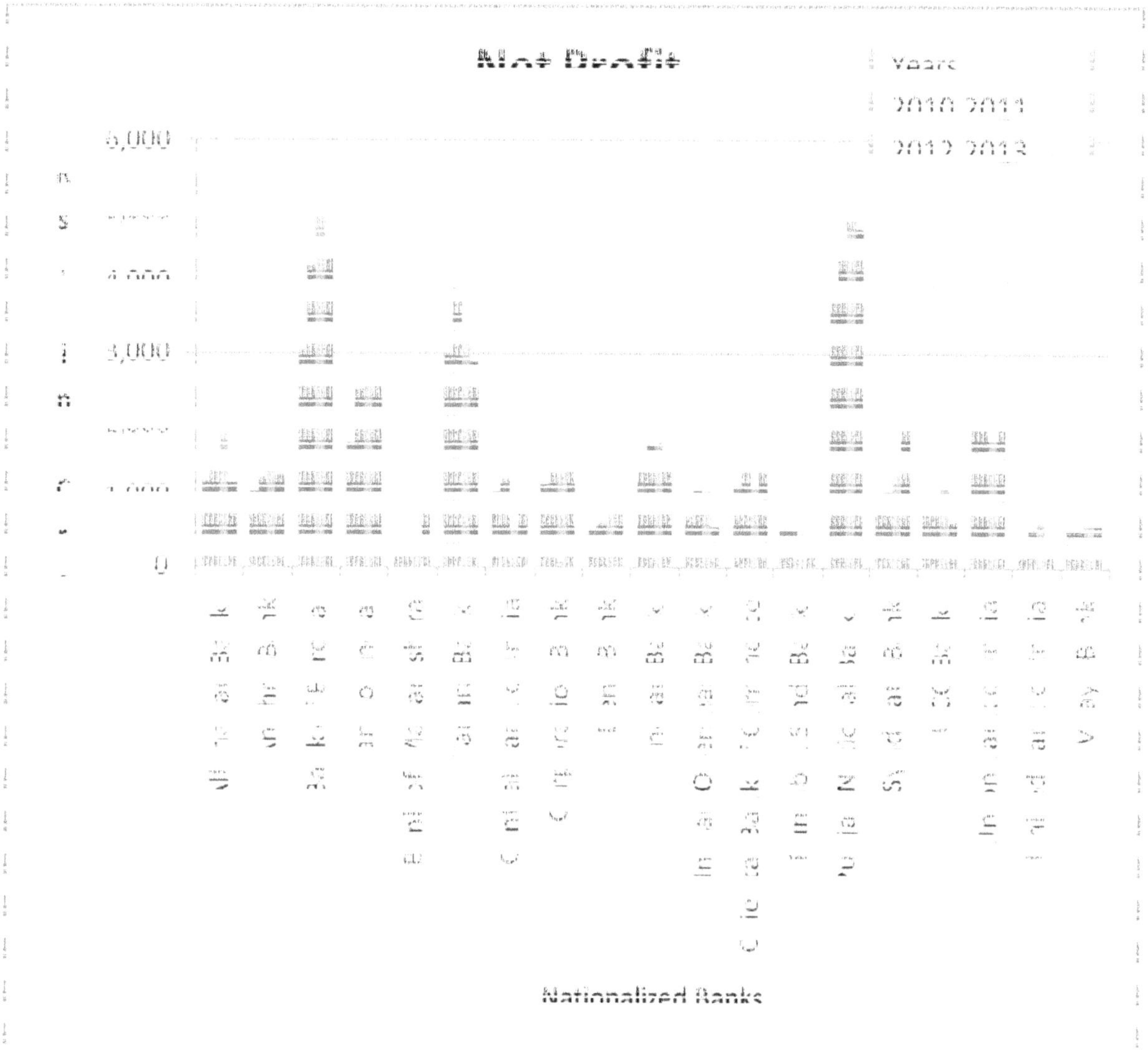

**Hypothesis Testing:** The researcher wanted to find out that if there is any significant difference regarding Net Profit Performance among all 19 Banks of Nationalized during 2009-10 to 2012-13.

**Null Hypothesis:** There would no significant difference regarding the performance of Net Profit among all 19 Banks of Nationalized during 2009-10 to 2012-13.

**Alternative Hypothesis:** There would significant difference regarding the performance of Net Profit among all 19 Banks of Nationalized during 2009-10 to 2012-13.

**Calculation:** N=76, K=4, T=120274,CF =190253718, $\sum_i\sum_j\sum X_{ij}2$ = 302390632, T.S.S = 112136914,$\sum T_i2$ =1184357705, S.S. Between (SSC):105835708.3, S.S. Within (SSE): 6301205.91

**Table No. 3.12.1 ANOVA of Net Profit of Nationalized Banks**

| Variation | d. f. | SS | MSS | F |
|---|---|---|---|---|
| **Between** | h-1=19-1 =18 | 105835708.3 | 5879762 | 53.18 |
| **Within** | N-h=76-19=57 | 6301205.91 | 110547.5 | |
| **Total** | N-1=76-1=75 | 112136914 | | |

**Fcal > Ftab = 53.18>1.70= Rejected**

The above ANOVA Table represents the calculated value of F-is 53.18 which is more than the table value of, 1.70, at 5% level of significance. So Null Hypothesis is rejected. It indicates that there is significant difference regarding the performance of Total Net Profit among all 19 Banks of Nationalized during 2009-10 to 2012-13.

## 3.17) Credit Deposit Ratio of Selected Nationalized Bank for last Three Years

There are two types of liquidity one is deposit liquidity which refers to the bank's ability to meet its deposit liabilities or demands for cash as they arise. Second types are loan liquidity which is bank's capacity to meet all the credit requirements of its customers. There are two ratios one is "Credit deposit ratio" It also called loan or advance to deposit ratio. And second is cash/cash plus liquid assets to deposit ratio. The higher this ratio, the lower is the liquidity position of the bank. Here, loans mean the amount which is paid to customer and deposits mean total amount of the bank which are mobilized from the people Moreover, the, Investment is an amount which is paid to any industry or company. Which may be short term investment or may be long term? The formula of the ratios is given below

$$\textbf{Credit Deposit Ratio} = \frac{\text{Advances}}{\text{Deposit}} \times 100$$

The Banker must safe guard his position by maintaining sufficient cash with him or with other banks or any liquid assets. Liquid assets include cash in hand, investment in Government and semi Government securities, money at call and short notice. The urgency of maintaining the liquid assets is recognized by banking regulation act- 1949, section 24 of an amount not less than 25 percent of its net demand and time liabilities.

**Table No.3.13 Credit Deposit Ratio**

| S.N. | NATIONALISED BANKS | Credit Deposit Ratio (%) | | | | |
|---|---|---|---|---|---|---|
| | | 2011 | 2012 | 2013 | Total | Avg. |
| 1 | Allahabad Bank | 70.99 | 69.64 | 72.45 | 213.08 | 71.03 |
| 2 | Andhra Bank | 77.52 | 78.62 | 79.46 | 235.60 | 78.53 |
| 3 | Bank of Baroda | 74.87 | 74.67 | 69.25 | 218.79 | 72.93 |
| 4 | Bank of India | 71.30 | 78.20 | 75.78 | 225.28 | 75.09 |
| 5 | Bank of Maharashtra | 70.13 | 73.25 | 80.00 | 223.39 | 74.46 |
| 6 | Canara Bank | 72.00 | 71.09 | 68.05 | 211.14 | 70.38 |
| 7 | Central Bank of | 72.33 | 75.20 | 76.06 | 223.59 | 74.53 |

| | | | | | | |
|---|---|---|---|---|---|---|
| | **India** | | | | | |
| **8** | **Corporation Bank** | 74.39 | 73.80 | 71.51 | 219.70 | 73.23 |
| **9** | **Dena Bank** | 69.82 | 73.47 | 67.67 | 210.95 | 70.32 |
| **10** | **Indian Bank** | 71.12 | 74.77 | 74.41 | 220.30 | 73.43 |
| **11** | **Indian Overseas Bank** | 77.00 | 78.87 | 79.34 | 235.21 | 78.40 |
| **12** | **Oriental Bank of Commerce** | 68.97 | 71.80 | 73.31 | 214.08 | 71.36 |
| **13** | **Punjab & Sind Bank** | 71.39 | 73.11 | 72.81 | 217.31 | 72.44 |
| **14** | **Punjab National Bank** | 77.38 | 77.39 | 78.84 | 233.61 | 77.87 |
| **15** | **Syndicate Bank** | 78.75 | 78.27 | 79.61 | 236.63 | 78.88 |
| **16** | **UCO Bank** | 68.19 | 75.02 | 73.97 | 217.19 | 72.40 |
| **17** | **Union Bank of India** | 74.58 | 79.81 | 78.90 | 233.29 | 77.76 |
| **18** | **United Bank of India** | 68.73 | 70.74 | 68.46 | 207.93 | 69.31 |
| **19** | **Vijaya Bank** | 66.51 | 69.72 | 71.91 | 208.14 | 69.38 |
| | **TOTAL** | **1375.96** | **1417.43** | **1411.81** | **4205.21** | **1401.74** |
| | **Avg.** | **72.42** | **74.60** | **74.31** | **221.33** | **73.78** |

(Various Bulletins of IBA)

The above Table shows Credit Deposit Ratios performance of 19 Nationalized Banks of the years 2011-12 to 20112-13. The Figures shows in ▪ Crore. The totals of 19 banks for the three years are 4205.21 with the overall average of 73.78 Percentage. The same things are represented through below Colum chart. The statically work for Hypothesis testing through ANOVA test is calculated below to understand its performance and consistency.

**Chart No.3.13 Credit Deposit Ratio**

**Hypothesis Testing:** The researcher wanted to find out that if there is any significant difference regarding Total Credit Deposit Ratio's

Performance among all 19 Banks of Nationalized during 2010-11 to 2012-13.

**Null Hypothesis:** There would no significant difference regarding the performance of Credit Deposit Ratio among all 19 Banks of Nationalized during 2010-11 to 2012-13.

**Alternative Hypothesis:** There would significant difference regarding the performance of Credit Deposit Ratio among all 19 Banks of Nationalized during 2010-11 to 2012-13.

**Calculation:** N=57, K=3, T=4205.21, CF =310241.509, $\sum_i\sum_j\sum X_{ij}2$ = 311025.83, T.S.S = 784.32, $\sum T_i2$ =932402.85, S.S. Between (SSC): 559.44, S.S. Within (SSE): 224.88

**Table No.3.13.1 ANOVA of Credit Deposit Ratio of Nationalized Banks**

| Variation | d. f. | SS | MSS | F |
|---|---|---|---|---|
| **Between** | h-1= 9-1 =18 | 559.44 | 31.08 | 5.25 |
| **Within** | N-h=57-19=38 | 224.88 | 5.91 | |
| **Total** | N-1=57-1=56 | 784.32 | | |

**Fcal > Ftab = 5.25>1.70= Rejected**

The above ANOVA Table represents the calculated value of F-is 5.25 which is more than the table value of, 1.79, at 5% level of significance. So Null Hypothesis is rejected. It indicates that there is significant difference regarding the performance of Credit Deposit Ratio among all 19 Banks of Nationalized during 2010-11 to 2012-13.

## 3.18) Investment Deposit Ratio of Selected Nationalized Bank for last Four Years

The higher this ratio, the lower is the liquidity position of the bank. Here, loans mean the amount which is paid to customer and deposits mean total amount of the bank which are mobilized from the people Moreover, the, Investment is an amount which is paid to any industry or company. Which may be short term investment or may be long term? The formula of the ratios is given below.

$$\text{Investment Deposit Ratio} = \frac{\text{Investment}}{\text{Deposit}} \times 100$$

The Banker must safe guard his position by maintaining sufficient cash with him or with other banks or any liquid assets. Liquid assets include cash in hand, investment in Government and semi Government securities, money at call and short notice. The urgency of maintaining the liquid assets is recognized by banking regulation act- 1949, section 24 of an amount not less than 25 percent of its net demand and time liabilities.

**Table No. 3.14 Investment Deposit Ratio**

| S.N. | NATIONALISED BANKS | Investment Deposit Ratio (%) | | | | | |
|---|---|---|---|---|---|---|---|
| | | 2010 | 2011 | 2012 | 2013 | Total | Avg. |
| 1 | Allahabad Bank | 36.23 | 32.79 | 34.01 | 32.62 | 135.66 | 33.91 |
| 2 | Andhra Bank | 26.88 | 26.26 | 27.99 | 30.40 | 111.53 | 27.88 |
| 3 | Bank of Baroda | 25.36 | 23.38 | 21.62 | 25.62 | 95.97 | 23.99 |
| 4 | Bank of India | 29.20 | 28.73 | 27.26 | 24.78 | 109.97 | 27.49 |
| 5 | Bank of Maharashtra | 33.68 | 33.65 | 34.02 | 33.32 | 134.66 | 33.67 |

| | | | | | | | |
|---|---|---|---|---|---|---|---|
| 6 | **Canara Bank** | 29.69 | 28.50 | 31.21 | 34.04 | 123.44 | 30.86 |
| 7 | **Central Bank of India** | 31.19 | 30.39 | 30.20 | 32.12 | 123.90 | 30.97 |
| 8 | **Corporation Bank** | 37.23 | 37.22 | 34.87 | 35.04 | 144.36 | 36.09 |
| 9 | **Dena Bank** | 30.57 | 29.23 | 29.84 | 35.33 | 124.97 | 31.24 |
| 10 | **Indian Bank** | 32.04 | 32.88 | 31.44 | 29.44 | 125.80 | 31.45 |
| 11 | **Indian Overseas Bank** | 33.98 | 33.47 | 31.14 | 30.38 | 128.98 | 32.24 |
| 12 | **Oriental Bank of Commerce** | 29.76 | 35.63 | 33.41 | 33.29 | 132.08 | 33.02 |
| 13 | **Punjab & Sind Bank** | 36.39 | 31.22 | 31.79 | 31.91 | 131.30 | 32.83 |
| 14 | **Punjab National Bank** | 31.17 | 30.41 | 32.33 | 33.17 | 127.09 | 31.77 |
| 15 | **Syndicate Bank** | 28.21 | 25.86 | 25.84 | 24.63 | 104.54 | 26.13 |
| 16 | **UCO Bank** | 35.55 | 29.55 | 29.72 | 30.12 | 124.95 | 31.24 |
| 17 | **Union Bank of India** | 31.99 | 28.84 | 27.98 | 30.65 | 119.47 | 29.87 |
| 18 | **United Bank of India** | 38.23 | 33.73 | 32.61 | 33.25 | 137.82 | 34.46 |
| 19 | **Vijaya Bank** | 34.08 | 34.32 | 34.49 | 32.25 | 135.14 | 33.78 |

| | | | | | | | |
|---|---|---|---|---|---|---|---|
| | **TOTAL** | **611.44** | **586.06** | **581.75** | **592.35** | **2371.61** | **592.90** |
| | **Avg.** | **32.18** | **30.85** | **30.62** | **31.18** | **124.82** | **31.21** |

(Various Bulletins of IBA)

The above Table shows Investment Deposit Ratios performance of 19 Nationalized Banks of the years 2010-11 to 20112-13. The Figures shows in Percentage **(%)**. The totals of 19 banks for the four years are 2371.61 with the average of 31.21 the same things are represented through below Colum chart. The statically work for Hypothesis testing through ANOVA test is calculated below to understand its performance and consistency.

**Chart No. 3.14 Investment Deposit Ratio**

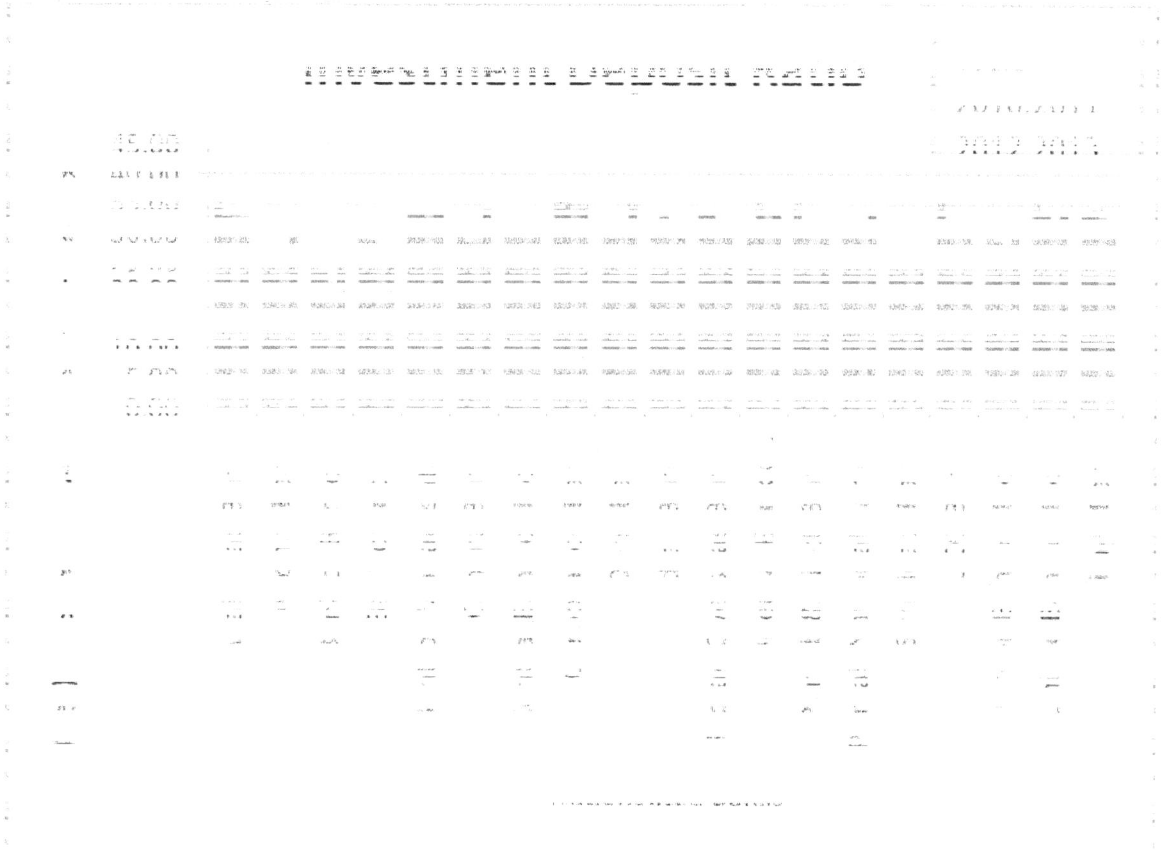

**Hypothesis Testing:** The researcher wanted to find out that if there is any significant difference regarding Investment Deposit Ratio's

Performance among all 19 Banks of Nationalized during 2009-10 to 2012-13.

**Null Hypothesis:** There would no significant difference regarding the performance of Investment Deposit Ratio's among all 19 Banks of Nationalized during 2009-10 to 2012-13.

**Alternative Hypothesis:** There would significant difference regarding the performance of Investment Deposit Ratio's among all 19 Banks of Nationalized during 2009-10 to 2012-13.

**Calculation:** N=76, K=4, T=2371.61, CF =74007.137, $\sum_i\sum_j\sum X_{ij}2$ = 74880.64, T.S.S = 873.50, $\sum T_i2$ =298690.35, S.S. Between (SSC):665.45, S.S. Within (SSE): 208.05

**Table No.3.14.1 ANOVA of Investment Deposit Ratio's of Nationalized Banks**

| Variation | d. f. | SS | MSS | F |
|---|---|---|---|---|
| **Between** | h-1=19-1 =18 | 665.45 | 36.96 | 10.12 |
| **Within** | N-h=76-19=57 | 208.05 | 3.64 | |
| **Total** | N-1=76-1=75 | 873.50 | | |

**Fcal > Ftab = 10.12>1.70= Rejected**

The above ANOVA Table represents the calculated value of F-is 10.12 which is more than the table value of, 1.70, at 5% level of significance. So Null Hypothesis is rejected. It indicates that there is significant difference regarding the performance of Total Investment Deposit Ratio's among all 19 Banks of Nationalized during 2009-10 to 2012-13.

**3.19) Spread as percentage (%) of Assets of Selected Nationalized Bank for last Four Years**

## Table No. 3.15 Spread as percentage (%) of Assets

| S. N. | NATIONALISED BANKS | Spread as % of Assets Percentage (%) | | | | | |
|---|---|---|---|---|---|---|---|
| | | 2010 | 2011 | 2012 | 2013 | Total | Avg. |
| 1 | Allahabad Bank | 2.18 | 2.66 | 2.82 | 2.38 | 10.04 | 2.51 |
| 2 | Andhra Bank | 2.43 | 2.96 | 3.02 | 2.57 | 10.97 | 2.74 |
| 3 | Bank of Baroda | 2.13 | 2.46 | 2.31 | 2.07 | 8.96 | 2.24 |
| 4 | Bank of India | 2.09 | 2.22 | 2.16 | 1.99 | 8.47 | 2.12 |
| 5 | Bank of Maharashtra | 1.82 | 2.58 | 2.76 | 2.59 | 9.75 | 2.44 |
| 6 | Canara Bank | 2.15 | 2.29 | 2.06 | 1.91 | 8.40 | 2.10 |
| 7 | Central Bank of India | 1.39 | 2.54 | 2.25 | 2.14 | 8.32 | 2.08 |
| 8 | Corporation Bank | 1.70 | 2.05 | 1.92 | 1.77 | 7.45 | 1.86 |
| 9 | Dena Bank | 1.91 | 2.49 | 2.40 | 2.10 | 8.90 | 2.23 |
| 10 | Indian Bank | 3.12 | 3.32 | 3.12 | 2.78 | 12.34 | 3.08 |
| 11 | Indian Overseas Bank | 2.42 | 2.35 | 2.28 | 2.15 | 9.20 | 2.30 |
| 12 | Oriental Bank of Commerce | 2.12 | 2.59 | 2.37 | 2.34 | 9.42 | 2.36 |
| 13 | Punjab & Sind Bank | 2.09 | 2.28 | 2.06 | 2.04 | 8.46 | 2.12 |

| | | | | | | | |
|---|---|---|---|---|---|---|---|
| **14** | **Punjab National Bank** | 2.86 | 3.12 | 2.93 | 3.10 | 12.01 | 3.00 |
| **15** | **Syndicate Bank** | 1.97 | 2.80 | 2.79 | 2.54 | 10.09 | 2.52 |
| **16** | **UCO Bank** | 1.69 | 2.35 | 2.16 | 2.31 | 8.51 | 2.13 |
| **17** | **Union Bank of India** | 2.15 | 2.63 | 2.59 | 2.42 | 9.79 | 2.45 |
| **18** | **United Bank of India** | 1.81 | 2.41 | 2.43 | 2.17 | 8.82 | 2.20 |
| **19** | **Vijaya Bank** | 2.06 | 2.37 | 1.99 | 1.69 | 8.12 | 2.03 |
| | **TOTAL** | **40.09** | **48.47** | **46.43** | **43.06** | **178.0** | **44.51** |
| | **Avg.** | **2.11** | **2.55** | **2.44** | **2.27** | **9.37** | **2.34** |

(Various Bulletins of IBA)

The above Table shows Spread as percentage (%) of Assets ratios performance of 19 Nationalized Banks of the years 2010-11 to 20112-13. The Figures shows in Percentage (**%**). The totals of 19 banks for the four years are 178.05 with the average of 2.34 the same things are represented through below Colum chart. The statically work for Hypothesis testing through ANOVA test is calculated below to understand its performance and consistency.

## Chart No. 3.15 Spread as percentage (%) of Assets

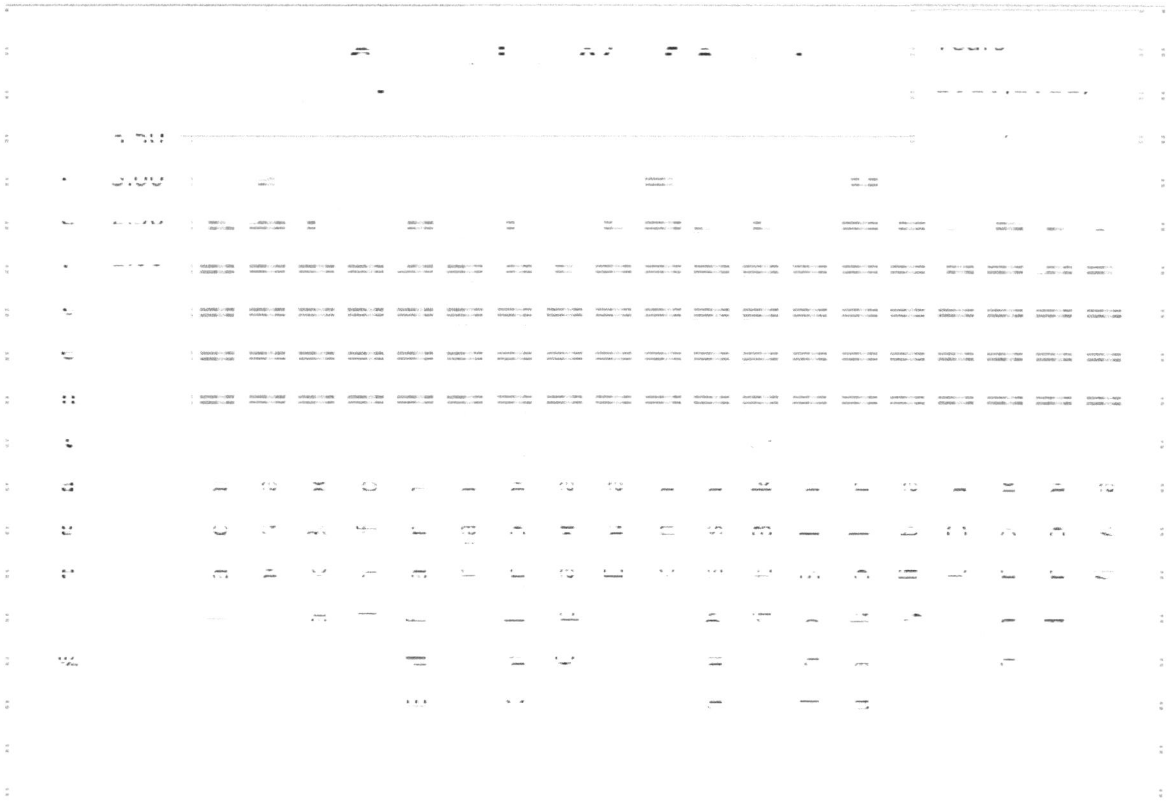

**Hypothesis Testing:** The researcher wanted to find out that if there is any significant difference regarding Spread as % of Assets Performance among all 19 Banks of Nationalized during 2009-10 to 2012-13.

**Null Hypothesis:** There would no significant difference regarding the performance of Spread as % of Assets among all 19 Banks of Nationalized during 2009-10 to 2012-13.

**Alternative Hypothesis:** There would significant difference regarding the performance of Spread as % of Assets among all 19 Banks of Nationalized during 2009-10 to 2012-13.

**Calculation:** N=76, K=4, T=178.05, CF =417.11, $\sum_i \sum_j \sum X_{ij}2$ = 428.59, T.S.S = 11.47, $\sum T_i2$ =1698.47,

S.S. Between (SSC):7.50, S.S. Within (SSE): 3.97

**Table No. 3.15.1 ANOVA of Investment Deposit Ratio's of Nationalized Banks**

| Variation | d. f. | SS | MSS | F |
|---|---|---|---|---|
| **Between** | h-1=19-1 =18 | 7.50 | 0.41 | 5.98 |
| **Within** | N-h=76-19=57 | 3.97 | 0.06 | |
| **Total** | N-1=76-1=75 | 11.47 | | |

**Fcal > Ftab = 5.98>1.70= Rejected**

The above ANOVA Table represents the calculated value of F-is 5.98 which is more than the table value of, 1.70, at 5% level of significance. So Null Hypothesis is rejected. It indicates that there is significant difference regarding the performance of Total Spread as % of Assets among all 19 Banks of Nationalized during 2009-10 to 2012-13.

## 3.20) Operating Expenses as % to Total Expenses of Selected Nationalized Bank for Last Three Years

**Table No. 3.16 Operating Expenses as % to Total Expenses**

| S.N. | NATIONALISED BANKS | Operating Expenses as % to Total Expenses Percentage (%) | | | | |
|---|---|---|---|---|---|---|
| | | 2011 | 2012 | 2013 | Total | Avg. |
| 1 | Allahabad Bank | 25.06 | 20.62 | 19.05 | 64.73 | 21.58 |
| 2 | Andhra Bank | 25.16 | 19.23 | 18.21 | 62.60 | 20.87 |
| 3 | Bank of Baroda | 26.14 | 20.88 | 19.74 | 66.76 | 22.25 |

| | | | | | | |
|---|---|---|---|---|---|---|
| 4 | **Bank of India** | 26.66 | 19.68 | 18.90 | 65.23 | 21.74 |
| 5 | **Bank of Maharashtra** | 31.38 | 25.91 | 21.45 | 78.74 | 26.25 |
| 6 | **Canara Bank** | 22.48 | 16.79 | 16.41 | 55.68 | 18.56 |
| 7 | **Central Bank of India** | 28.78 | 21.15 | 20.79 | 70.72 | 23.57 |
| 8 | **Corporation Bank** | 20.95 | 15.30 | 14.36 | 50.61 | 16.87 |
| 9 | **Dena Bank** | 24.71 | 19.75 | 16.63 | 61.09 | 20.36 |
| 10 | **Indian Bank** | 26.57 | 21.87 | 22.70 | 71.13 | 23.71 |
| 11 | **Indian Overseas Bank** | 24.58 | 19.71 | 18.10 | 62.39 | 20.80 |
| 12 | **Oriental Bank of Commerce** | 19.31 | 16.64 | 17.01 | 52.96 | 17.65 |
| 13 | **Punjab & Sind Bank** | 22.59 | 18.89 | 16.42 | 57.90 | 19.30 |
| 14 | **Punjab National Bank** | 29.54 | 23.29 | 23.19 | 76.03 | 25.34 |
| 15 | **Syndicate Bank** | 26.50 | 21.65 | 21.41 | 69.56 | 23.19 |
| 16 | **UCO Bank** | 21.62 | 16.08 | 15.17 | 52.87 | 17.62 |

| | | | | | | |
|---|---|---|---|---|---|---|
| **17** | **Union Bank of India** | 27.84 | 21.88 | 20.42 | 70.15 | 23.38 |
| **18** | **United Bank of India** | 23.75 | 20.15 | 18.19 | 62.09 | 20.70 |
| **19** | **Vijaya Bank** | 26.89 | 16.49 | 15.97 | 59.34 | 19.78 |
| | **Total** | **480.50** | **375.97** | **354.10** | **1,210.57** | **403.52** |
| | **Avg.** | **25.29** | **19.79** | **18.64** | **63.71** | **21.24** |

(Various Bulletins of IBA)

The above Table shows Operating Expenses As % To Total Expenses ratios performance of 19 Nationalized Banks of the years 2011-12 to 2012-13. The Figures shows in Percentage **(%)**. The totals of 19 banks for the three years are 1210.57 with the average of 21.24 the same things are represented through below Colum chart. The statically work for Hypothesis testing through ANOVA test is calculated below to understand its performance and consistency.

**Chart No. 3.16 Operating Expenses as % to Total Expenses**

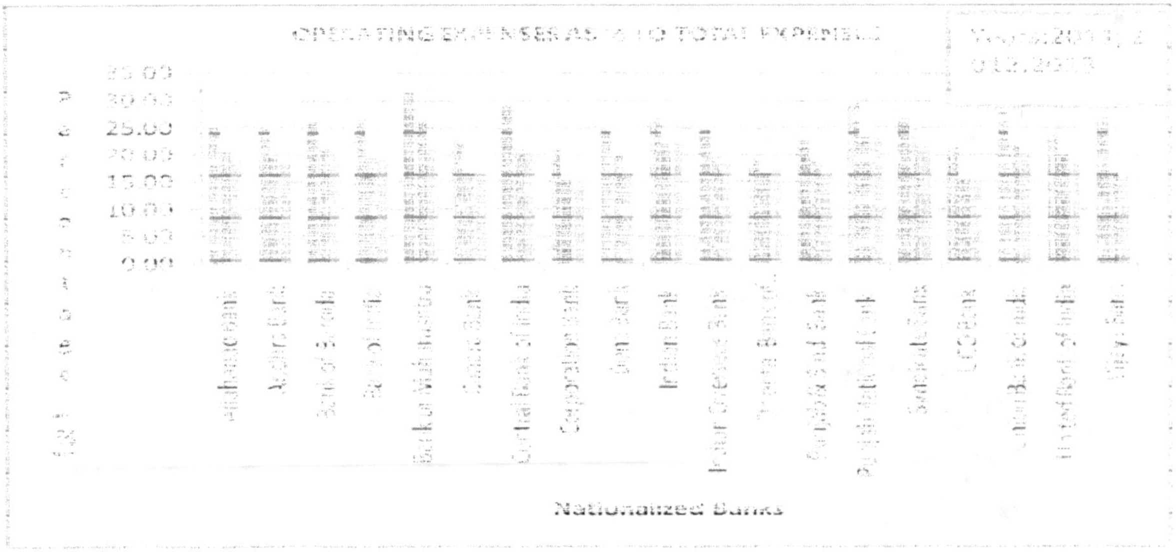

**Hypothesis Testing:** The researcher wanted to find out that if there is any significant difference regarding Operating Expenses as % to Total Expenses Performance among all 19 Banks of Nationalized during 2010-11 to 2012-13.

**Null Hypothesis:** There would no significant difference regarding the performance of Operating Expenses as % to Total Expenses among all 19 Banks of Nationalized during 2010-11 to 2012-13.

**Alternative Hypothesis:** There would significant difference regarding the performance of Operating Expenses as % to Total Expenses among all 19 Banks of Nationalized during 2010-11 to 2012-13.

**Calculations** =57, K=3, T=1210.57, CF =25710.21, $\sum_i\sum_j\sum X_{ij}2$ = 26606.90, T.S.S = 896.68, $\sum T_i2$ =78235.60, S.S. Between (SSC):368.31, S.S. Within (SSE): 528.36

**Table No. 3.16.1 ANOVA of Operating Expenses as % to Total Expenses of Nationalized Banks**

| Variation | d. f. | SS | MSS | F |
|---|---|---|---|---|
| **Between** | h-1 = 19-1 =18 | 368.31 | 20.46 | 1.47 |
| **Within** | N-h = 57-19=38 | 528.36 | 13.90 | |
| **Total** | N-1=57-1=56 | 896.68 | | |

**Fcal > Ftab = 1.47<1.79= Accepted**

The above ANOVA Table represents the calculated value of F-is 1.47 which is less than the table value of, 1.79, at 5% level of significance. So Null Hypothesis is accepted. It indicates that there is no significant difference regarding the performance of Operating Expenses as % to Total Expenses among all 19 Banks of Nationalized during 2010-11 to 2012-13.

## 3.21) Return on Assets of Selected Nationalized Bank for Last Four Years

Below ratio are indicators to measure profitability. How much return achieved on the assets, is an important factor. The formula of this ratio is

$$\text{Return on Assets} = \frac{\text{Net Profit}}{\text{Net worth}} \times 100 \quad \text{or} \quad \frac{\text{Net profit}}{\text{Total Assts}} \times 100$$

**Net Profit:** The Net profit will be achieved by deducting provisions and contingencies from operating profit.

**Net Worth:** Net worth will be achieved by deducting total liability from Total Assets. The Bank's long term solvency can be measured with the use of net worth. In my calculation, we have calculated with total assets instead of net worth.

**Table No. 3.17 Return on Assets**

| S.N. | NATIONALISED BANKS | Return on Assets Percentage (%) | | | | | |
|---|---|---|---|---|---|---|---|
| | | 2010 | 2011 | 2012 | 2013 | Total | Avg. |
| 1 | Allahabad Bank | 1.16 | 1.11 | 1.02 | 0.64 | 3.93 | 0.98 |
| 2 | Andhra Bank | 1.39 | 1.36 | 1.19 | 0.99 | 4.93 | 1.23 |
| 3 | Bank of Baroda | 1.21 | 1.33 | 1.24 | 0.90 | 4.68 | 1.17 |
| 4 | Bank of India | 0.70 | 0.82 | 0.72 | 0.65 | 2.89 | 0.72 |
| 5 | Bank of Maharashtra | 0.72 | 0.47 | 0.55 | 0.74 | 2.48 | 0.62 |
| 6 | Canara Bank | 1.30 | 1.42 | 0.95 | 0.77 | 4.44 | 1.11 |
| 7 | Central Bank of | 0.66 | 0.70 | 0.26 | 0.44 | 2.06 | 0.52 |

| | | | | | | | |
|---|---|---|---|---|---|---|---|
| | India | | | | | | |
| 8 | Corporation Bank | 1.28 | 1.21 | 1.06 | 0.88 | 4.43 | 1.11 |
| 9 | Dena Bank | 1.01 | 1.00 | 1.08 | 0.85 | 3.94 | 0.99 |
| 10 | Indian Bank | 1.67 | 1.53 | 1.31 | 1.02 | 5.53 | 1.38 |
| 11 | Indian Overseas Bank | 0.53 | 0.71 | 0.52 | 0.24 | 2.00 | 0.50 |
| 12 | Oriental Bank of Commerce | 0.91 | 1.03 | 0.67 | 0.71 | 3.32 | 0.83 |
| 13 | Punjab & Sind Bank | 1.05 | 0.90 | 0.65 | 0.44 | 3.04 | 0.76 |
| 14 | Punjab National Bank | 1.44 | 1.34 | 1.19 | 1.00 | 4.97 | 1.24 |
| 15 | Syndicate Bank | 0.62 | 0.76 | 0.81 | 1.07 | 3.26 | 0.82 |
| 16 | UCO Bank | 0.87 | 0.66 | 0.69 | 0.33 | 2.55 | 0.64 |
| 17 | Union Bank of India | 1.25 | 1.05 | 0.79 | 0.79 | 3.88 | 0.97 |
| 18 | United Bank of India | 0.45 | 0.66 | 0.70 | 0.38 | 2.19 | 0.55 |
| 19 | Vijaya Bank | 0.76 | 0.72 | 0.66 | 0.59 | 2.73 | 0.68 |
| | Total | **18.98** | **18.78** | **16.06** | **13.43** | **67.25** | **16.81** |
| | Avg. | **1.00** | **0.99** | **0.85** | **0.71** | **3.54** | **0.88** |

(Various Bulletins of IBA)

The above Table shows Return on assets ratios performance of 19 Nationalized Banks of the years 2010-11 to 2012-13. The Figures shows in Percentage **(%)**. The totals of 19 banks for the four years are 67.25 with the average of 0.88 the same things are represented through below Colum chart. The statically work for Hypothesis testing through ANOVA test is calculated below to understand its performance and consistency.

**Chart No. 3.17 Return on Assets**

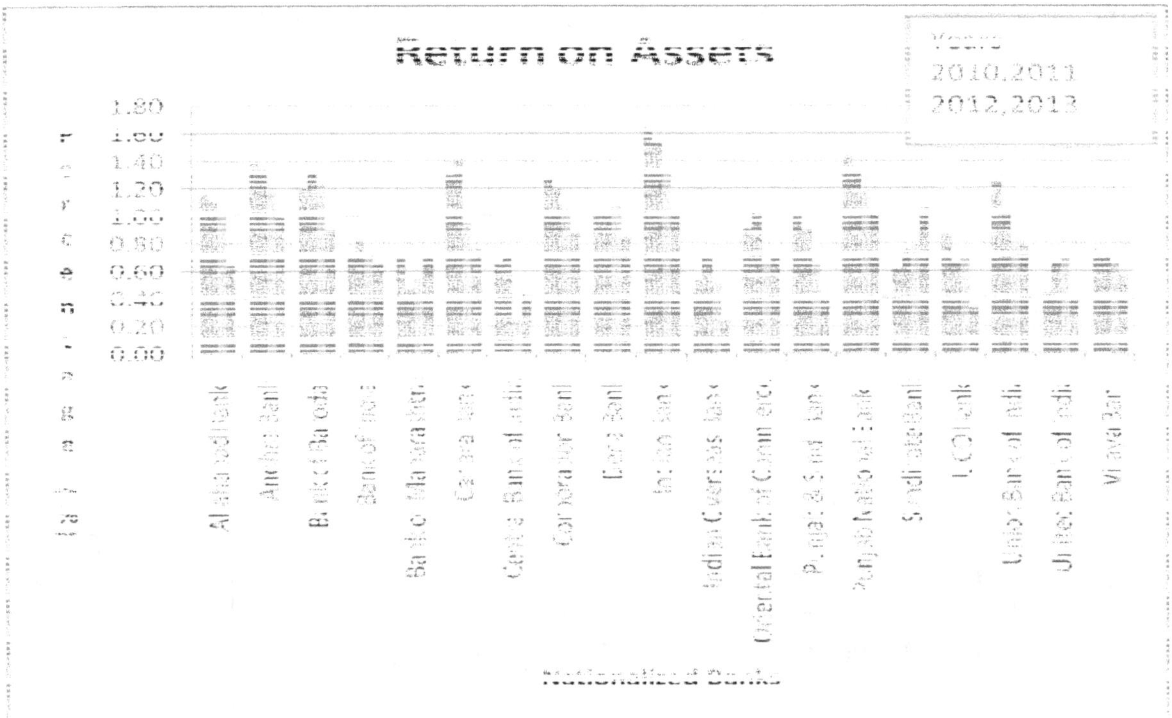

**Hypothesis Testing:** The researcher wanted to find out that if there is any significant difference regarding Return on Assets Performance among all 19 Banks of Nationalized during 2009-10 to 2012-13.

**Null Hypothesis:** There would no significant difference regarding the performance of Return on Assets among all 19 Banks of Nationalized during 2009-10 to 2012-13.

**Alternative Hypothesis:** There would significant difference regarding the performance of Return on Assets among all 19 Banks of Nationalized during 2009-10 to 2012-13.

**Calculation:** N=76, K=4, T=67.25, CF =59.507, $\sum_i\sum_j\sum X_{ij}2$ =67.03, T.S.S = 7.53, $\sum T_i2$ =259.23, S.S. Between (SSC):5.30, S.S. Within (SSE): 2.22

**Table No. 3.17.1 ANOVA of Return on Assets of Nationalized Banks**

| Variation | d. f. | SS | MSS | F |
|---|---|---|---|---|
| **Between** | h-1=19-1 =18 | 5.30 | 0.294 | 7.53 |
| **Within** | N-h=76-19=57 | 2.22 | 0.039 | |
| **Total** | N-1=76-1=75 | 7.53 | | |

**Fcal > Ftab = 7.53>1.70= Rejected**

The above ANOVA Table represents the calculated value of F-is 7.53 which is more than the table value of, 1.70, at 5% level of significance. So Null Hypothesis is rejected. It indicates that there is significant difference regarding the performance of Return on Assets among all 19 Banks of Nationalized during 2009-10 to 2012-13.

## 3.22) Capital Adequacy Ratio- Basel -I of Selected Nationalized Bank for Last Four Years

The basic committee report on the convergence of capital and standards in 1988 passed a directive that CAR of 8% was necessary for bank. Then, the Narasimaham committee recommendation that all Indian Banks should achieve CAR of 8% by March 1996 was implemented by RBI. The Narasimham committee on banking sector reforms proposed an increase in the CAR of Banks. Consequently a CAR target of 9% by March 2000 was fixed. Then the RBI has proposed to increase CAR to 10% by March 2002. The CAR is 9% fixed by 2006 for all the banks. Capital adequacy is indicated by a minimum numerical ratio which the banks are expected to maintain to ensure stability and strength.

Formula: -

$$\text{Capital to Risk Assets Ratio (CRAR)} = \frac{\text{Capital Funds}}{\text{Risk Weight Assets}} \times 100$$

Capital funds will calculate tier-I capital (shareholder's equity + retained profit) and tier-II capital (supplementary capital and Tier-III capital (subordinated debt with a minimum maturity of two year this criteria is suggested by Basle-II committee, which is implemented by 2005. Funds risk weight assets are calculated, e.g. on balance sheet items and non funded risk assets e.g. off balance sheets items. As per the prudential norms, the commercial banks are required to achieve 9% capital to risk weighted assets ratio (CRAR) by 31st march, 2000. And by September 2006, 9% of capital to risk weighted assets ratio has implemented in all the Indian banks.

**Table No. 3.18 Capital Adequacy Ratio- Basel -I**

| S. N. | NATIONALISED BANKS | Capital Adequacy Ratio - Basel -I Percentage (%) | | | | | |
|---|---|---|---|---|---|---|---|
| | | 2010 | 2011 | 2012 | 2013 | Total | Avg. |
| 1 | Allahabad Bank | 12.98 | NA | NA | NA | 12.98 | 3.24 |

| | | | | | | | |
|---|---|---|---|---|---|---|---|
| **2** | **Andhra Bank** | 13.30 | 13.48 | 12.34 | 11.26 | 50.38 | 12.59 |
| **3** | **Bank of Baroda** | 12.84 | 13.02 | NA | NA | 25.86 | 6.46 |
| **4** | **Bank of India** | 12.63 | 11.42 | 11.57 | 11.35 | 46.97 | 11.74 |
| **5** | **Bank of Maharashtra** | 11.33 | 11.75 | 11.25 | 11.72 | 46.05 | 11.51 |
| **6** | **Canara Bank** | 11.47 | NA | NA | NA | 11.47 | 2.86 |
| **7** | **Central Bank of India** | 10.82 | 10.74 | 11.96 | 11.33 | 44.85 | 11.21 |
| **8** | **Corporation Bank** | 15.00 | 12.90 | 11.94 | 11.38 | 51.22 | 12.805 |
| **9** | **Dena Bank** | 10.65 | 11.04 | NA | NA | 21.69 | 5.42 |
| **10** | **Indian Bank** | 12.16 | 12.83 | 12.67 | 11.59 | 49.25 | 12.31 |
| **11** | **Indian Overseas Bank** | 14.26 | 13.28 | 11.95 | 10.74 | 50.23 | 12.55 |
| **12** | **Oriental Bank of Commerce** | 10.88 | 12.30 | 11.01 | 10.75 | 44.94 | 11.235 |
| **13** | **Punjab & Sind Bank** | 11.74 | 11.94 | 12.81 | 12.71 | 49.2 | 12.3 |
| **14** | **Punjab National Bank** | 12.97 | 11.76 | 11.59 | 12.28 | 48.6 | 12.15 |
| **15** | **Syndicate Bank** | 11.20 | 11.20 | 10.81 | 11.12 | 44.33 | 11.08 |
| **16** | **UCO Bank** | 11.35 | 11.87 | 11.03 | 12.48 | 46.73 | 11.68 |

| | | | | | | | |
|---|---|---|---|---|---|---|---|
| **17** | **Union Bank of India** | 11.61 | NA | NA | NA | 11.61 | 2.90 |
| **18** | **United Bank of India** | 12.80 | 11.16 | 10.48 | 9.77 | 44.21 | 11.05 |
| **19** | **Vijaya Bank** | 11.79 | 12.59 | 10.96 | 9.58 | 44.92 | 11.23 |
| | **Total** | **231.78** | **193.28** | **162.37** | **158.06** | **745.49** | **186.37** |
| | **Avg.** | **12.19** | **10.17** | **8.54** | **8.31** | **39.24** | **9.81** |

(Various Bulletins of IBA)

The above Table shows Capital Adequacy Ratios Basel-I performance of 19 Nationalized Banks of the years 2010-11 to 2012-13. The Figures shows in Percentage (%). The totals of 19 banks for the four years are 475.49 with the average of 9.81. the same things are represented through below Colum chart. The statically work for Hypothesis testing through ANOVA test is calculated below to understand its performance and consistency.

**Chart No. 3.18 Capital Adequacy Ratio- Basel –I**

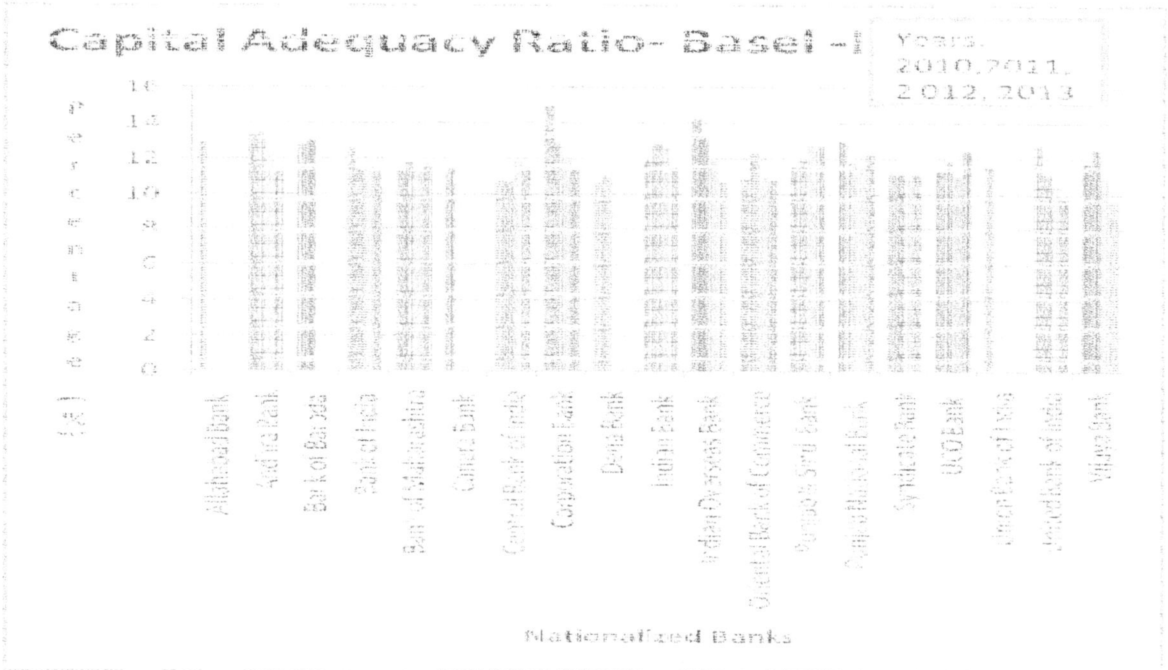

**Hypothesis Testing:** The researcher wanted to find out that if there is any significant difference regarding Capital Adequacy Ratio-Basel -I Performance among all 19 Banks of Nationalized during 2009-10 to 2012-13.

**Null Hypothesis:** There would no significant difference regarding the performance of Capital Adequacy Ratio- Basel -I among all 19 Banks of Nationalized during 2009-10 to 2012-13.

**Alternative Hypothesis:** There would significant difference regarding the performance of Capital Adequacy Ratio- Basel -I among all 19 Banks of Nationalized during 2009-10 to 2012-13.

**Calculations:** N=76, K=4, T=745.49, CF =7312.57, $\sum_i \sum_j \sum X_{ij}2$ =8883.37, T.S.S = 1570.80, $\sum T_i 2$ =32945.96, S.S. Between (SSC):923.91, S.S. Within (SSE): 646.89

**Table No. 3.18.1 ANOVA of Capital Adequacy Ratio- Basel -I of Nationalized Banks**

| Variation | d. f. | SS | MSS | F |
|---|---|---|---|---|
| Between | h-1 = 19-1 =18 | 923.91 | 51.32 | 4.52 |
| Within | N-h= 76-19=57 | 646.89 | 11.34 | |
| Total | N-1=76-1=75 | 1570.80 | | |

**Fcal > Ftab = 4.52>1.70= Rejected**

The above ANOVA Table represents the calculated value of F-is 4.52 which is more than the table value of, 1.70, at 5% level of significance. So Null Hypothesis is rejected. It indicates that there is significant difference regarding the performance of regarding Capital Adequacy Ratio- Basel -I among all 19 Banks of Nationalized during 2009-10 to 2012-13.

### 3.23) Capital Adequacy Ratio- Basel -II of Selected Nationalized Bank for Last Four Years

**Table No. 3.19 Capital Adequacy Ratio- Basel -II**

| S. N. | NATIONALISED BANKS | Capital Adequacy Ratio - Basel- II Percentage (%) | | | | | |
|---|---|---|---|---|---|---|---|
| | | 2010 | 2011 | 2012 | 2013 | Total | Avg. |
| 1 | Allahabad Bank | 13.62 | 12.96 | 12.83 | 11.03 | 50.44 | 12.61 |
| 2 | Andhra Bank | 13.93 | 14.38 | 13.18 | 11.76 | 53.25 | 13.31 |
| 3 | Bank of Baroda | 14.36 | 14.52 | 14.67 | 13.30 | 56.85 | 14.21 |
| 4 | Bank of India | 12.94 | 12.17 | 11.95 | 11.02 | 48.08 | 12.02 |
| 5 | Bank of Maharashtra | 12.78 | 13.35 | 12.43 | 12.59 | 51.15 | 12.78 |
| 6 | Canara Bank | 13.43 | 15.38 | 13.76 | 12.40 | 54.97 | 13.74 |
| 7 | Central Bank of India | 12.24 | 11.64 | 12.40 | 11.49 | 47.77 | 11.94 |

| 8 | Corporation Bank | 15.37 | 14.11 | 13.00 | 12.33 | 54.81 | 13.70 |
|---|---|---|---|---|---|---|---|
| 9 | Dena Bank | 12.77 | 13.41 | 11.51 | 11.03 | 48.72 | 12.18 |
| 10 | Indian Bank | NA | 13.56 | 13.47 | 13.08 | 40.11 | 10.027 |
| 11 | Indian Overseas Bank | 14.78 | 14.55 | 13.32 | 11.85 | 54.5 | 13.62 |
| 12 | Oriental Bank of Commerce | 12.54 | 14.23 | 12.69 | 12.04 | 51.5 | 12.87 |
| 13 | Punjab & Sind Bank | 13.10 | 12.94 | 13.26 | 12.91 | 52.21 | 13.05 |
| 14 | Punjab National Bank | 14.16 | 12.42 | 12.63 | 12.72 | 51.93 | 12.98 |
| 15 | Syndicate Bank | 12.70 | 13.04 | 12.24 | 12.59 | 50.57 | 12.64 |
| 16 | UCO Bank | 13.21 | 13.71 | 12.35 | 14.22 | 53.49 | 13.37 |
| 17 | Union Bank of India | 12.51 | 12.95 | 11.85 | 11.45 | 48.76 | 12.19 |
| 18 | United Bank of India | 13.05 | 13.05 | 12.69 | 11.66 | 50.45 | 12.61 |
| 19 | Vijaya Bank | 12.50 | 13.88 | 13.06 | 11.32 | 50.76 | 12.69 |
| | Total | **239.99** | **256.25** | **243.29** | **230.79** | **970.32** | **242.58** |
| | Avg. | **12.63** | **13.48** | **12.80** | **12.14** | **51.06** | **12.76** |

(Various Bulletins of IBA)

The above Table shows Capital Adequacy Ratios Basel-II performance of 19 Nationalized Banks of the years 2010-11 to 2012-13. The Figures shows in Percentage (%). The totals of 19 banks for the four years are 970.32 with the average of 12.76 the same things are represented through below Colum chart. The statically work for Hypothesis testing through ANOVA test is calculated below to understand its performance and consistency.

**Chart No. 3.19 Capital Adequacy Ratio- Basel -II**

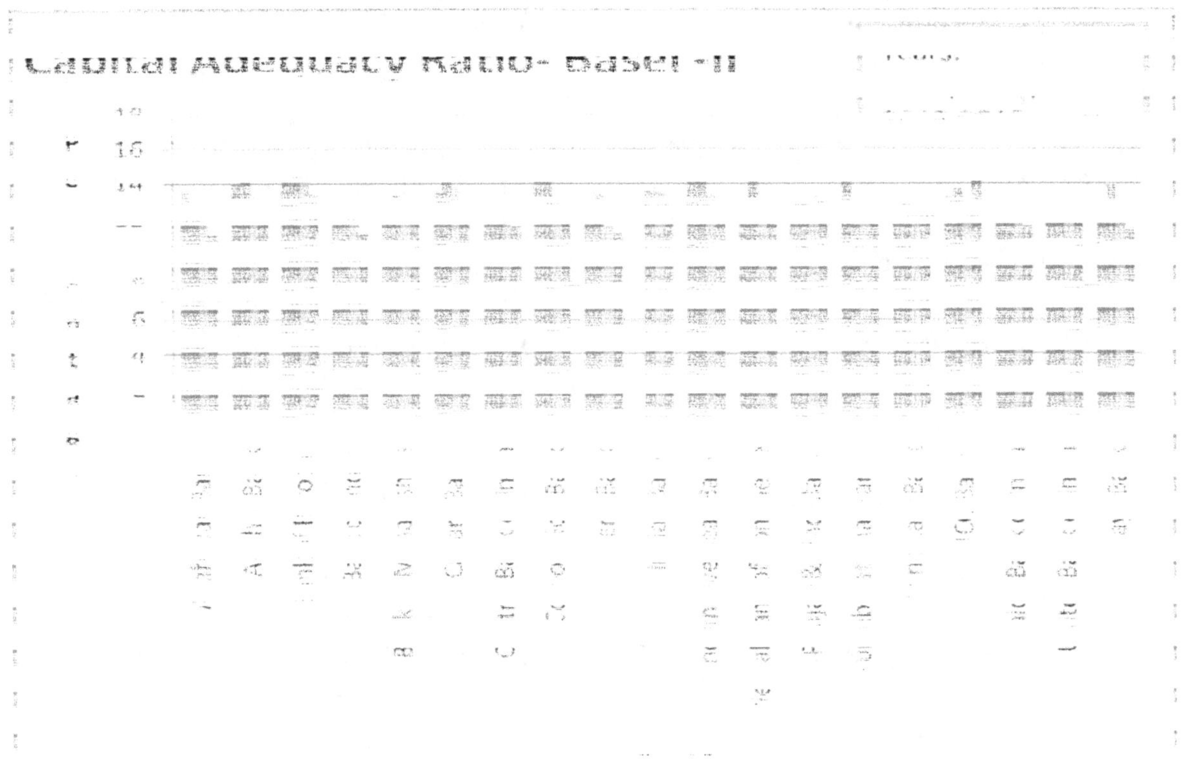

**Hypothesis Testing:** The researcher wanted to find out that if there is any significant difference regarding Capital Adequacy Ratio-Basel -II Performance among all 19 Banks of Nationalized during 2009-10 to 2012-13.

**Null Hypothesis:** There would no significant difference regarding the performance of Capital Adequacy Ratio- Basel -II among all 19 Banks of Nationalized during 2009-10 to 2012-13.

**Alternative Hypothesis:** There would significant difference regarding the performance of Capital Adequacy Ratio- Basel -II among all 19 Banks of Nationalized during 2009-10 to 2012-13.

**Calculations:** N=76, K=4, T=970, CF =12388.43, $\sum_i\sum_j\sum X_{ij}2$ =12626.12, T.S.S = 237.69, $\sum T_i2$ =49792.88, S.S. Between (SSC):59.78, S.S. Within (SSE): 177.90

**Table No. 3.19.1 ANOVA of Capital Adequacy Ratio-Basel -II of Nationalized Banks**

| Variation | d. f. | SS | MSS | F |
|---|---|---|---|---|
| **Between** | h-1=19-1 =18 | 59.78 | 3.32 | 1.064 |
| **Within** | N-h=76-19=57 | 177.90 | 3.12 | |
| **Total** | N-1=76-1=75 | 237.69 | | |

**Fcal > Ftab = 1.064<1.70= Accepted**

The above ANOVA Table represents the calculated value of F-is 1.064 which is less than the table value of, 1.70, at 5% level of significance. So Null Hypothesis is accepted. It indicates that there is no significant difference regarding the performance of Capital Adequacy Ratio- Basel -II among all 19 Banks of Nationalized during 2009-10 to 2012-13.

### 3.24) Net NPA to Net Advance Ratio of Selected Nationalized Bank for Last Four Years

The ratio of "Net NPA to advance ratio" is a credit efficiency parameter if the ratio is lower, it is a sign of credit efficiency. There is a big problem of NPAs for all the banks now a day. The high ratio of NPA is not good for any Bank or Business. This ratio indicates in ability of recovery from advances. For getting more business, some banks advances on higher risk. Afton giving advances, no efficiency to recover that money, can be seen in Nationalized Banks.

$$\text{Net NPA to Advance Ratio} = \frac{\text{Net non- performing Assets}}{\text{Advance}} \times 100$$

If the ratio is lower, it is a very good sign of credit efficiency of a bank. The higher ratio leads to weak performance of a bank NPA is the latest debatable and manageable issue now a day for every bank.

**Table No. 3.20 Net NPA to advance Ratio**

| S. N. | Nationalized Banks | Net NPA to Net Advance Ratio Percentage (%) | | | | | |
|---|---|---|---|---|---|---|---|
| | | 2010 | 2011 | 2012 | 2013 | Total | Avg. |
| 1 | Allahabad Bank | 0.66 | 0.79 | 0.98 | 3.19 | 5.62 | 1.41 |
| 2 | Andhra Bank | 0.17 | 0.38 | 0.91 | 2.45 | 3.91 | 0.98 |
| 3 | Bank of Baroda | 0.34 | 0.35 | 0.54 | 1.28 | 2.51 | 0.63 |
| 4 | Bank of India | 1.31 | 0.91 | 1.47 | 2.06 | 5.75 | 1.44 |
| 5 | Bank of Maharashtra | 1.64 | 1.32 | 0.84 | 0.52 | 4.32 | 1.08 |
| 6 | Canara Bank | 1.06 | 1.1 | 1.46 | 2.18 | 5.80 | 1.45 |
| 7 | Central Bank of India | 0.69 | 0.65 | 3.09 | 2.9 | 7.33 | 1.83 |
| 8 | Corporation Bank | 0.31 | 0.46 | 0.87 | 1.19 | 2.83 | 0.71 |
| 9 | Dena Bank | 1.21 | 1.22 | 1.01 | 1.39 | 4.83 | 1.21 |
| 10 | Indian Bank | 0.23 | 0.53 | 1.33 | 2.26 | 4.35 | 1.09 |
| 11 | Indian Overseas | 2.52 | 1.19 | 1.36 | 2.51 | 7.58 | 1.90 |

| | **Bank** | | | | | | |
|---|---|---|---|---|---|---|---|
| **12** | **Oriental Bank of Commerce** | 0.87 | 0.98 | 2.21 | 2.25 | 6.31 | 1.58 |
| **13** | **Punjab and Sind Bank** | 0.36 | 0.56 | 1.19 | 2.16 | 4.27 | 1.07 |
| **14** | **Punjab National Bank** | 0.53 | 0.85 | 1.52 | 2.34 | 5.24 | 1.31 |
| **15** | **Syndicate Bank** | 1.07 | 0.97 | 0.96 | 0.76 | 3.76 | 0.94 |
| **16** | **UCO Bank** | 1.17 | 1.84 | 1.96 | 3.17 | 8.14 | 2.04 |
| **17** | **Union Bank of India** | 0.81 | 1.19 | 1.7 | 1.61 | 5.31 | 1.33 |
| **18** | **United Bank of India** | 1.84 | 1.42 | 1.71 | 2.86 | 7.83 | 1.96 |
| **19** | **Vijaya Bank** | 1.40 | 1.52 | 1.72 | 1.3 | 5.94 | 1.49 |
| | **Total** | **18.19** | **18.23** | **26.83** | **38.38** | **101.63** | **25.41** |
| | **Avg.** | **0.95** | **0.95** | **1.41** | **2.02** | **5.35** | **1.34** |

(Various Bulletins of IBA)

The above Table shows Net NPA to Net Advance Ratio performance of 19 Nationalized Banks of the years 2010-11 to 2012-13. The Figures shows in ▪ Crore. The totals of 19 banks for the four years are 101.63 with the average of 1.34 the same things are represented through below Colum chart. The statically work for

Hypothesis testing through ANOVA test is calculated below to understand its performance and consistency.

**Chart No. 3.20 Net NPA to advance Ratio**

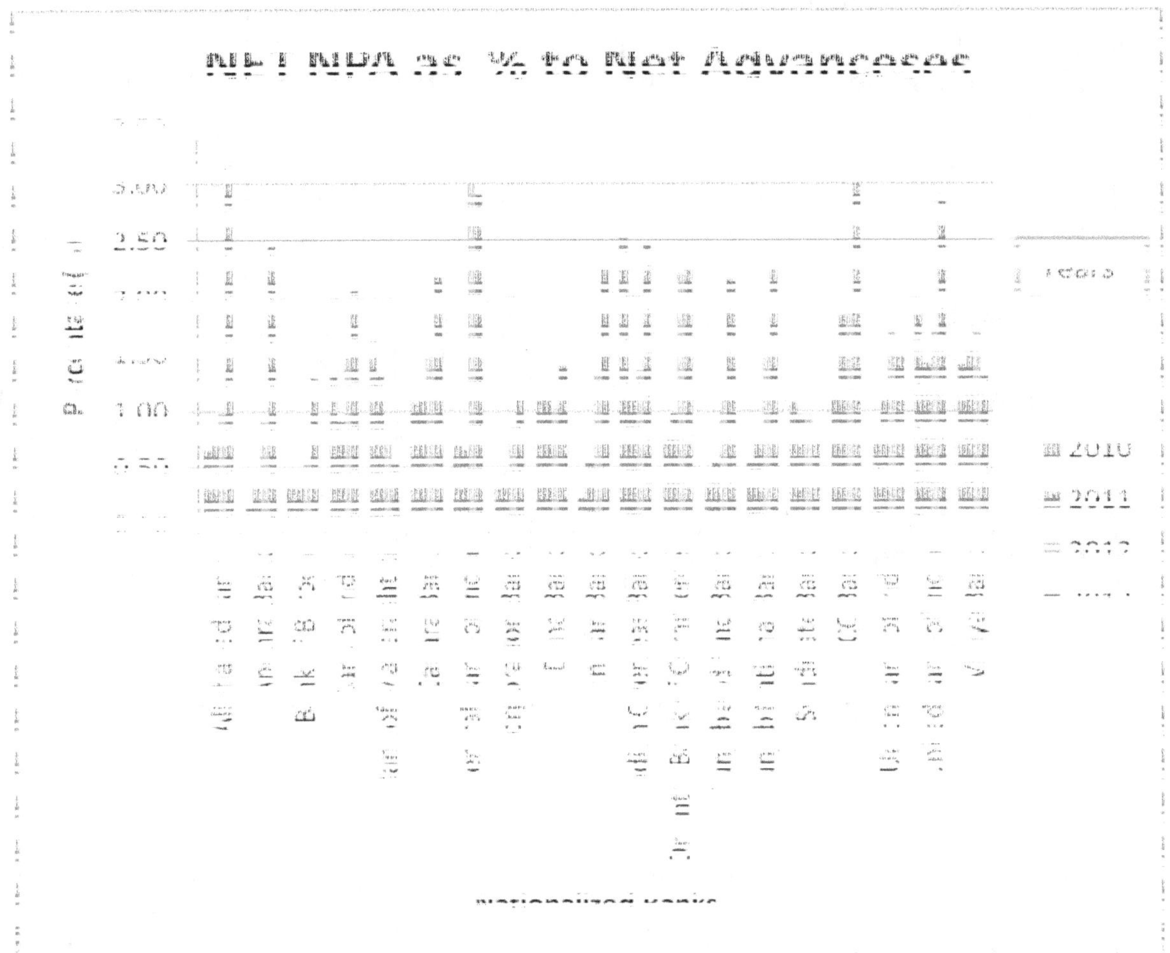

**Hypothesis Testing:** The researcher wanted to find out that if there is any significant difference regarding Net NPA to Net Advances Ratio Performance among all 19 Banks of Nationalized during 2009-10 to 2012-13.

**Null Hypothesis:** There would no significant difference regarding the performance of Net NPA to Net Advances Ratio among all 19 Banks of Nationalized during 2009-10 to 2012-13.

**Alternative Hypothesis:** There would significant difference regarding the performance of Net NPA to Net Advances Ratio among all 19 Banks of Nationalized during 2009-10 to 2012-13.

**Calculations:** N=76, K=4, T=101.63, CF =135.90, $\sum_i\sum_j\sum X_{ij}2$ =177.4981, T.S.S = 41.58, $\sum T_i2$ =590.6755, S.S. Between (SSC):11.76, S.S. Within (SSE): 29.811

**Table No. 3.20.1 ANOVA of Net NPA to Net Advances Ratio of Nationalized Banks**

| Variation | d. f. | SS | MSS | F |
|---|---|---|---|---|
| **Between** | h-1 = 19-1 =18 | 11.76 | 0.6538 | 1.250 |
| **Within** | N-h= 76-19=57 | 29.811 | 0.523 | |
| **Total** | N-1=76-1=75 | 41.58 | | |

**Fcal > Ftab = 1.250<1.70= Accepted**

The above ANOVA Table represents the calculated value of F-is 1.250 which is less than the table value of, 1.70, at 5% level of significance. So Null Hypothesis is accepted. It indicates that there is no significant difference regarding the performance of regarding Net NPA to Net Advances Ratio among all 19 Banks of Nationalized during 2009-10 to 2012-13.

## 3.25) Business per Employee Ratio of Selected Nationalized Bank for Last Four Years

Business is equal to aggregate of depends plus aggregate advances. In my study, "Business per employee" is a productivity parameter. It comes in Rs. Crores. This ratio is an indicator of degree of employee's productivity of banks. If the ratio is higher, it indicates more productivity of labour in banks. It also proves the managerial efficiency regarding staffing activities.

$$\text{Business per Employee (in Rs)} = \frac{\text{Business}}{\text{No. of Employee}}$$

**Table No. 3.21 Business per Employee**

| S. N. | Nationalized Banks | Business Per Employee (Spread as % 0f) | | | | | |
|---|---|---|---|---|---|---|---|
| | | 2010 | 2011 | 2012 | 2013 | Total | Avg. |
| 1 | Allahabad Bank | 8.45 | 10.63 | 12.17 | 13.73 | 44.98 | 11.25 |
| 2 | Andhra Bank | 9.39 | 11.65 | 12.62 | 13.55 | 47.21 | 11.80 |
| 3 | Bank of Baroda | 9.81 | 12.29 | 14.66 | 16.89 | 53.65 | 13.41 |
| 4 | Bank of India | 10.11 | 12.84 | 13.60 | 15.82 | 52.37 | 13.09 |
| 5 | Bank of Maharashtra | 7.62 | 8.25 | 9.67 | 12.56 | 38.10 | 9.53 |
| 6 | Canara Bank | 9.82 | 11.99 | 13.74 | 14.20 | 49.75 | 12.44 |
| 7 | Central Bank of India | 7.11 | 8.35 | 8.62 | 9.73 | 33.81 | 8.45 |
| 8 | Corporation Bank | 12.69 | 15.73 | 17.13 | 19.21 | 64.76 | 16.19 |
| 9 | Dena Bank | 8.27 | 10.77 | 12.84 | 14.31 | 46.19 | 11.55 |
| 10 | Indian Bank | 7.61 | 9.30 | 11.14 | 13.01 | 41.06 | 10.27 |
| 11 | Indian Overseas Bank | 7.12 | 10.05 | 11.76 | 12.88 | 41.81 | 10.45 |
| 12 | Oriental Bank of | 13.31 | 14.18 | 14.62 | 16.20 | 58.31 | 14.58 |

| | Commerce | | | | | | |
|---|---|---|---|---|---|---|---|
| 13 | Punjab & Sind Bank | 9.63 | 11.90 | 13.02 | 13.70 | 48.25 | 12.06 |
| 14 | Punjab National Bank | 8.08 | 10.18 | 11.32 | 11.65 | 41.23 | 10.31 |
| 15 | Syndicate Bank | 7.47 | 8.75 | 10.74 | 12.57 | 39.53 | 9.88 |
| 16 | UCO Bank | 8.64 | 10.69 | 11.64 | 11.89 | 42.86 | 10.72 |
| 17 | Union Bank of India | 8.53 | 10.43 | 10.70 | 12.15 | 41.81 | 10.45 |
| 18 | United Bank of India | 7.14 | 8.60 | 9.71 | 10.83 | 36.28 | 9.07 |
| 19 | Vijaya Bank | 8.36 | 9.28 | 11.28 | 12.40 | 41.32 | 10.33 |
| | Total | **169.16** | **205.86** | **230.98** | **257.28** | **863.28** | **215.82** |
| | Avg. | **8.90** | **10.83** | **12.15** | **13.54** | **45.44** | **11.36** |

(Various Bulletins of IBA)

The above Table shows Business per employee performance of 19 Nationalized Banks of the years 2010-11 to 20112-13. The amount is shows in Crores of rupees. The totals of 19 banks for four years are Rs.863.28 with the average of Rs.11.36 the same things are represented through below Colum chart. The statically work for Hypothesis testing through ANOVA test is calculated below to understand its performance and consistency.

**Chart No. 3.21 Business per Employee**

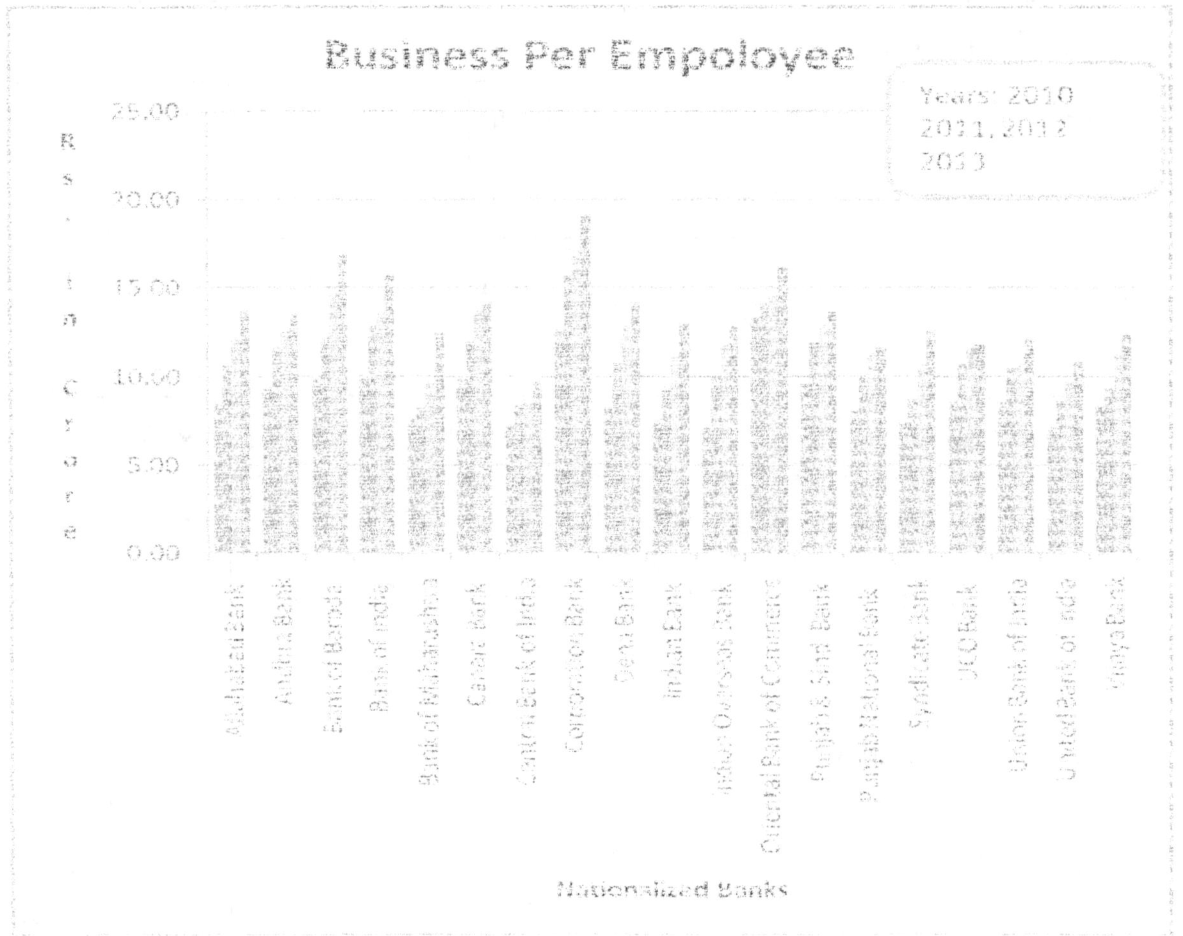


**Hypothesis Testing:** The researcher wanted to find out that if there is any significant difference regarding Business per Employee Performance among all 19 Banks of Nationalized during 2009-10 to 2012-13.

**Null Hypothesis:** There would no significant difference regarding the performance of Business per Employee among all 19 Banks of Nationalized during 2009-10 to 2012-13.

**Alternative Hypothesis:** There would significant difference regarding the performance of Business per Employee among all 19 Banks of Nationalized during 2009-10 to 2012-13.

**Calculations:** N=76, K=4, T=863.28, CF =9805.95, $\sum_i \sum_j \sum X_{ij}2$ =10320.97, T.S.S = 515.01, $\sum T_i 2$ =40303.73, S.S. Between (SSC):269.98, S.S. Within (SSE): 245.02

**Table No. 3.21.1 ANOVA of Business per Employee of Nationalized Banks**

| Variation | d. f. | SS | MSS | F |
|---|---|---|---|---|
| **Between** | h-1 = 19-1 =18 | 269.98 | 14.99 | 3.49 |
| **Within** | N-h= 76-19=57 | 245.02 | 4.29 | |
| **Total** | N-1=76-1=75 | 515.01 | | |

**Fcal > Ftab = 3.49>1.70= Rejected**

The above ANOVA Table represents the calculated value of F-is 3.49 which is more than the table value of, 1.70, at 5% level of significance. So Null Hypothesis is rejected. It indicates that there is significant difference regarding the performance of regarding Business per Employee among all 19 Banks of Nationalized during 2009-10 to 2012-13.

### 3.26) Profit per Employee Ratio of Selected Nationalized Bank for Last Four Years. (Profit per Employee)

Another ratio is "profit per employee" shows the labour productivity of banks with the angle of profit. Net profit per employee can be obtained in rupees. It indicates the profitability and productivity per employee for the bank positive and higher ratio indicates higher labour productivity.

$$\text{Profit per Employee (In Rs)} = \frac{\text{Net Profit}}{\text{No. of Employee}}$$

In this ratio the higher position indicates higher labour productivity and profitability per employee for the bank.

**Table No. 3.22 Profit per Employee**

| S.N. | Nationalized Banks | Profit per Employee (Spread as % 0f) | | | | | |
|---|---|---|---|---|---|---|---|
| | | 2010 | 2011 | 2012 | 2013 | TOTAL | AVG. |
| 1 | Allahabad Bank | 5.76 | 6.70 | 8.36 | 5.25 | 26.07 | 6.52 |
| 2 | Andhra Bank | 7.00 | 9.00 | 9.00 | 9.00 | 34.00 | 8.50 |
| 3 | Bank of Baroda | 8.00 | 11.00 | 12.00 | 10.00 | 41.00 | 10.25 |
| 4 | Bank of India | 4.39 | 6.20 | 6.40 | 6.44 | 23.43 | 5.86 |
| 5 | Bank of Maharashtra | 3.21 | 2.38 | 3.12 | 5.59 | 14.30 | 3.58 |
| 6 | Canara Bank | 7.35 | 9.76 | 8.21 | 6.96 | 32.28 | 8.07 |
| 7 | Central Bank of India | 3.30 | 3.96 | 1.51 | 2.83 | 11.60 | 2.90 |
| 8 | Corporation Bank | 9.52 | 10.92 | 10.90 | 9.68 | 41.02 | 10.26 |
| 9 | Dena Bank | 4.86 | 6.15 | 7.87 | 7.31 | 26.19 | 6.55 |
| 10 | Indian Bank | 7.92 | 8.88 | 9.30 | 8.38 | 34.48 | 8.62 |
| 11 | Indian Overseas Bank | 2.63 | 4.16 | 3.84 | 1.99 | 12.62 | 3.16 |
| 12 | Oriental Bank of Commerce | 7.39 | 9.04 | 6.21 | 7.03 | 29.67 | 7.42 |
| 13 | Punjab & Sind | 6.00 | 6.00 | 6.00 | 4.00 | 22.00 | 5.50 |

| | | | | | | | |
|---|---|---|---|---|---|---|---|
| | **Bank** | | | | | | |
| **14** | **Punjab National Bank** | 7.31 | 8.35 | 8.42 | 8.06 | 32.14 | 8.04 |
| **15** | **Syndicate Bank** | 3.18 | 3.99 | 5.29 | 8.11 | 20.57 | 5.14 |
| **16** | **UCO Bank** | 4.43 | 4.19 | 5.09 | 2.72 | 16.43 | 4.11 |
| **17** | **Union Bank of India** | 7.47 | 8.00 | 6.00 | 7.00 | 28.47 | 7.12 |
| **18** | **United Bank of India** | 2.11 | 3.48 | 4.08 | 2.53 | 12.20 | 3.05 |
| **19** | **Vijaya Bank** | 4.50 | 6.30 | 5.00 | 5.00 | 20.80 | 5.20 |
| | **Total** | **106.33** | **128.46** | **126.60** | **117.88** | **479.27** | **119.82** |
| | **Avg.** | **5.59** | **6.76** | **6.66** | **6.20** | **25.22** | **6.31** |

(Various Bulletins of IBA)

The above Table shows Business per employee performance of 19 Nationalized Banks of the years 2010-11 to 20112-13. The amount is shows in Lakh of rupees. The totals of 19 banks for four years are Rs.479.27 with the average of Rs.6.31 the same things are represented through below Colum chart. The statically work for Hypothesis testing through ANOVA test is calculated below to understand its performance and consistency.

**Chart No. 3.22 Profit per Employee**

**Hypothesis Testing:** The researcher wanted to find out that if there is any significant difference regarding Profit per Employee Performance among all 19 Banks of Nationalized during 2009-10 to 2012-13.

**Null Hypothesis:** There would no significant difference regarding the performance of regarding Profit per Employee among all 19 Banks of Nationalized during 2009-10 to 2012-13.

**Alternative Hypothesis:** There would significant difference regarding the performance of regarding Profit per Employee among all 19 Banks of Nationalized during 2009-10 to 2012-13.

**Calculations:** N=76, K=4, T=479.27, CF =3022.36, $\sum_i\sum_j\sum X_{ij}2$ =3487.99, T.S.S = 465.6250, $\sum T_i2$ =13645.7287, S.S. Between (SSC):389.072, S.S. Within (SSE): 76.552

**Table No. 3.22.1 ANOVA of Profit per Employee of Nationalized Banks**

| Variation | d. f. | SS | MSS | F |
|---|---|---|---|---|
| **Between** | h-1=19-1 =18 | 389.072 | 21.61 | 16.13 |
| **Within** | N-h=76-19=57 | 76.552 | 1.34 | |
| **Total** | N-1=76-1=75 | 465.6250 | | |

**Fcal > Ftab = 16.13>1.70= Rejected**

The above ANOVA Table represents the calculated value of F-is 16.13 which is more than the table value of, 1.70, at 5% level of significance. So Null Hypothesis is rejected. It indicates that there is significant difference regarding the performance of regarding Profit per Employee among all 19 Banks of Nationalized during 2009-10 to 2012-13. This Chapter covers statically work and the finding in details which can helpful for banks for the better and smooth operation discussed in chapter five.

# CHAPTER NO. 4

# BASEL-I, II AND III

This work is covers the major developments in the efforts towards harmonization of bank capital standards by the Basel Committee on Banking Supervision (BCBS) viz., the Basel Accord of 1988, the 1996 amendment to the Basel Accord, the Basel II framework and the subsequent refinements and Basel -III. Though capital regulation in banking had existed in some form or the other even before the signing of Basel Accord in 1988, the Accord marked a watershed in the efforts towards harmonization of bank capital regulation across nations. More than 100 countries adopted the Basel I regulatory requirement of capital at eight per cent of risk-weighted assets. The high pace of financial innovations, however, brought into light the deficiencies of Basel I framework and the need for a more flexible and more risk-sensitive capital standards. After years of intense consultations and modifications, the revised capital framework, popularly known as Basel II was released by the BCBS in June 2004. While the implementation of Basel II is in progress in several countries across the globe, soundness and stability of the international banking has been severely challenged by the outbreak of the sub-prime crisis in the US mortgage market in 2007. The crisis has spread across sectors and across nations without showing any sign of abatement and by now has taken the shape of an international financial market crisis. This has brought into sharp focus the need for faster implementation of Basel II. At the same time, further refinements in the Basel II framework are being mooted with a view to ensuring that the banking sector serves its traditional role as a shock absorber to the financial system, rather than an amplifier of risk between the financial sector and the real economy. The issues being re-examined include inter alia strengthening the risk capture on trading book and off-balance sheet exposures, dampening procyclicality, strengthening framework to assess liquidity at banks, and globally coordinated supervisory follow-up exercises. The Basel framework on capital regulation thus continues to evolve in response to the changing circumstances, and has come to be established at the core of the assessment of soundness and stability of the banking system.

The forces of globalization and deregulation brought about sweeping changes in the banking sector across countries. While new vistas opened up for augmenting revenues of banks, increased competition in the wake of new products, new processes and technological progress exposed banking to higher risks. This gave renewed emphasis to efforts towards harmonization of international capital standards which gained momentum under the aegis of Bank for International Settlement (BIS). The setting up of the Basel Committee on Banking Supervision (BCBS) in 1975, following the failure of Bankhus I. D. Herstatt in Cologne, Germany, was a significant contribution of the BIS towards international harmonization of supervisory standards. The BCBS contributed to supervisory standards through issuance of 'best practices' papers. Although these standards are not legally binding, they have made substantial impact on banking supervision, in general, and bank capital regulation, in particular. Robust risk management and strong capital position have come to be recognized to be crucial to ensuring safety and soundness of individual banking organizations as also for fostering stability in the financial system.

Though capital regulation in banking existed even before the Basel Accord of 1988, there were vast variations in the method and timing of its adoption in different countries. In the pre-Basel phase, the use of capital ratios to establish minimum regulatory requirements was being tested for more than a century. In the US, between 1864 and 1950s, the supervisors: (i) tried to make use of a variety of capital adequacy measures such as static minimum capital requirements based on the population of each bank's service area, ratios of capital-to-total deposits and capital-to-total assets; (ii) adjusted assets for risk; and (iii) created capital-to-risk-assets ratios, but none was universally accepted at that time. Even the banking sector was in favour of a more subjective system where the regulators could decide which capital requirements were suited for a particular bank as a function of its risk profile. The emergence of more bank failures and diminishing bank capital triggered a regulatory response in 1981 when, for the first time, the federal banking agencies in the US introduced explicit numerical regulatory capital requirements. The adopted standards employed a leverage ratio of primary capital (which consisted mainly of equity and loan loss reserves) to average total assets. However, each regulator had a different view as to what exactly constituted bank capital.

Over the next few years, regulators worked to converge upon a uniform measure. The inadequate capitalisation of Japanese banks and differing banking structures (universal banks of Germany vis-à-vis narrow banks of US) and varying risk profile of individual banks made agreement on capital standards difficult. The Congress in the US passed legislations in 1983, directing the federal banking agencies to issue regulations addressing capital adequacy. The legislation provided the impetus for a common definition of regulatory capital and final uniform capital requirements in 1985. By 1986, regulators in the US were concerned about the failure of primary capital ratio to differentiate among risks and not providing an accurate measure of the risk exposures associated with innovative and expanding banking activities, most notably off-balance-sheet activities at larger institutions. Regulators in the US began studying the risk-based capital frameworks of other countries – France, the UK and West Germany had implemented risk-based capital standards in 1979, 1980 and 1985, respectively. The agencies also revisited the earlier studies of risk-based capital ratios. Leading the initiative in 1987, the US joined the UK in announcing a bilateral agreement on capital adequacy, soon to be joined by Japan (buoyed by a booming stock market in raising capital). Subsequently in December 1987 'international convergence of capital measures and capital standards' was achieved. In July 1988, the Basel I Capital Accord was created.

As regards banking companies, the primary functions of capital are to support banks' operations by absorbing losses and changes in asset values, and thereby maintaining solvency. A comfortable bank capital level boosts depositors' confidence, encourages shareholders' interest in governance of bank and provides protection to creditors in the event of liquidation. Bank capital acts as an insurance against uncertainty.

The Basel Core Principles, as a framework of minimum standards for sound supervisory practices considered universally applicable, emphasise capital adequacy and risk management process as one of the significant prudential regulation and requirements. According to the BCBS core principles, supervisors must set prudent and appropriate minimum capital adequacy requirements for banks that reflect the risks that the bank undertakes, and must define the components of capital, bearing in mind its ability to absorb losses. At least for internationally active banks, these requirements must not be less than those established in the applicable Basel requirement. Supervisors must be satisfied that banks and banking groups have in place a comprehensive risk management process (including Board and senior management oversight) to identify, evaluate, monitor and control or mitigate all material risks and to assess their overall capital adequacy in relation to their risk profile. These processes should be commensurate with the size and complexity of the institution.

The supervisory and regulatory framework governing the capital adequacy of international banks as evolved by the BCBS over the years. The paper is organized into four sections. Section 1 elaborates the Basel Accord of 1988, and the 1996 amendment relating to market risk, which was the most important modification in the Basel norms on capital regulation before the introduction of Basel II framework. Section 4.1 deals with the criticisms of the Basel Capital Accord, 1988. Section 4.2 presents the Basel II framework, followed by a discussion of a few conceptual and implementation issues relating to the new capital adequacy framework and outlines the initiatives taken by the Basel Committee in response to the recent financial turmoil. Section-4.3 covers Indian Banking Sector – Road towards Basel III.

## Section 4.1: The Basel I Framework

### 4.1.1 The Basel Capital Accord, 1988

As discussed earlier, the BCBS has been making efforts over the years to secure international convergence of supervisory regulations governing the capital adequacy of international banks. The Committee adopted a consultative process wherein the proposals are circulated not only to the central bank Governors of G-10 countries, but also to the supervisory authorities worldwide. The major milestones in the Basel norms of capital measurement and capital standards are: Capital Accord of 1988, market risk amendment of January 1996, New Capital Adequacy framework of June 2004. The two fundamental objectives of the Committee's work on regulatory convergence are: (i) the framework should serve to strengthen the soundness and stability of the international banking system; and (ii) the framework should be fair and have a high degree of consistency in its application to banks in different countries with a view to diminishing an existing source of competitive inequality among international banks.

The Basel Accord was endorsed by 12 countries (all G-10 countries plus Luxembourg and Switzerland) in July 1988 under the chairmanship of W P Cooke (Bardos, 1988). As many banks were undercapitalized at that time, a target of 7.25 per cent was set to be met by the end of 1990, and the 8 per cent requirement was to be achieved by the end of 1992. Since then, the Basel Accord has been subjected to several amendments and has itself been evolving under a consultative framework. The Accord has been endorsed by many countries other than G-10 countries, and applied to many banks other than those conducting significant international business. The Accord was phased in by January 1993, and currently more than hundred countries have adopted the Basel Norms.

The main features of Basel- I are documented in 'International Convergence of Capital Measurement and Capital Standards 'over three sections (BCBS, 1998). While the first two describe the framework in terms of the constituents of capital and the risk weighting system, the third section deals with the target ratio. The framework provides a framework for fair and reasonable degree of consistency in the application of capital standards in different countries, on a shared definition of capital. The central focus of this framework is credit risk and, as a further aspect of credit risk, country transfer risk.

Capital as per Basel Accord, better known as regulatory capital, is sum of Tier I and Tier II capital which a bank is required to maintain in relation to its risk-weighted assets. Under both Basel I and Basel II, the regulatory definition of capital is comprised of three levels (or 'tiers') of capital. An item qualifies for a given tier if it satisfies the specific criteria. Tier 1 Capital (or 'core capital') comprises only those elements which have the highest capacity for absorbing losses on an ongoing basis. Tier 2 Capital (or 'supplementary capital') is made up of a broad mix of near equity components and hybrid capital/debt instruments, the total of which is limited to 100 per cent of Tier 1 Capital. It is subdivided into two categories: (i) Upper Tier 2 comprises items closer to common equity, like perpetual subordinated debt; (ii) Lower Tier 2 comprises items closer to debt than of equity. It also includes various types of reserves whose values and/or availability are more uncertain than disclosed reserves. Tier 3 Capital (or 'additional supplementary capital') was added in 1996 and can only be used to meet capital requirements for market risk.

The Committee recommended a weighted risk ratio in which capital is related to different categories of asset or off-balance-sheet exposure, weighted according to broad categories of relative riskiness, as the preferred method for assessing the capital adequacy of banks -other methods of capital measurement are considered to be supplementary to the risk-weighted approach. The risk weighted approach has been preferred over a simple gearing ratio approach because: (i) it provides a fairer basis for making international comparisons between banking systems whose structures may differ; (ii) it allows off-balance-sheet exposures to be incorporated more easily into the measure; (iii) it does not deter banks from holding liquid or other assets which carry low risk. There were inevitably some broad-brush judgments in deciding which weight should apply to different types of asset and the framework of weights has been kept as simple as possible with only five weights being used for on balance-sheet items i.e., 0, 10, 20, 50 and 100 per cent (Table 4.1). Government bonds of the countries that were members of the Organization for Economic Cooperation and Development (OECD) (which includes all members of the Basel Committee) were assigned a zero risk weight, all short-term interbank loans and all long-term interbank loans to banks headquartered in OECD countries a 20 per cent risk weight, home mortgages a 50 per cent risk weight, and most other loans a 100 per cent risk weight.

**Table No. 4.1: Risk Weights by Category of On-balance Sheet Assets**

| Risk Weight | Categories of Asset |
|---|---|
| **0%** | (a) Cash<br>(b) Claims on central governments and central banks denominated in national currency and funded in that currency<br>(c) Other claims on OECD, central governments, and central banks<br>(d) Claims collateralized by cash of OECD central-government securities or guaranteed by OECD central governments |
| **0, 10, 20 or 50%** (at national | Claims on domestic public-sector entities, excluding central government, and loans guaranteed by or collateralized by securities issued by such entities |

| | |
|---|---|
| discretion) | |
| **20%** | (a) Claims on multilateral development banks (IBRD, IADB, AsDB, AfDB, EIB, EBRD) and claims guaranteed by, or collateralized by securities issued by such banks<br>(b) Claims on banks incorporated in the OECD and claims guaranteed by OECD incorporated banks<br>(c) Claims on securities firms incorporated in the OECD subject to comparable supervisory and regulatory arrangements, including in particular risk-based capital requirements,6 and claims guaranteed by these securities firms<br>(d) Claims on banks incorporated in countries outside the OECD with a residual maturity of up to one year and claims with a residual maturity of up to one year guaranteed by banks incorporated in countries outside the OECD<br>(e) Claims on non-domestic OECD public-sector entities, excluding central government, and claims guaranteed by or collateralized by securities issued by such entities<br>(f) Cash items in process of collection |
| **50%** | Loans fully secured by mortgage on residential property that is or will be occupied by the borrower or that is rented |
| **100%** | (a) Claims on the private sector |

| | |
|---|---|
| | (b) Claims on banks incorporated outside the OECD with a residual maturity of over one year<br>(c) Claims on central governments outside the OECD (unless denominated in national currency - and funded in that currency)<br>(d) Claims on commercial companies owned by the public sector<br>(e) Premises, plant and equipment and other fixed assets<br>(f) Real estate and other investments (including non-consolidated investment participations in other companies)<br>(g) Capital instruments issued by other banks (unless deducted from capital) All other assets |

Off-balance sheet contingent contracts, such as letters of credit, loan commitments and derivative instruments, which are traded over the counter, needed to be first converted to a credit equivalent and then assigned appropriate risk weights (Table 4.2).

The initial standards required internationally active banks to meet two minimum capital ratios, both computed as a percentage of the risk-weighted (both on- and off-balance sheet) assets. The minimum Tier 1 ratio was 4 per cent of risk-weighted assets, while total capital (tiers 1 and 2) had to exceed 8 per cent of risk-weighted assets. The three major principles of the Basel Accord are as follows:

(1) A bank must hold equity capital to at least a fixed per cent (8 per cent) of its risk-weighted credit exposures as well as capital to cover market risks in the bank's trading account.

(2) When capital falls below this minimum requirement, shareholders may be permitted to retain control, provided that they recapitalize the bank to meet the minimum capital ratio.

(3) If the shareholders fail to do so, the bank's regulatory agency is empowered to sell or liquidate the bank.

**Table No. 4.2: Credit Conversion Factors for Off-balance Sheet Items**

| | Instruments | Credit Conversion Factors (%) |
|---|---|---|
| 1. | Direct credit substitutes, for example, general guarantees of indebtedness (including standby letters of credit serving as financial guarantees for loans and securities) and acceptances (including endorsements with the character of acceptances) | 100 |
| 2. | Certain transaction-related contingent items (for example, performance bonds, bid bonds, warranties and standby letters of credit related to particular transactions) | 50 |
| 3. | Short-term self-liquidating trade-related contingencies (such as documentary credits collateralized by the underlying shipments) | 20 |
| 4. | Sale and repurchase agreements and asset sales with recourse,1 where the credit risk remains with the bank | 100 |
| 5. | Forward asset purchases, forward deposits and partly-paid shares and securities, which represent commitments with certain drawdown | 100 |
| 6. | Note issuance facilities and revolving underwriting facilities | 50 |
| 7. | Other commitments (for example, formal standby facilities and credit lines) with an original maturity of over one year | 50 |
| 8. | Similar commitments with an original maturity of up to one year, or which can be unconditionally cancelled at any time | 0 |

Capital adequacy is just one of the several factors for assessing the strength of banks, and therefore capital ratios, judged in isolation, may provide a misleading guide to relative strength. Much also depends on the quality of a bank's assets and, importantly, the level of provisions a bank may be holding outside its capital against assets of doubtful value. Recognising the close relationship between capital and provisions, monitoring the provisioning policies by banks in member countries and convergence of policies in this field as well has come to engage the attention of the Basel Committee. The fiscal treatment and accounting presentation for tax purposes of certain classes of provisions for losses and of capital reserves derived from retained earnings, which differ for different countries, may to some extent distort the comparability of the real or apparent capital positions of international banks. Convergence in tax regimes, though desirable, lies outside the purview of the Committee, though tax considerations also need to be reviewed to the extent that they affect the comparability of the capital adequacy. Another issue of relevance is the ownership structures and the position of banks within financial conglomerate groups. The capital requirement should be applied to banks on a consolidated basis, including subsidiaries undertaking banking and financial business. The ownership structures should not be such as to weaken the capital position of the bank or expose it to risks stemming from other parts of the group.

Most regulatory authorities have adopted allocation of capital to risk assets ratio system as the basis of assessment of capital adequacy which takes into account the element of risk associated with various types of assets reflected in the balance sheet as well as in respect of off-balance sheet assets.

With due regard to particular features of the existing supervisory and accounting systems in individual member countries, the capital adequacy framework allowed for a degree of national discretion in the way in which it is applied. It also provided for a transitional period so that the existing circumstances in different countries can be reflected in flexible arrangements that allow time for adjustment.

### 4.1.2 The 1996 Amendment to the Basel Accord

The Basel Capital Accord of July 1988 was amended in January 1996 with the objective of providing an explicit capital cushion for the price risks to which banks are exposed, particularly those arising from their trading activities (BCBS, 1998). The amendment covers market risks arising from banks' open positions in foreign exchange, traded debt securities, traded equities, commodities and options. A companion paper describing the way in which G-10 supervisory authorities plan to use 'backtesting' (i.e., ex-post comparisons between model results and actual performance) in conjunction with banks' internal risk measurement systems as a basis for applying capital charges was also released.

The novelty of this amendment lied in the fact that it allowed banks to use, as an alternative to the standardized measurement framework originally put forward in April 1993, their internal models to determine the required capital charge for market risk. The standard approach defines the risk charges associated with each position and specifies how these charges are to be aggregated into an overall market risk capital charge. The minimum capital requirement is expressed in terms of two separately calculated charges, one applying to the 'specific risk' of each security, whether it is a short or a long position, and the other to the interest rate risk in the portfolio (termed 'general market risk') where long and short positions in different securities or instruments can be offset.

The internal models approach, in contrast, allows a bank to use its proprietary in-house models to estimate the value-at-risk (VaR) in its trading account, that is, the maximum loss that the portfolio is likely to experience over a given holding period with a certain probability. The market risk capital requirement is then set based on the VaR estimate as the higher of the following two: (i) the previous day's value-at-risk; and (ii) three times the average of the daily value-at-risk of the preceding sixty business days. This amendment also defined a Tier 3 capital to cover market risks, and allowed banks to count subordinated debt (with an original maturity of at least two years) in this tier.

### 4.1.3 Basel-I Drawbacks

The major achievement of the Basel Capital Accord 1988 has been introduction of discipline through imposition of risk-based capital standards both as measure of the strength of banks and as a trigger device for supervisors' intervention under the scheme of prompt corrective action (PCA). The fundamental objective of the 1988 Accord has been to develop a framework that would further strengthen the soundness and stability of the international banking system while maintaining sufficient consistency that capital adequacy regulation will not be a significant source of competitive inequality among internationally active banks. The design of the

Accord, however, has met with severe criticisms which are discussed in detail in this Section.

First, the standards have not been able to meet one of the central objectives, viz., to make the competitive playing field more even for international banks. For example, in a comparison of the competitiveness of banks in the United States and Japan after the implementation of Basel Accord, it was found that the Accord had no impact on competitiveness. The authors also showed that other factors such as taxes, accounting requirements, disclosure laws, implicit and explicit deposit guarantees, social overhead expenditures, employment restrictions, and insolvency laws, also affect the competitiveness of an institution. Consequently, imposing the same capital standard on all institutions that differ with regard to those other factors is unlikely to enhance competitive equity.

The other fundamental objective of the Accord in terms of increasing the soundness and stability of the banking system need not necessarily be met. Capital adequacy regulation in some contexts could even accentuate systemic risk. Therefore, under international financial integration, a simple coordination on some parts of banking regulation (uniform capital requirements), but not others (the forbearance in supervisor's closure policies), could give rise to international negative externalities that destabilize the global system. Furthermore, a design of capital adequacy requirements, based only on individual bank risk, as the actual proposed in the Basel Accord, is showed to be suboptimal in both papers. All the above arguments suggest the need for an analysis of how banks set their capital to assets ratio.

The bank capital adequacy regulation as in Basel I is also criticised for imposing the same rules on all banks even within a country. The simple 'one-size-fits-all' standard under Basel I encouraged transactions using securitisation and off-balance sheet exposures, whose principal aim was to arbitrage bank capital. The Basel rules encouraged some banks to move to high quality assets off their balance sheet, thereby reducing the average quality of bank loan portfolios. Furthermore, banks took large credit risks in the least creditworthy borrowers who had the highest expected returns in a risk-weighted class.

Perhaps the most fundamental problem with the Basel I standards stems from the fact that they attempt to define and measure bank portfolio risk categorically by placing different types of bank exposures into separate 'buckets'. Banks are then required to maintain minimum capital proportional to a weighted sum of the amounts of assets in the various risk buckets. That approach incorrectly assumes, however, that risks are identical within each bucket and that the overall risk of a bank's portfolio is equal to the sum of the risks across the various buckets. But, most of the times, the risk-weight classes did not match realised losses. In an examination of loan charge-offs and delinquency rates for banks, it was found that the 1988 Capital Accord risk weights did not accurately track the credit experience in the US. Collateralized loans had the least risk. Commercial loans appear to be under-burdened by the Basel I weights and mortgages were overburdened. All activities or loans within a particular category do not have the same market-based credit risk. For example, not all mortgages are exactly or even approximately half as risky as all commercial loans (reflecting the assigned risk weights).

Securitization of banks' credit portfolios has become a widespread phenomenon in industrialized countries. At first, banks used to sell their mortgage loans, for such loans represented accurately evaluated risks. But since the advent of e-finance, it is now possible to expand this activity to other types of loans, including those made to small businesses. This type of activity also allows banks to have a much more liquid credit-risk portfolio and, in theory, to adjust their capital ratio to an optimal economic level rather than sticking to the ratio decreed by the Basel Committee.

Moreover, diversification of a bank's credit-risk portfolio is not taken into account in the computation of capital ratios. The aggregate risk of a bank is not equal to the sum of its individual risks -diversification through the pooling of risks can significantly reduce the overall portfolio risk of a bank. Indeed, a well-established principle of finance is that the combination in a single portfolio of assets with different risk characteristics can produce less overall risk than merely adding up the risks of the individual assets. The Accord does not take into account the benefits of portfolio diversification.

The standards have also been criticized for failing to assign 'correct' risk weights and for failing to promote bank safety effectively. Although the risk weights attempt to reflect credit risk, they are not based on market assessments but instead favour claims on banks headquartered in OECD countries and OECD Governments, and on residential mortgages. The 1988 standards also assign a zero risk weight to all sovereign debt issued by countries belonging to the OECD. Although sovereign debt was not at the centre of the Asian financial crises, it played a central role in the earlier Mexican financial and currency crisis of 1994-1995. Illustratively, Mexico and South Korea, both of which experienced substantial bank insolvencies, are now members of the OECD; and hence, the bonds issued by their Governments are subject to the zero risk weight.

Cosmetic changes in bank capital are possible because the measures of both capital and risk are imperfect proxies for the economically relevant variables. Regulators cannot construct perfect measures as long as bank managers have private information about the value or risk of their portfolios. However, even granting the impossibility of perfect measures, the crudeness of current measures offers substantial measures for cosmetic changes in capital ratios. Capital-to-total asset measures (leverage standards) are easily defeated by reducing low-risk, high-liquidity assets and substituting a smaller quantity of higher risk, lower liquidity assets. The existing risk-based standards are slightly more sophisticated, but numerous flaws remain. The standards (i) require that most commercial and consumer loans carry the same risk weighting and do not allow for differential asset quality within asset classes, (ii) do not allow for risks other than credit risks and (iii) do not account for diversification across different types of risk or even across credit risks. Banks, can therefore, exploit accounting conventions by accelerating the recognition of gains on assets with market value greater than book value, while slowing the recognition of losses on assets with market value less than book value.

The problems are compounded by the fact that the Basel standards are computed on the basis of book-value accounting measures of capital, not market values. Accounting practices vary significantly across the G-10 countries and often produce results that differ markedly from market assessments.

The Subgroup of the Shadow Financial Regulatory Committees of Europe, Japan, Latin America and the United States observed that problems inherent in assigning risk weights in the Basel standards are compounded by the inappropriate division of bank capital into different 'tiers'. In the process, the Basel Committee implicitly favours equity over other forms of capital, specifically, subordinated debt. The preference for equity not only is unwarranted but also may be counterproductive since subordinated debt, which is included in Tier 2 capital, but not in Tier 1, often can be superior to equity from a regulatory standpoint.

The financial crises of the 1990s involving international banks have highlighted several additional weaknesses in the Basel standards that permitted and in some cases even encouraged, excessive risk taking and misallocations of bank credit. Notably, Asian banks' short-term borrowing of foreign currencies was a major source of vulnerability in the country's most seriously affected by the Asian financial crisis. The current Basel standards contributed to that problem by assigning a relatively favourable 20 per cent risk weight to short-term interbank lending - only one-fifth as large as the weight assigned to longer-term lending or to lending to most private non-bank borrowers. Putting aside the important issue of whether the standards should have assigned different risk weights for short-term lending to banks in the developed and in the developing world–a distinction not captured by the current system of weighting asset risks– it is clear that the much lower risk weight given to interbank lending than to other types of bank loans encouraged some large internationally active banks to lend too much for short durations to banks in Southeast Asia. Those banks re-loaned the funds in domestic currency at substantially higher rates and assumed large foreign exchange rate risk. One would expect those distortions to be most pernicious for banks that are capital-constrained. Therefore, it is not surprising that Japanese banks, which have been weakly capitalized throughout the 1990s, had accumulated the heaviest concentrations of claims on faltering Asian banks. As noted in the document itself, the risk weights do not attempt to take account of risks other than credit risk, viz., market risks, liquidity risk and operational risks that may be important sources of insolvency exposure for banks. The Basel Committee itself has recognized the validity of many of the above-mentioned criticisms. These shortcomings seem to have distorted the behaviour of banks and this makes it much more complicated to monitor them. In fact, it is not even clear that the higher capital ratios observed since the introduction of this new form of capital regulation necessarily lower risks.

### 4.1.4 BASEL-I: ACCORD 1988 in Briefs

- Response to Banking Sector Distress
- Focus on Credit Risk
- Provided definition of Capital &
- Structure of Risk Weights
- Tier I Capital Ratio= Tier I Capital/All RWAs
- Total Capital Ratio= [Tier I+ Tier II Capital]/All RWAs
- Leverage Ratio= Total Capital/ Average Total Assets
- India implemented Basel I in April 1992
- All the banks were asked to achieve CRAR of 4 per cent by March 1993 and 8 percent by March 1996.
- Relatively simple structure
- Provided competitive equality among internationally active banks
- Introduced disciplined management of capital
- Market and operational risks excluded for capital adequacy assessment
- In assessment of credit risk, no differentiation among debtors of different quality and rating
- Not able to assess risk assessment of new financial instruments

## Section 4.2: The Revised Framework: Basel II

The Basel II framework entails a more comprehensive measure and minimum standard for capital adequacy that national supervisory authorities are working to implement through domestic rule-making and adoption procedures. It seeks to improve on the existing rules by aligning regulatory capital requirements more closely to the underlying risks that banks face, i.e., trend towards convergence of the regulatory and economic capital, which is especially evident in the advanced approaches. In addition, the Basel II framework is intended to promote a more forward-looking approach to capital supervision, one that encourages banks to identify the risks they may face, today and in the future, and to develop or improve their ability to manage those risks. As a result, it is intended to be more flexible and better able to evolve with advances in markets and risk management practices.

The fundamental objective of the Committee's work to revise the 1988 Accord has been to develop a more comprehensive approach towards addressing risks, and, thereby, improve the way regulatory capital requirements reflect underlying risks, i.e., better risk sensitivity. The review of the Accord was designed to better address the financial innovations that have occurred in recent years, for example, asset securitization structures. The review was also aimed at recognizing the improvements in risk measurement and control that have occurred.

In June 1999, the BCBS released for comments its proposal to introduce a new capital adequacy framework for International Convergence of Capital Measurement and Capital Standards, more popularly known as the Basel II. The BCBS held three quantitative impact studies apart from several rounds of consultations and discussions with the member countries, and the final version of the New Basel Norms was released by the BIS on June 26, 2004, which would replace the 1988 Capital Accord by year-end 2007. In March 2005, the Basel Committee on Banking Supervision re-discussed the schedules for national rule-making processes within member countries and decided to review the calibration of the Basel II framework in spring 2006. In November 2005, the Committee issued an updated version of the revised framework incorporating the additional guidance set forth in the Committee's paper, 'The Application of Basel II to Trading Activities and the Treatment of Double Default Effects' (July 2005). In July 2006, the Committee issued a comprehensive version of the Basel II framework, which is a compilation of the (i) June 2004 Basel II framework, (ii) the elements of the 1988 Accord that were not revised during the Basel II process, (iii) the 1996 Amendment to the Capital Accord to Incorporate Market Risks, and (iv) the 2005 paper on the Application of Basel II to Trading Activities and the Treatment of Double Default Effects. No new elements have been introduced in this compilation. The key elements of the 1988 capital adequacy framework that were retained in the revised framework include the general requirement for banks to hold total capital equivalent to at least 8 per cent of their risk-weighted assets and the definition of eligible capital. The Committee also proposed to develop capital charges for risks not taken into account by the 1988 Accord, such as interest rate risk in the banking book and operational risk. The greater risk sensitivity under Basel II would be achieved by linking each bank's capital requirements to empirically based measures of credit and operational risk as determined in part by risk parameters estimated by that organization, such as a loan's probability of default and its expected loss given default.

Basel II consists of three mutually reinforcing pillars: minimum capital requirements, supervisory review process and market discipline. Within the three pillar approach, minimum capital requirement seeks to develop and expand on the standardized rules set forth in the 1988 Accord, supervisory review of a bank's capital adequacy and internal assessment process, and effective use of market discipline as a lever to strengthen disclosure and encourage safe and sound banking practices, has been designed to strengthen the international financial architecture.

### 4.2.1 The First Pillar – Minimum Capital Requirements

In the revised capital framework, the importance of minimum regulatory capital requirements continues to be recognized as the first pillar of the framework[5]. The measures for credit risk are more complex, market risk is the same, while operational risk is new.

### 4.2.2 Credit Risk

With regard to minimum capital requirements for credit risk, a modified version of the existing Accord has come to be known as the 'standardised' approach. The alternative methodology, which is subject to the explicit approval of the bank's supervisor, would allow banks to use their internal rating systems for credit risk. For some sophisticated banks, use of internal credit ratings and, at a later stage, portfolio models could contribute to a more accurate assessment of a bank's capital requirement in relation to its particular risk profile. The capital treatment of a number of important credit risk mitigation techniques, risk reducing effects of guarantees, credit derivatives, and securitisation, is also provided under Pillar 1, thus improving regulatory capital incentive for banks to hedge portfolio credit risks.

### 4.2.3 The Standardized Approach

Under the standardized approach, one of the main innovations relative to the 1988 Accord is the use of external ratings agencies to set the risk weights for corporate, bank and sovereign claims. More specifically, the new proposals include tables defining ‘buckets’ of ratings for corporate and for sovereign credits to translate a particular rating into a risk weight. The approach is most clear for corporates. The rules for claims on banks are slightly more complex than those of corporates. One alternative allows banks to be rated one notch worse (i.e., one risk weight category higher) than the sovereign but with a cap at a risk.

For sovereigns, there are slightly different buckets in the basic approach but there are also some special rules that apply. For example, at national discretion, there is a special rule for claims on the sovereign of the country where the bank is incorporated where the claim is denominated in the currency of the sovereign and also funded in that currency (i.e., loans to sovereigns funded and lent in the domestic currency). At first sight this allows banks in emerging countries to lend to their Governments (or hold bonds in an investment account) with a zero or low capital charge. However, in many emerging countries such loans and bonds are often expressed in dollars or other non -local currencies, and these would not then attract this special treatment. In this case, credit extended to a Government of an emerging country would attract the capital charge given the rating of the sovereign. It is not entirely clear what the treatment would be in Ecuador, El Salvador or Panama (3 dollarized countries) or for that matter for the countries of EMU. If the special treatment exists because the 'credit risk' of a local currency claim will, in general, be less than that of a foreign currency claim when there is a devaluation or sharp depreciation of the local currency then this suggests the special treatment should not be extended to dollarized countries or members of EMU and this takes as a given that any currency risk mismatch is treated in an appropriate manner separately. The view that local currency claims are different because of the existence of a lender of last resort appears to confuse 'credit risk' with liquidity considerations and suggests that banks' capital requirements should explicitly reflect the fact that Governments would deflate away debts that goes against any credible commitment to, say, an inflation target.

### 4.2.4 Internal Rating Approach

Under the internal rating approach banks may employ their own opinions regarding borrowers in setting capital requirements. More specifically, there are a set of basic parameters that banks may estimate and then feed into a formula to determine actual risk weights. Two crucial parameters required are the probability of default (PD) and the loss given default (LGD). Two alternative approaches are proposed (1) a foundation and (2) an advanced approach. Under the foundation approach banks determine the probability of default and all other parameters are essentially set by supervisory rules. Under the advanced approach, banks may also determine the loss given default (LGD). Other parameters also important for the calculation of the actual risk weight, including in some cases the maturity of the transaction and the exposure at default (EAD) are determined by supervisory rules under both alternatives.

Besides, proposals to develop a capital charge for interest rate risk in the banking book for banks, where interest rate risk is significantly above average, have also been provided.

**4.2.5 Operational risk**

Operational risk has been defined as the risk of loss resulting from inadequate or failed internal processes, people and systems or from external events. This definition includes legal risk, but excludes strategic and reputational risk, whereby legal risk includes, but is not limited to, exposures to fines, penalties, or punitive damages resulting from supervisory actions, as well as private settlements. The framework outlines three methods for calculating operational risk capital charges in a continuum of increasing sophistication and risk sensitivity: (i) the Basic Indicator Approach; (ii) the Standardised Approach; and (iii) Advanced Measurement Approaches (AMA). Banks are encouraged to move along the spectrum of available approaches as they develop more sophisticated operational risk measurement systems and practices.

**4.2.6 The Second Pillar – Supervisory Review Process**

Pillar 2 (Supervisory Review Process) requires banks to implement an internal process for assessing their capital adequacy in relation to their risk profiles as well as a strategy for maintaining their capital levels, i.e., the Internal Capital Adequacy Assessment Process (ICAAP). On the other hand, Pillar 2 also requires the supervisory authorities to subject all banks to an evaluation process and to impose any necessary supervisory measures based on the evaluations. A significant innovation of the revised framework is the greater use of assessments of risk provided by banks' internal systems as inputs to capital calculations. Each supervisor is expected to develop a set of review procedures for ensuring that banks' systems and controls are adequate to serve as the basis for the capital calculations. There are three main areas that might be particularly suited to treatment under Pillar 2: risks considered under Pillar 1 that are not fully captured by the Pillar 1 process (e.g. credit concentration risk); those factors not taken into account by the Pillar 1 process (e.g. interest rate risk in the banking book, business and strategic risk); and factors external to the bank (e.g. business cycle effects). A further important aspect of Pillar 2 is the assessment of compliance with the minimum standards and disclosure requirements of the more advanced methods in Pillar 1, in particular the internal rating based (IRB) framework for credit risk and the advanced measurement approaches for operational risk. Supervisors must ensure that these requirements are being met, both as qualifying criteria and on a continuing basis. Four key principles of supervisory review were identified, based on the Core Principles for Effective Banking Supervision and the Core Principles Methodology. First, banks should have a process for assessing their overall capital adequacy in relation to their risk profile and a strategy for maintaining their capital levels. Second, supervisors should review and evaluate banks' internal capital adequacy assessments and strategies, as well as their ability to monitor and ensure their compliance with regulatory capital ratios.

Supervisors should take appropriate supervisory action if they are not satisfied with the result of this process. Third, supervisors should expect banks to operate above the minimum regulatory capital ratios and should have the ability to require banks to hold capital in excess of the minimum. Fourth, supervisors should seek to intervene at an early stage to prevent capital from falling below the minimum levels required to support the risk characteristics of a particular bank and should require rapid remedial action if capital is not maintained or restored.

### 4.2.7 The Third Pillar – Market Discipline

The third pillar is a set of disclosure requirements included in the Basel II framework to allow market participants assess the capital adequacy of the institution based on information on the scope of application, capital, risk exposures, risk assessment processes, etc. Such disclosures are of particular relevance keeping in view the greater discretion allowed to banks in using internal methodologies for assessing capital requirements under Pillar 1. Supervisors have different powers available to them under Pillar 2, ranging from 'moral suasion' to reprimands or financial penalties, that they can use to make banks to make such disclosures. Market discipline can contribute to a safe and sound banking environment, and complement the minimum capital requirements (Pillar 1) and the supervisory review process (Pillar 2).

Banks should have a formal disclosure policy approved by the board of directors that addresses the bank's approach regarding the disclosures they make, and the internal controls over the disclosure process. In addition, banks should implement a process for assessing the appropriateness of their disclosures, including validation and frequency. Several key banking risks to which banks are exposed, such as credit risk, market risk, interest rate risk and equity risk in the banking book and operational risk, and the techniques that banks use to identify, measure, monitor and control those risks such as disclosures relating to credit risk mitigation and asset securitisation, both of which alter the risk profile of the institution, are important factors market participants consider in their assessment of an institution.

### 4.2.8 Basel II: An Evaluation

Even though implementation of Basel II is in progress with approximately 57 countries adopting all or parts of the framework by end-2008, the major advantages and deficiencies in Basel II have been discussed widely by the practitioners, policymakers and academicians. The main incentives for adoption of Basel II are (a) it is more risk sensitive; (b) it recognises developments in risk measurement and risk management techniques employed in the banking sector and accommodates them within the framework; and (c) it aligns regulatory capital closer to economic capital. These elements of Basel II take the regulatory framework closer to the business models employed in several large banks. In Basel II framework, banks' capital requirements are more closely aligned with the underlying risks in the balance sheet. Basel II compliant banks can also achieve better capital efficiency as identification, measurement and management of credit, market and operational risks have a direct bearing on regulatory capital relief. Operational risk management would result in continuous review of systems and control mechanisms. Capital charge for better managed risks is lower and banks adopting risk-based pricing are able to offer a better price (interest rate) for better risks. This helps banks not only to attract better business but also to formulate a business strategy driven by efficient risk-return parameters. Marketing of products, thus, becomes more focused/ targeted.

The movement towards Basel II has prompted banks to make necessary improvement in their risk management and risk measurement systems. Thus, banks would be required to adopt superior technology and information systems which aid them in better data collection, support high quality data and provide scope for detailed technical analysis. For instance, the framework requires fundamental improvement in the data supporting the probability of default (PD), exposure at default (EAD) and loss given default (LGD). Basel II incorporates much of the latest 'technology' in the financial arena for managing risk and allocating capital to cover risk.

Basel II goes beyond merely meeting the letter of the rules. Under Pillar 2, when supervisors assess economic capital, they are expected to go beyond banks' systems. Pillar 2 of the framework provides greater scope for bankers and supervisors to engage in a dialogue, which ultimately will be one of the important benefits emanating from the implementation of Basel II. The added transparency in Pillar 3 should also generate improved market discipline for banks, in some cases forcing them to run a better business. Indeed, market participants play a useful role by requiring banks to hold more capital than implied by minimum regulatory capital requirements - or sometimes their own economic capital models - and by demanding additional disclosures about how risks are being identified, measured, and managed. A strong understanding by the market of Pillars 1 and 2 would make Pillar 3 more comprehensible and market discipline a more reliable tool for supervisors and the market.

According to a survey published by Ernst & Young, processes and systems are expected to change significantly, along with the ways in which risks are managed. Over three-quarters of respondents believed that Basel II will change the competitive landscape for banking. Those organizations with better risk systems are expected to benefit at the expense of those which have been slower to absorb change. Eighty-five per cent of respondents believed that economic capital would guide some, if not all, pricing. Greater specialization was also expected, due to increased use of risk transfer instruments. A majority of respondents (over 70 per cent) believe that portfolio risk management would become more active, driven by the availability of better and more timely risk information as well as the differential capital requirements resulting from Basel II. This could improve the profitability of some banks relative to others, and encourage the trend towards consolidation in the sector.

### 4.2.9 Restrictions of Basel II

The Basel II framework also suffers from several limitations, especially from the angle of implementation in emerging economies. In its attempt to strive for more accurate measure of risks in banks, the simplicity of the 1988 Capital Accord has been replaced by a highly complex methodology which needs the support of highly sophisticated MIS/data processing capabilities. The complexity of Basel II also arises from several options available. The complexity and sophistication essential for banks for implementing the New Capital Accord restricts its universal application. Consequently, many of the countries that have voluntarily adopted Basel I also view these issues with considerable caution. While it is true that the Basel II framework is more complex, at the same time, it has also been argued that this complexity is largely unavoidable mainly because the banking system and related instruments that have evolved in recent times are inherently complex in nature. The risk management system itself has become more sophisticated over the time and applying equal risk weights (as done in the Basel I accord) may not be realistic anymore.

The more sophisticated risk measures unfairly advantage the larger banks that are able to implement them and, from the same perspective, that the developing countries generally also do not have these banks and that Basel II will disadvantage the economically marginalized by restricting their access to credit or by making it more expensive.

In the standardized approach for credit risk measurement, rating agencies have been assigned a crucial role. Rating agencies move slowly, and changes in ratings, lag changes in actual credit quality, so that the ratings have a questionable ability to predict default (Altman and Saunders, 2001). Moreover, rating agencies have limited penetration in many emerging countries. In the absence of reliable ratings for different assets, banking industry will not be able to fully exploit the flexibility of Basel II and most credit risks will tend to end up in the unrated 100 per cent category and as a result there will be little change in capital requirements relative to Basel I. It has also been argued that in the case of standardized approach, unrated borrowers will have a lower risk weight (100 per cent) as compared to the lowest graded borrower (150 per cent) and this may lead to moral hazard problem with lower grade borrowers preferring to remain unrated. This may also lead to adverse selection. Concerns have also been expressed about the quality of rating agencies' judgments. Even in the developed economies, the recent sub-prime crisis has highlighted the problems relating to the role of rating agencies which is discussed in the following section.

Under the IRB approaches, greater reliance on banks' own internal risk ratings may be an improvement, but this is also not free from difficulties. Specifically, the proposal does not indicate how regulators will evaluate the accuracy of banks' own internal credit-risk ratings or how they would be translated into capital requirements. Nor does it explain how it would achieve comparability across the variety of internal rating systems in different banks. Most important, the proposal does not explain how regulators will enforce the ratings that banks produce or impose sanctions if the ratings turn out to be inaccurate and capital is insufficient or depleted. In any event, even if an effective enforcement mechanism is put in place, summing across risk buckets is just as deficient when the risk buckets are determined by internal ratings as when they are determined by external risk ratings or the current arbitrary regulatory distinctions.

The interactions between regulatory and accounting approaches at both the national and international level to reduce, wherever possible, inappropriate disparities between regulatory and accounting standards which can have significant consequences for the comparability of the resulting measures of capital adequacy and for the costs associated with the implementation of these approaches. Keeping this in view, changes in the treatments of unexpected and expected losses, credit risk mitigation, treatment of securitization exposures and qualifying revolving retail exposures, among others, are being incorporated.

A more serious criticism is that the operation of Basel II will lead to a more pronounced business cycle. This criticism arises because the credit models used for Pillar 1 compliance typically use a one year time horizon. This would mean that, during a downturn in the business cycle, banks would need to reduce lending as their models forecast increased losses, increasing the magnitude of the downturn. Regulators should be aware of this risk and can be expected to include it in their assessment of the bank models used. That the risk-based capital requirements are pro-cycle in nature (more capital is required in recessions because credit risk in banks' portfolios increases in cyclical downturns) was also recognized by the Basel Committee on Banking Supervision (BCBS). In a Consultative Paper issued by the BCBS in 1999, the Financial Stability Forum had raised the question whether several features of the new capital framework discussed by the BCBS could increase the cyclical fluctuations in the economy. In response, the BCBS confirmed that risk-based capital requirements were inevitably pro-cyclical, but could be addressed by different instruments. During the course of consultation, the Basel Committee maintained that various features of the risk weights of the IRB approach under Pillar 1 can be expected to mitigate its pro-cyclical impact. For example, the length of the observation period mandated for estimating PD is at least five years and that for LGD and EAD seven years, with the qualification that if the observations for any of the sources used span a longer period, then the latter should be used. Basel II requires banks to estimate long run average PD and downturn LGD, which to a great extent reduced the variability of capital requirement with respect to business cycles. The greater allowance for eligible provisions can also be expected to reduce the importance in risk-weighted assets of defaulted loans during cyclical downturns, when such loans increase as a proportion of banks' portfolios. The Committee further recommended that national supervisors could also promote the use of internal models leading to lower pro-cyclicality. Measures such as through-the-cycles rating methodologies could also 'filter-out' the Impact of business cycle on borrower rating. Supervisors could also prescribe additional capital under Pillar 2 during a business cycle expansion.

### 4.2.10 Challenges to Effective Implementation of Basel II

Apart from certain deficiencies of Basel II, its implementation presents several challenges, especially in emerging market economies. Data limitation is a key impediment to the design and implementation of credit risk models. Most credit instruments are not marked to market; hence, the predictive nature of a credit risk model does not derive from a statistical projection of future prices based on comprehensive historical experience. The scarcity of the data required to estimate credit risk models also stems from the infrequent nature of default events and the longer term time horizons used in measuring credit risk. Thus, in specifying model parameters, credit risk models require the use of simplifying assumptions and proxy data. One of the major challenges is the availability of long-time series and reliable data and information as also sophisticated IT resources. In view of these constraints, banks in emerging economies are forced to adopt the standardised approach.

Banks need to put in place sound and efficient operational risk management framework since this will be a focus under the Pillar 2. The most important Pillar 2 challenge relates to acquiring and upgrading the human and technical resources necessary for the review of banks' responsibilities under Pillar 1 by the supervisors. Other areas of concern include coordination of home and host supervisors in the cross-border implementation of Basel II; issues relating to outsourcing; common reporting templates for easy comparability; and external benchmarks to be made available by the regulator, and to be used for comparison/self-evaluation for the risk components/ operational losses.

Aligning supervisory disclosures under Pillar 3 with international and domestic accounting standards has emerged as a major challenge. There are also issues relating to (i) reporting framework/disclosures in the context of risk appetite for the stated business objectives and risk management systems in place; and (ii) providing information, on the risks and the risk management systems in place, in the public domain which could be used for comparison among banks. Market discipline is not possible if counterparties and rating agencies do not have good information about banks' risk positions and the techniques used to manage those positions.

Full implementation of Basel II would require upgradation of skills both at the level of supervisory authority and the banks. Banks would be required to use fully scalable state of the art technology, ensure enhanced information system security and develop capability to use the central database to generate any data required for risk management as well as reporting. The emphasis on improved data standards in the revised accord is not merely a regulatory capital requirement, but rather it is a foundation for risk-management practices that will strengthen the value of the banking franchise.

The validation of credit risk models is also fundamentally more difficult than the back testing of market risk models. Where market risk models typically employ a horizon of a few days, credit risk models generally rely on a timeframe of one year or more. The longer holding period, coupled with the higher target loss quintiles used in credit risk models, presents problems to model-builders in assessing the accuracy of their models. A quantitative validation standard similar to that in the Market Risk Amendment would require an impractical number of years of data, spanning multiple credit cycles.

The costs associated with Basel II implementation, particularly costs related to information technology and human resources, are expected to be quite significant for both banks and supervisors. Even in the absence of Basel II, well managed financial institutions and regulatory authorities would have continued to update and improve their IT systems and risk management practices simply to keep pace with the evolving practices in the marketplace. However, Basel II has pushed banks and supervisors for development of human resource skills and IT upgradation. In this context, the challenge that banks are likely to face will have many facets, viz., assessing requirements, identifying and bridging the gaps, identifying talents, putting the available talents to optimum use, attracting fresh talents, retention of talents and change management.

Though, the Basel II framework aims to achieve common standards, its implementation also requires closer cooperation, information sharing and co-ordination of policies among supervisors. The existence of separate supervisory bodies to regulate different segments of the markets within a jurisdiction may create challenges in implementation of Basel II not only within a jurisdiction but also across jurisdictions. This is because when different market participants are regulated by separate supervisors, it is difficult to maintain comparable quality of policy formulation and vigilance. In many developing countries, only the banks are coming under the ambit of Basel II and not other financial services providers, thus creating some scope for regulatory arbitrage. As the main objective of the New Accord is to ensure competitive equality and providing a reasonable degree of consistency in application, it is necessary that supervisors across the globe should have a common definition of internationally active banks. Basel Committee may, therefore, define what constitute internationally active banks. For example, in Indian conditions, those banks with cross-border business exceeding 20-25 per cent of their total business may be classified as internationally active banks. The foreign banks in EMEs are the ones which would be implementing the advanced approaches of Basel II on a world-wide consolidated basis. However, the home-host regulatory and supervisory issues would get accentuated due to the greater scope for multiple regulatory treatments as also the several unresolved cross-border issues under the different Basel II approaches.

The risk weights/implied correlations for different exposures under standardised or IRB approaches are based upon certain assumptions which may not be applicable in the context of emerging economies. For instance, 35 per cent risk weight for mortgage lending is based upon PD estimates and LGD of developed European/US markets and may not be adequate as the losses in secured real estate lending in countries like Taiwan, Thailand and Indonesia have at times exceeded 35 per cent. Thus, the regulators in developing countries need to independently assess whether all the assumptions of Basel II framework are applicable to their domestic markets and modify them suitably, if required.

Countries that have already adopted Basel I and are complying with the reasonable minimum BCP (Basel Core Principles of Effective Banking Supervision), are in a better position to choose among the various alternatives offered under Basel II. In environments where banking supervision is weak as reflected in a poor BCP compliance, implementing sophisticated methods of calculating bank capital may pose challenges for the supervisors that far outweigh the benefits derived from more accurate calculation of bank risk and capital prescribed under Basel II. Furthermore, the thin regulatory resources have a tendency to deflect away from the priority areas. Such countries would need to adopt the BCP more fully and are advised to focus primarily on Basel Pillars 2 and 3. Though there is enough room for country specific adaptations, it should be borne in mind that such adaptations should not take away the essence of a 'standard'. The IMF (jointly with the World Bank), as a part of its financial sector assessment programs, have reviewed countries' compliance with the Basel Core Principles (BCP). In the course of 71 confidential assessments covering 12 advanced, 15 transition and 44 emerging economies, it was found that all advanced economies under consideration complied with the core principles regarding market risk and risk management. In contrast, 66 per cent of emerging economies and 53 per cent of transition economies did not comply with such principles. Given this level of compliance, the challenges that are likely to be faced by the emerging economies in implementing the Basel II framework is daunting indeed.

As countries are moving forward with Basel II implementation, supervisors are closely monitoring its impact on overall bank capital levels. A capital monitoring exercise is in place to track minimum capital requirements, actual capital buffers above the minimum and how the minimum requirements compare to Basel II floors. Analysis of the first data submissions will be available to the BCBS in the first quarter of 2009, and data will continue to be collected on an ongoing semi-annual basis.

**4.2.11 Basel II in the light of the Current Financial Turmoil**

In light of recent financial market turbulence, the importance of implementing Basel II capital framework and strengthening supervision and risk management practices, and improving the robustness of valuation practices and market transparency for complex and less liquid products, have assumed greater significance. Moreover, it has become indispensable to have robust and resilient core firms at the centre of the financial system operating on safe and sound risk management practices. The Basel II plays an important role in this respect by ensuring the robustness and resilience of these firms through a sound global capital adequacy framework along with other benefits including greater operational efficiencies, better capital allocation and greater shareholder value through the use of improved risk models and reporting capabilities.

The recent financial turmoil exhibited that even such technical analysis have their limitations, such as incomplete data or assumptions that have not been tested across business cycles.

Therefore, quantitative assessment of risks also needs to be supplemented by qualitative measures and sound judgment.

The Financial Stability Forum (FSF) made comprehensive proposals that were ratified in early April 2008 by the G-7 to be implemented over the next 100 days. The proposals include inter alia full and prompt disclosure of risk exposures; urgent action by setters of accounting standards and other relevant standard setters to improve accounting and disclosure standards for off-balance sheet or entities and to enhance guidance on fair value accounting, particularly on valuing financial instruments in periods of stress; strengthening of risk management practices, supported by supervisors' oversight, including rigorous stress testing; and strengthening of capital positions as needed. In addition, the FSF emphasized on a number of proposals for implementation by end-2008 which include inter alia strengthening prudential oversight of capital, liquidity, and risk management under Basel II, especially for complex structured credit instruments and off-balance sheet vehicles; enhancing transparency and valuation for off-balance sheet entities, securitization exposures, and liquidity commitments under the Basel Committee's guidance; enhancing due diligence in the use of ratings.

As part of its capital monitoring exercise, the BCBS would be tracking on an ongoing basis the impact of Basel II on bank capital levels. This will shed light on the effects of the proposed amendments to Basel II and help determine whether additional efforts are needed to strengthen capital in the banking system. In addition, BCBS members regularly exchange information on how supervisors are implementing the various aspects of Basel II and conducting model approvals in practice. The BCBS has also launched a joint undertaking with the FSF to examine the impact of Basel II on the cyclicality of capital requirements and possible measures for mitigating it. The FSF will report to the G7 on progress with this work in April 2009. The BCBS announced a comprehensive strategy on November 20, 2008 to address the fundamental weaknesses revealed by the financial market crisis related to the regulation, supervision and risk management of internationally-active banks. The primary objective was to strengthen capital buffers and help contain leverage in the banking system arising from both on- and off-balance sheet activities. The key building blocks of the Committee's strategy include the following:

• strengthening the risk capture of the Basel II framework (in particular for trading book and off-balance sheet exposures);

• enhancing the quality of Tier 1 capital;

• building additional shock absorbers into the capital framework that can be drawn upon during periods of stress and dampen procyclicality;

• evaluating the need to supplement risk-based measures with simple gross measures of exposure in both prudential and risk management frameworks to help contain leverage in the banking system;

• strengthening supervisory frameworks to assess funding liquidity at cross-border banks;

• leveraging Basel II to strengthen risk management and governance practices at banks;

• strengthening counterparty credit risk capital, risk management and disclosure at banks; and

• promoting globally coordinated supervisory follow-up exercises to ensure implementation of supervisory and industry sound principles.

Under Basel II, though liquidity risk is not reckoned explicitly as Pillar 1 risk, it is provided that a bank's Pillar 2 assessment should cover the full range of risks facing an institution, including liquidity risks. Effective liquidity risk management usually emerges as a challenge during periods of financial stress, when many markets become less liquid, making it difficult for some entities to fund themselves. In recent months, some of the well-known challenges associated with liquidity risk management became evident in the light of the US sub-prime crisis and the failure of the Northern Rock bank in the UK. Even banks with strong capital base experienced liquidity problems as they did not have a strong liquidity risk management system in place. The adequate stress and scenario testing for potential asset expansions arising from liquidity shocks becomes crucial to communicate to market participants about their risk profiles. The BCBS has already initiated the process of assessment of the weaknesses identified by the recent crisis with a view to setting global standards for liquidity risk management and supervision, and integrating it more closely with other risk management disciplines. After issuing a public consultation document in June, the BCBS released in September

Principles for Sound Liquidity Risk Management and Supervision. The Principles materially raise standards for sound liquidity risk management and measurement – including the capture of off-balance sheet exposures, securitization activities and other contingent liquidity risks that were not well managed during the turmoil. The Principles underscore the importance of establishing a robust liquidity risk management framework that is well integrated into the bank-wide risk management process. Key elements of a bank's governance of its liquidity risk management are also emphasized. Moreover, the document sets out principles to strengthen the measurement and management of their liquidity risk, which include inter alia, the requirement of a bank to: (i) maintain a cushion of unencumbered, high quality liquid assets as insurance against a range of stress scenarios; (ii) actively manage its intraday liquidity positions and risks to meet payment and settlement obligations on a timely basis under both normal and stressed conditions, and thus contribute to the smooth functioning of payment and settlement systems; (iii) conduct regular stress tests for a variety of short-term and protracted institution-specific and market-wide stress scenarios and use the outcomes to develop robust and operational contingency funding plans; and (iv) ensure the alignment of risk-taking incentives of individual business lines with the liquidity risk exposures the activities create.

The Principles highlight the key role of supervisors, including the responsibility to intervene to require effective and timely remedial action by a bank to address liquidity risk management deficiencies. The Principles also stress the need for regular communication with other supervisors and public authorities, both within and across national borders. They also recommend regular public disclosure that enables market participants to make an informed judgment about the soundness of a bank's liquidity risk management framework and liquidity position. The guidance focuses on liquidity risk management at medium and large complex banks, but the sound principles have broad applicability to all types of bank. The document notes that implementation of the sound principles by both banks and supervisors should be tailored to the size, nature of business and complexity of a bank's activities. Other factors that a bank and its supervisors should consider include the bank's role and systemic importance in the financial sectors of the jurisdictions in which it operates. The BCBS expects banks and supervisors to implement the Principles thoroughly and quickly, and will assess progress in this area. It will also start to examine possible steps to promote more robust and internationally consistent liquidity approaches for cross-border banks. This will include assessing the scope for further convergence of liquidity supervision.

The Basel Committee on Banking Supervision issued a package of consultative documents to strengthen the Basel II capital framework on January 16, 2009. These enhancements are part of a broader effort the Committee has undertaken to strengthen the regulation and supervision of internationally active banks in light of weaknesses revealed by the financial markets crisis. The proposed changes to capital requirements cover: (i) trading book exposures, including complex and illiquid credit products; (ii) certain complex securitizations in the banking book [for example, collateralized debt obligations (CDOs) of asset backed securities (ABS)]; and (iii) exposures to off-balance sheet vehicles (i.e., asset-backed commercial paper conduits).

The Committee is also proposing standards to promote more rigorous supervision and risk management of risk concentrations, off-balance sheet exposures, securitisations and related reputation risks. Through the supervisory review process, the Committee is promoting improvements to valuations of financial instruments, the management of funding liquidity risks and firm-wide stress testing practices. In addition, the Committee is proposing enhanced disclosure requirements for securitisations and sponsorship of off-balance sheet vehicles, which should provide market participants with a better understanding of an institution's overall risk profile.

The Committee proposes that the capital requirements for the trading book be implemented in December 2010 while the other improvements, including those related to risk management and disclosures, be introduced by the end of 2009.

The BCBS is developing for consultation by end-2008 proposed guidance to further strengthen Pillar 3 disclosure requirements under Basel II for securitisation and re-securitisation exposures, sponsorship of off-balance sheet vehicles, liquidity commitments to ABCP conduits, valuations with regard to securitisation exposures and pipeline and warehousing risks. This effort is well underway and is also drawing from leading practice risk disclosures that banks are providing in response to the FSF recommendations. The BCBS plans to issue final guidance in 2009.

The BCBS is developing guidance to enhance the supervisory assessment of corporate governance and controls over banks' valuation processes and related risk management and capital adequacy issues. The guidance will reinforce sound bank valuation practices and address approaches supervisors should take when deficiencies are identified. The drafting effort is well underway and further dialogue is planned with securities markets regulators as part of the development process. Furthermore, the BCBS plans to address improved valuation disclosures as part of proposed amendments to the disclosure requirements of Pillar 3 of Basel II. These proposed changes are part of the Committee's broader work programme, as set out in its November 20, 2008 press release, to strengthen in a fundamental way bank capital adequacy, risk management and supervision. In particular, this includes assessing ways to mitigate procyclicality, for example, by promoting capital buffers above the regulatory minimum that can be drawn upon during periods of stress. These efforts are in support of the April 2008 recommendations of the Financial Stability Forum and the G-20's November 2008 action plan.

## Section 4.3: INDIAN BANKING SECTOR – ROAD TOWARDS BASEL III

The Reserve Bank of India (RBI) on 27 March 2014 extended the deadline for Indian banks to meet capital requirements under the so-called Basel III norms by a year to 31 March 2019. Earlier this norm was to be implemented by 31 March 2018. The norms of Basel –III are 1) Basel III is a comprehensive set of reform measures, developed by the Basel Committee on Banking Supervision, to strengthen the regulation, supervision and risk management of the banking sector. 2) Under Basel III norms, being implemented in phases between April 2013 and March 2019, banks need to have a core capital ratio of 8% and a total capital adequacy ratio of 11.5% against 9% now. Capital adequacy is a measure of a bank's financial strength expressed as a ratio of capital to risk-weighted assets. With implementation of this norm, the banks are expected to face some cash crunch and consequential impact on the performance/profitability of the banks.

**4.3.1 Basel-II Accord 2004**

- International Convergence of Capital Measurement and Capital Standards: A revised framework
- G 20 Economies
- To protect the international financial system
- To maintain consistency of regulations

- Considers Credit risk, Market Risk and Operational Risk for capital adequacy
- Total CRAR=[Eligible total capital funds]/[Credit RWAs+ Market RWAs + Operational RWAs]
- Tier I CRAR= [ Eligible Tier I Capital funds]/ [Credit RWAs+ Market RWAs + Operational RWAs]
- Basel recommend – 8% CRAR & 4% Tier I CRAR
- RBI Guideline – 9% CRAR & 6% Tier I CRAR
- BCBS issued a comprehensive framework in June 2006
- More risk sensitive approach to capital requirements

**4.3.2 Risk:** The possibility of outcome not occurring as expected In financial terms- the possibility of financial loss Classified as Credit risk, Market risk, Interest Rate Risk, Operational risk and Systematic Risk

1) **Credit Risk:** Risk that a party to a contractual agreement or transaction will be unable to meet their obligations or will default on commitments
2) **Market Risk:** a) Risk of loss arising from movements in market prices or rates away from the rates or prices set out in a transaction or agreement b) Interest Rate Risk c) Exchange Rate Risk d) Commodity Price Risk e) Equity Price Risk

**4.3.3 Interest Rate Risk**

- Risk that the financial value of assets or liabilities (inflows/outflows) will be altered because of fluctuation in interest rates

- Mismatch/Gap Risk – arises out of mismatches in maturities, volumes and the mix of these two in various items of assets and liabilities
- Basis Risk – the risk arising out of exposure to various types of instruments in both the assets and liabilities and the different degrees to which interest rates change in respect of these instruments (fixed vs. floating, Domestic vs. Libor etc.)
- Yield Curve Risk – arises from the variation in spread between two instruments (based on the yields of which a pair of assets and liability is priced) in a composite yield curve.
- Embedded Option Risk – arises on account of pre mature withdrawal of funds by the lenders, pre payment option in a loan contract, cash credit system etc.
- Price Risk – is the result of change in the price of various instruments due to changes in interest rates
- Reinvestment Risk – the risk that the periodic coupons may have to be reinvested at a lower rate if interest rate decline

**4.3.4 Operational Risk**

- The risk of direct or indirect loss resulting from inadequate or failed internal processes, people and systems or from external events
- Failure of operating system due to fraudulent activities, natural disaster, human error, omission or sabotage

**Systemic Risk**

- Failure of one financial institution spreads as chain reaction to threaten the financial stability of the financial system as a whole

- RBI mandated Foreign banks operating in India and Indian banks having presence outside India to migrate to Revised Framework by- March 31, 2008
- All other commercial banks (excl. LABs & RRBs)- March 31, 2009
- Revised Capital Adequacy norms applicable uniformly to all Commercial Banks at the solo level as well as at the Consolidated level

### 4.3.6 Minimum Capital Requirement (Pillar I )

Computation of CRAR

- Eligible Total Capital Funds – Tier I (Core) & Tier II (additional or supporting ) Capital
- Risk Weighted Assets are a bank's assets or off balance sheet exposures, weighted according to risk. Weighting is based upon the credit rating of asset type as a measure of its relative level of risk. Better quality asset reduces capital requirement as they are subject to lesser risk weights Capital Requirement for Various Risk Areas

**Table No. 4.3 a case of ICICI BANK as of March 31, 2013**

| Particulars | Rs. In billion |
|---|---|
| I. Capital required for credit risk | 377.18 |
| - For portfolio subject to Standardized approach | 376.44 |
| - For Securitization exposure | 0.74 |
| II. Capital required for market risk | 32.46 |
| -For Interest rate risk | 26.65 |

| | |
|---|---|
| - For foreign exchange (including Gold ) risk | 0.79 |
| -For equity position risk | 5.02 |
| III. Capital required for Operational risk | 27.49 |
| Total Capital requirement (I+II+III) | 437.13 |
| Total Capital funds of the bank | 956.51 |
| Total Risk Weighted Assets | 4,856.98 |
| Capital Adequacy Ratio | 19.69 % |
| Minimum Capital Adequacy Ratio | 9.00 % |

(www.icici.com)

### 4.3.7 Computing Capital required for Credit Risk

- Standardized Approach
- Foundation Internal Rating Based – April 1, 2012
- Advanced Internal Rating Based – April 1,2012

### 4.3.8 Tier I Capital Covers:

1) Paid up capital 2) Statutory Reserves
3) Disclosed Free Reserves 4) Capital Reserves

**Tier II Capital Covers:**

1) Undisclosed Reserves 2) Revaluation Reserves 3) General Provision and Loss Reserves 4) Computing Capital required for Market Risk 5) Standardized Approach 6) Internal Model Approach – April 1,2010 7) Computing Capital required for Operational Risk 8) Basic Indicator Approach 9) Standardized Approach – April 1,2010 10) Advanced Measurement Approach – April 1, 2012

### 4.3.9Supervisory Review & Evaluation Process (Pillar II)

- Important principles of developing and implementing better risk management techniques for monitoring and managing all the risk exposures of banks and ensuring adequate capital and their review by the supervisory authority

- Banks should have a process for assessing their overall capital adequacy in relation to their risk profiles and a strategy for maintaining their capital levels.
- Supervisors should review and evaluate banks' internal capital adequacy assessments and strategies
- Supervisors should expect banks to operate above the minimum regulatory capital ratios and should have the ability to require banks to hold capital in excess of the minimum.
- Supervisors should seek to intervene at an early stage to prevent capital from falling below the minimum levels required to support the risk characteristics of a particular bank.
- Banks are required to establish a well defined internal assessment process through which they assure the RBI that adequate capital is indeed held towards the various risks to which they are exposed. For the purpose, the RBI has issued broad guidelines to establish Internal Capital Adequacy Assessment Process **(ICAAP)** which shall be operationalised w.e.f. March, 2008 for foreign banks and from March, 2009 by all other commercial banks, excluding the Local Area Banks and Regional Rural Banks.

### 4.3.10 Market Discipline (Pillar III)

- To encourage market discipline by developing a set of disclosure requirements which allow market participants to assess key areas of information on the scope of application, capital, risk exposures, risk assessment processes and the capital adequacy of the institution.

- To provide information that are based on a common framework is an effective means of informing the market about a bank's exposure to various risks and to provide a consistent and comprehensive disclosure framework that enhances comparability.
- Banks, including consolidated banks, are required to provide both quantitative and qualitative disclosures as at March end each year along with the annual financial statements. Banks with capital funds of Rs.100 crore or more should make interim disclosures on the qualitative aspects, on a standalone basis, on their respective websites. All banks with capital funds of Rs.500 crore or more, and their subsidiaries, must disclose their Tier I Capital, Total capital, total required capital and Tier I ratio, on a quarterly basis. The disclosures on the websites should be made in a web page titled Basel II Disclosures.
- Banks are required to have a formal disclosure policy duly approved by the Board of Directors stating the bank's approach for determination of content and format of disclosures keeping into consideration the materiality and proprietary issues. The first of the disclosures as per these guidelines were required to be made as on the effective dates of migration to the revised framework by banks as applicable to them i.e. $31^{st}$ March, 2008/2009.

**4.3.11Basel III Capital Regulations 2010**

- Financial crisis of 2008

- G 20 Leaders- Pittsburg Summit 2009
- To improve the banking sector's ability to absorb shocks arising from financial and economic stress
- To reduce the risk of spill over from the financial sector to real economy
- To strengthen the regulatory system for banks and other financial firms
- Basel III : A global regulatory framework for more resilient banks and banking system
- BCBS and FSB (Financial Stability Board) joint project addressing various macro and micro economic policy deficiencies leading to global crisis
- G 20 – a major force in international economic policy making leading to
- Quick stabilization of financial markets 2. Ensuring smooth flow of capital 3. Removing deficiencies in financial regulatory and supervisory policy framework
- IMF has identified India as a one of the jurisdictions having systematically important financial sector
- FSAP ( Financial Stability & Assessment Programme) – a regular & mandatory part of surveillance in India
- RBI has established FSU (Financial Stability Unit) with a mandate to assess & publish FSR (Financial Stability Report)
- FSR covers reporting of various Banking Stability Measures (BSMs) such as Banking Stability Index, Toxicity Index & Vulnerability Index.
- RBI issued guidelines in May 2012

- To be implemented from April 1, 2013 in phases and will be fully implemented as on March 31, 2018
- Continue to be based on three mutually reinforcing Pillars 1) Minimum Capital Requirements 2) Supervisory Review & Evaluation Process (SREP) 3) Market Discipline

## 4.3.12 Minimum Capital Requirements

1) Common Equity (Tier I) = $\frac{\text{Common Equity Tier I Capital}}{\text{Credit Risk WA+ Market Risk WA+ Operational Risk WA}}$

2) Tier I Capital Ratio = $\frac{\text{Eligible Equity Tier I Capital}}{\text{Credit Risk WA+ Market Risk WA+ Operational Risk WA}}$

3) Total CRAR = $\frac{\text{Eligible Total Capital}}{\text{Credit Risk WA+ Market Risk WA+ Operational Risk WA}}$

Tier I Capital (Going concern capital)

1) Common Equity Tier I

2) Additional Tier I and Tier II Capital (Gone concern capital)

- Going concern capital – which can absorb losses without triggering bankruptcy of the bank
- Gone concern capital – which will absorb losses only in a situation of liquidation of the bank

**Table No. 4.4. Regulatory Capital as percentage to RWAs**

| S. N. | Regulatory Capital | As % to RWAs |
|---|---|---|
| 1. | Minimum Common Equity Tier I Ratio | 5.5 |
| 2 | Capital Conservation Buffer | 2.5 |

| | (comprised of Common Equity) | |
|---|---|---|
| 3 | Minimum Common Equity Tier I Ratio plus Capital Conservation Buffer (1+2) | **8.0** |
| 4 | Additional Tier I Capital | **1.5** |
| 5 | Minimum Tier I Capital Ratio (1+4) | **7.0** |
| 6 | Tier II Capital | **2.0** |
| 7 | Minimum Total Capital Ratio (MTC) (5+6) | **9.0** |
| 8 | Minimum Total Capital Ratio plus Capital Conservation Buffer (2+7) | **11.5** |

### 4.3.13 Extended deadline of Basel III.

Indian banking industry is presently going through a rough patch as weak economic growth, high interest costs and stalled projects that crimped cash flows have made it difficult for many corporate borrowers to repay their debts. The economy grew 4.5% in the year to 31 March 2013, and is forecast by the government to expand by less than 5% in the current year. The extension of Basel III deadline is expected to give breathing space for the banking sector to take care of their growth capital needs given that the industry is current facing difficulties in terms of rise in bad loans. More time to achieve Basel III requirements means that the capital burden of banks, both in terms of bad loan provisioning and mandatory capital requirements will be eased a bit.

According to a 6 March 2014 report by Kotak Institutional Equities, public sector banks would need another $17 billion (around Rs.1.02 trillion) to comply with Basel III requirements between fiscal 2015 and fiscal 2018. However, the government has been struggling to fund state-run banks, which control two-thirds of the assets in India's Rs.83 trillion banking sector.

**Table No. 4.5 Minimum Capital Ratio Up to March 31, 2018**

| Minimum Capital Ratio | Apr. 1, 2013 | Mar. 31 2014 | Mar.31 2015 | Mar.31 2016 | Mar.31 2017 | Mar.31 2018 |
|---|---|---|---|---|---|---|
| Minimum Common Equity Tier I-CET 1 | 4.5 | 5.0 | 5.5 | 5.5 | 5.5 | 5.5 |
| Capital Conservation Buffer | -- | -- | 0.625 | 1.25 | 1.875 | 2.5 |
| Minimum CET 1+CCB | 4.5 | 5.0 | 6.125 | 6.75 | 7.375 | 8.0 |
| Minimum Tier I Capital | 6.0 | 6.5 | 7.0 | 7.0 | 7.0 | 7.0 |
| Minimum Total Capital | 9.0 | 9.0 | 9.0 | 9.0 | 9.0 | 9.0 |
| Minimum Total Capital +CCB | 9.0 | 9.0 | 9.625 | 10.25 | 10.875 | 11.5 |

### 4.3.14 Capital Conservation Buffer

- To enable banks to absorb losses during period of financial and economic distress
- To be introduced in phased manner between January 1, 2016 and March 31, 2019
- During the period of stress, the bank will be allowed to access the buffer to meet the minimum requirement of core capital such an access shall activate certain restrictions on usage of bank's earnings for discretionary payouts such as dividends and share buy backs.

### 4.3.15 Counter cyclical Buffer

- An important macro-prudential measure
- To achieve the broader macro prudential goal of protecting the banking sector from the periods of excess credit growth as per BCBS guidance, it will be the discretion of national jurisdictions to determine the range of buffer (0-2.5 percent of RWAs)
- RBI has constituted a Working group to examine various issues involved in operationalisation of the countercyclical capital buffer

### 4.3.16 Liquidity Coverage Ratio (LCR)

To ensure that a bank maintains an adequate level of unencumbered, high quality assets those are convertible into cash to meet its liquidity needs for a 30 day time horizon under an acute liquidity stress scenario.

LCR= Stock of high quality liquid assets/ Net Cash outflow over a 30 day period

A credible supplementary measure to the risk based capital requirement.

**4.3.17 Net Stable Funding Ratio (NSFR)**

- To act as a minimum enforcement mechanism to complement the Liquidity Coverage Ratio
- To avoid short term funding mismatches and moving towards more stable, long term funding of assets and business activities

NSFR= Available Stable Funding/ Required Stable Funding

A minimum acceptable amount of stable funding based on liquidity characteristics of a bank's assets and business activities over a one year time horizon.

# CHAPTER NO. 5 FINDINGS, SUGGESTIONS AND RECOMMENDATIONS

I have covered four points in this chapter from my study. The first point 5.1 related to findings which covers results of all hypotheses tested and what banks should implements for the betterment. The second point 5.2 focuses on General Suggestions for the betterment of banking activities. The Third point 5.3 covers concluding remarks regarding Basel-I, II and III. Which reflects the road map regarding implementations of Basel in India. And last point 5.4. emphasis on Recommendations Regarding Selected Nationalized Banks. Following is given details for the same.

## 5.1. Finding:

- Bank of Baroda has generated assets and secured first Positions in the selected 19 nationalized banks while the second position is secured by Punjab national bank and third position secured by bank of India. Same way the worth performance in **Net assets** Dena bank is at last positions, Bank of Maharashtra is at second last position and Vijya bank is at third last positions. With the base year 2010 Net Assets is Avg. 147105 cr. Total if I Consider This Amt. as 100% than it is increased in year 2011 – 23.18 %(Net 123.18%), year 2012- 42.32% (Net 142.32%) and in year 2013-63.63% (Net 163.63%). The result of Hypothesis testing shows that there is significant difference in the performance of Net Assets generation. And all banks were not generating net assets at equal level. So ideal those banks which were poor in performance they should pay attention to the generating more Net Assets because it increases the business of entity and satisfy more and more customers.

- **Gross NPA** is lesser show the good performance of the bank. Here the Punjab & Sind Bank at first, Dena Bank stand at second and Corporation Bank at third position in the lowest Gross NPA in the selected 19 nationalized banks while the worth performance in Gross NPA Punjab National Bank at first position, Bank of India at second position and Central Bank of India at third position in higher rate of Gross NPA Performance. With the base year 2010 Gross NPA is Avg. 1803 cr. Total if I Consider This Amt. as 100% than it is increased in year 2011 – 21.07 %( Net 121.07%), year 2012- 88.29% (Net 188.29%) and in year 2013-177.98% (Net 277.98%). that is shows not good performance for the banking industries. The result of Hypothesis testing shows that there is significant difference in the performance of Gross NPA. It is recommended that those bank whose Gross NPA is Higher they should try to reduce their Gross NPA. Less NPA provides sufficient funds and benefits to the Banks. It increases the banks business and providing more funds to potential customers.
- **Net** NPA is lesser show the good performance of the bank. Here the Punjab & Sind Bank at first, Bank of Maharashtra stand at second and Dena Bank at third position in the lowest Net NPA in the selected 19 nationalized banks while the worth performance in Net NPA Punjab National Bank at first position,

Bank of India at second position and Canara bank at third position in higher rate of Net NPA Performance. With the base year 2010 Gross NPA is Avg. 811 cr. Total if I Consider This Amt. as 100% than it is increased in year 2011 – 27.12 %(Net 127.12%), year 2012- 133.66% (Net 233.66%) and in year 2013-281.25 % (Net 381.25%). that is shows not good performance for the banking industries. The result of Hypothesis testing shows that there is significant difference in the performance of Gross NPA. It is recommended that those bank whose Gross NPA is Higher they should try to reduce their Gross NPA. Less NPA provide sufficient fund and benefits to the Banks. It increases the banks business and providing more funds to potential customers.

- Interest income is higher shows the good performance of Bank. It is income on landed amt. to the customer in the form of loan, borrowing funds etc. here Canara bank at first, Bank of Baroda at second and Bank of India has secured the third position in interest income generation. While the worth performance Punjab & Sind Bank at first, Dena Bank stand at second and Bank of Maharashtra at third position in generation of interest income for the study of 19 selected banks for the year 2010 to 2013. With the base year 2010 Interest income is Avg. 10146 cr. Total if I Consider This Amt. as 100% than it is increased in year 2011 – 23.33%(Net 123.33%), year 2012- 64.86% (Net 164.86%) and in year 2013-89.87% (Net 189.87%). The result of Hypothesis testing shows that there is significant difference regarding the performance of Interest Income. Banks should try to generate more income through this source.

- Other income is higher shows the good performance of Bank. here Bank of Baroda at first, Bank of India at second and Canara bank has secured the third position in other income generation. While the worth performance Punjab & Sind Bank at first, Vijya Bank stand at second and Dena Bank at third position in generation of other income for the study of 19 selected banks for the year 2010 to 2013. With the base year 2010 other income is Avg. 1484 cr. total if I Consider this Amt. as 100% than it is decreased in year 2011 – 5.73%(Net 94.27%), year 2012- 7% (Net 107.00%) and in year 2013-19.94% (Net 119.94%). The result of Hypothesis testing shows that there is significant difference regarding the performance of other Income. Banks should try to generate more income through this source.
- Total income is higher shows the good performance of Bank. Here Punjab national Bank at first, Canara bank at second and Bank of Baroda has secured the third position in total income generation. While the worth performance Punjab & Sind Bank at first, Dena Bank stand at second and Bank of Maharashtra at third position in generation of total income for the study of 19 selected banks for the year 2010 to 2013. With the base year 2010 total income is Avg. 11630 cr. Total if I Consider This Amt. as 100% than it is increased in year 2011 – 19.63%(Net 119.63%), year 2012- 57.59% (Net 157.59%) and in year 2013-80.95% (Net 180.95%). The result of Hypothesis testing shows that there is significant difference regarding the

performance of Total Income. Banks should try to generate more income through this source.

- Interest expended higher show high expense is not good.
  And lower expenses show good position of bank. Here higher expenses amt. Punjab National Bank at first, Bank of India at second and Bank of Baroda has secured the third position in interest Expended. While the Lower expenses of Punjab & Sind Bank at first, Dena Bank stand at second and Bank of Maharashtra at third position in the interest expended for the study of 19 selected banks for the year 2010 to 2013. With the base year 2010 expended income is Avg. 6985 cr. Total if I Consider This Amt. as 100% than it is increased in year 2011 – 12.92%(Net 112.92%), year 2012- 166.45% (Net 166.45%) and in year 2013-97.19% (Net 197.19%). The result of Hypothesis testing shows that there is significant difference regarding the performance of Interest Expended. Banks should try to reduce this type of expenses.
- Operating expended higher show high expense that is not
  good. And lower expenses show good position of bank. Here higher expenses amt. Punjab National Bank at first, Bank of Baroda at second and Bank of India has secured the third position in interest Expended. While the Lower expenses of Punjab & Sind Bank at first, Dena Bank stand at second and Bank of Maharashtra at third position in the operating expenses for the study of 19 selected banks for the year 2010 to 2013. With the base year 2010 expenses is Avg. 2051 cr. Total if I Consider This Amt. as 100% than it is increased in year 2011 –

32.32%(Net 132.32%), year 2012- 140.66% (Net 140.66%) and in year 2013-57.82% (Net 157.82%). The result of Hypothesis testing shows that there is significant difference regarding the performance of operating Expenses. Banks should try to reduce this type of expenses.

- Total expenditure higher show high expense is not good. And lower expenses show good position of bank. Here higher expenses amt. Punjab National Bank at first, Canara at second and Bank of India has secured the third position in total Expenses. While the Lower expenses of Punjab & Sind Bank at first, Dena Bank stand at second and Bank of Maharashtra at third position in the Total expenses for the study of 19 selected banks for the year 2010 to 2013. With the base year 2010 expenses is Avg. 9035 cr. Total if I Consider This Amt. as 100% than it is increased in year 2011 – 17.33%(Net 117.33%), year 2012- 60.61% (Net 160.61%) and in year 2013-88.27% (Net 188.27%). The result of Hypothesis testing shows that there is significant difference regarding the performance of total Expenses. Banks should try to reduce this type of expenses.
- Operating Profit is higher shows the good performance of Bank. Here Punjab national bank at first, Bank of Baroda at second and Bank of India has secured the third position in Operating Profit generation. While the worth performance Punjab & Sind Bank at first, Vijya Bank stand at second and Dena Bank at third position in generation of operating profit for the study of 19 selected banks for the year 2011 to 2013. With the base year 2011 Operating Profit is Avg. 3312 cr. total if I

Consider this Amt. as 100% than it is increased in year 2012-15.21% (Net 115.21%) and in year 2013-21.79% (Net 121.79%). The result of Hypothesis testing shows that there is significant difference regarding the performance of Operating Profit. Banks should try to generate more profit through this source.

- Provisions and Contingencies means savings (investments) funds (amount) for future uncertainty and problems. Its higher performance shows wise decision for the Bank. Here Punjab national bank at first, Bank of Baroda at second and Bank of India has secured the third position Provisions and Contingencies generation. While the worth performance Punjab & Sind Bank at first, Vijya Bank stand at second and Dena Bank at third position in generation of Provisions and Contingencies for the study of 19 selected nationalized banks for the year 2010 to 2013. With the base year 2010 Provisions and Contingencies is Avg. 1237 cr. total if I Consider this Amt. as 100% than it is increased in year 2011 – 34.19%(Net 134.19%), year 2012-71.70% (Net 171.70%) and in year 2013-94.26% (Net 194.26%). The result of Hypothesis testing shows that there is significant difference regarding the performance of Provisions and Contingencies. Banks should try to generate more and more Provisions and Contingencies for future securities and uncertainty.
- Net Profit is higher shows the good performance of the Bank. Here Punjab national bank at first, Bank of Baroda at second and Canara Bank has secured the third position Net Profit generation. While the worth performance Punjab & Sind

Bank at first, United Bank of India stand at second and Vijya Bank at third position in generation of Net Profit for the study of 19 selected nationalized banks for the year 2010 to 2013. With the base year 2010 Net Profit is Avg. 1358 cr. total if I Consider this Amt. as 100% than it is increased in year 2011 – 21.64%(Net 121.64%), year 2012- 24.59% (Net 124.59%) and in year 2013- its decreased in compare to year 2012 by 5% and in comparison with year 2010 it is increased with 19.80 (Net 119.80%). The result of Hypothesis testing shows that there is significant difference regarding the performance of Provisions and Contingencies. Banks should try to generate more and more Net Profit through its various Operations in future.

- Credit Deposit Ratio shows the lower is the liquidity position of the bank. Here the higher performances of the banks are Syndicate Bank at first, Andhra Bank at second and Indian Overseas Bank has secured the third position in Credit Deposit Ratio. While the lower performance United Bank of India at first, Vijaya Bank stand at second and Allahabad Bank at third position in the calculation of Credit Deposit Ratio for the study of 19 selected nationalized banks for the year 2011 to 2013. The Avg. ratio for year 2011 is 72.42%, in the year 2012- 74.60 (increased by 2.12%) and in year 2013is 74.31% (decreased by 0.29%). The result of Hypothesis testing shows that there is significant difference regarding the performance of Credit Deposit Ratio. Banks should try to reduce this ratio because it's creating more liquid position for bank and bank easily meets its routing operation.

- Investment Deposit Ratio shows the higher the ratio, the lower is the liquidity position of the bank. Here the higher ratio rates of the banks are Corporation Bank at first, Allahabad Bank at second and Bank of Maharashtra has secured the third position in Credit Deposit Ratio. While the lower performance Bank of Baroda at first, Syndicate Bank stand at second and Andhra Bank at third position in the calculation of Investment Deposit Ratio for the study of 19 selected nationalized banks for the year 2010 to 2013. The Avg. ratio for year 2010 is 32.18%, in the year 2011- 30.85 (decreased by 1. 33%), in the year 2012- 30.62 (decreased by 0.23%) and in the year 2013is 31.18% (Increased by 0.56%). The result of Hypothesis testing shows that there is significant difference regarding the performance of Investment Deposit Ratio. Banks should try to reduce this ratio because it's creating more liquid position for bank and bank simply meets its routing operation.
- Spread As Percentage (%) Of Assets Ratio means Net interest spread is similar to net interest margin; net interest spread expresses the nominal average difference between borrowing and lending rates, without compensating for the fact that the amount of earning assets and borrowed funds may be different. Its show effective use of assets for generates net interest income. (Interest income –interest expenses)The higher the ratio shows good performance of bank. Here the higher ratio rates of the banks are Indian Bank at first, Punjab National Bank at second and Andhra Bank has secured the third position in Spread as percentage (%) of Assets Ratio.

While the lower ratio rates Corporation Bank at first, Vijaya Bank stand at second and Bank of India & Punjab & Sind Bank at third position in Spread as percentage (%) of Assets Ratio for the study of 19 selected nationalized banks for the year 2010 to 2013. The Avg. ratio for year 2010 is 2.11 %, in the year 2011- 2.55% (Increased by 0.44%), in the year 2012- 2.44 (decreased by 0.11%) and in the year 2013is 2.27% (Decreased by 0.17%). The result of Hypothesis testing shows that there is significant difference regarding the performance of Spread as percentage (%) of Assets Ratio. Banks should try to increase this ratio because it's creating more income through its efficient use of Operations.

- Operating Expenses as % to Total Expenses means contributions of operating expenses in to total expenses. Here the higher ratio rates of the banks are Bank of Maharashtra at first, Punjab National Bank at second and Indian Bank has secured the third position in this expenses calculation. While the lower ratio rates banks are Corporation Bank at first, UCO Bank stand at second and Oriental Bank of Commerce at third position in operating expenses ratio for the study of 19 selected nationalized banks for the year 2011 to 2013. The Avg. ratio for year 2011 is 25.29 %, in the year 2012- 19.79% (Decreased by 5.50 %), and in the year 2013- 18.64 (decreased by 1.13%) The result of Hypothesis testing shows that there is no significant difference regarding the performance of Spread as percentage (%) of Assets Ratio. Means all selected Banks have common operating expenses as % to total expenses. Banks should maintain Decreasing level of this ratio because it's creating more Expenses of banking Operations.

- Return on Assets Percentage (%) means net profit divided to net assets (after deducting provisions and contingency) the higher ratio indicate good position of the bank. Here the higher ratio rates of the banks are Indian Bank at first, Punjab National Bank at second and Andhra Bank has secured the third position in this ratio calculation. While the lower ratio rates banks are Indian Overseas Bank at first, Central Bank of India stand at second and United Bank of India at third position in Return on Assets Ratio for the study of 19 selected nationalized banks for the year 2011 to 2013. The Avg. ratio for year 2010 is 1.00 %, in the year 2011- 0.99% (Decreased by 0.01 %), in the year 2012- 0.85% (decreased by 0.14%) and in the year 2013- 0.71% (decreased by 0.14%) The result of Hypothesis testing shows that there is significant difference regarding the performance of Return on Assets percentage (%) Ratio. All Banks should try to Increase this ratio because it generates more profit through the banking Operations.
- Capital Adequacy Ratio - Basel -I Percentage (%) Capital adequacy is indicated by a minimum numerical ratio which the banks are expected to maintain to ensure stability and strength. As per RBI All banks must maintained 9 % rate for it. In this study of 19 selected nationalized banks for the year 2011 to 2013 all banks has maintained the rate. The higher ratio rates of the banks are Punjab & Sind Bank at first, UCO Bank at second and Punjab National Bank has secured the third position in this

ratio computation as per year 2013. While the lower ratio rates banks is Vijaya Bank at first, United Bank of India stand at second and Indian Overseas Bank at third position in as per year 2013 data ratio computation. The result of Hypothesis testing shows that there is significant difference regarding the performance of Capital Adequacy Ratio. All banks should follow RBI Guidelines and try to increase this ratio rate.

- Capital Adequacy Ratio - Basel -II Percentage (%) Capital adequacy is indicated by a minimum numerical ratio which the banks are expected to maintain to ensure stability and strength. As per RBI All banks must maintained 9 % rate for it. In this study of 19 selected nationalized banks for the year 2011 to 2013 all banks has maintained the rate. The higher Avg. ratio rates of the banks are Bank of Baroda at first, Canara Bank at second and Corporation Bank has secured the third position in this ratio computation. While the lower Avg. ratio rates banks is Indian Bank at first, Bank of India stand at second and Union Bank of India at third position computation. The result of Hypothesis testing shows that there is significant difference regarding the performance of Capital Adequacy Ratio. All banks should follow RBI Guidelines and try to increase this ratio rate.
- Net NPA to Net Advance Ratio The ratio of "Net NPA to advance ratio" is a credit efficiency parameter if the ratio is lower, it is a sign of credit efficiency. There is a big problem of NPAs for all the banks now a day. The high ratio of NPA is not good for any Bank or Business. This ratio indicates in ability of

recovery from advances. The higher Avg. ratio rates of the banks are UCO Bank at first, United Bank of India second and Central Bank of India has secured the third position in this ratio computation. While the lower Avg. ratio rates banks are Bank of Baroda at first, Corporation Bank stand at second and Syndicate Bank at third position computation. The result of Hypothesis testing shows that there is no significant difference regarding the performance of Net NPA to Net Advance Ratio. All banks should try to decrease this ratio rate.

- Business per Employee ratio is an indicator of degree of employee's productivity of banks. If the ratio is higher, it indicates more productivity of labour in banks. It also proves the managerial efficiency regarding staffing activities. The higher Avg. ratio rates of the banks are Corporation Bank at first, Oriental Bank of Commerce second and Bank of Baroda has secured the third position in this ratio computation. While the lower Avg. ratio rates banks are Central Bank of India at first, United Bank of India stand at second and Bank of Maharashtra at third position computation. The result of Hypothesis testing shows that there is significant difference regarding the performance of Business per Employee Ratio. All banks should try to Increase this ratio rate.
- Profit per Employee ratio shows the labour productivity of banks with the angle of profit. Net profit per employee can be obtained in rupees. It indicates the profitability and productivity per employee for the bank positive and higher ratio indicates higher labour productivity. The higher Avg. ratio

rates of the banks are Corporation Bank at first, Bank of Baroda second and Indian Bank has secured the third position in this ratio computation. While the lower Avg. ratio rates of the banks are Central Bank of India at first, United Bank of India stand at second and Bank of Maharashtra at third position computation. The result of Hypothesis testing shows that there is significant difference regarding the performance of Profit per Employee Ratio. All banks should try to Increase this ratio rate.

## 5.2. Suggestions

- To enhance the growth rate in agriculture to 4.0 per cent, Manufacturing to 10.0 per cent and Real GDP of 8.2 per cent as envisaged in the Approach to the Twelth Five Year Plan, and improving its robustness would require substantial investment in irrigation and water management technologies, diversification and boosting productivity of different crops through improved seeds and plant-care practices. The move towards inclusive growth is a big challenge for the financial system of the country, including commercial banks. Banks would need to adopt an innovative, customer-friendly approach to increase their effective reach so that the share of organised finance increases. A participatory and partnership-based model for financial inclusion, coupled with community-linked financial initiatives is the need of the hour. In the near future customer-friendly products, delivery channels, relationship banking, dependency on IT systems and competitive pricing would be the driving forces. Banks will to move to high-tech banking. The Internet would be the engine of the banking revolution in the decades to come and e-commerce would be its fuel. Therefore, the key to survival of banks in future will be the retention of customer loyalty by providing value-added services tailored to their needs.

- First, traditionally banks have viewed rural areas as a segment purely in need of upliftment. This was based on the underlying philosophy of a social obligation. However, the future lays with those who see the poor as their customers, namely, financial inclusion. By 'financial inclusion' is meant the provision by the financial system, of financial products and services at an affordable price, to those who have been financially excluded. As banking services are in the nature of a public utility service, it is essential that banking and payment services are provided to the entire population without discrimination. The harsh reality is that the spread of banking facilities in India is uneven, with a substantial portion of the households, especially in the rural areas, still outside the coverage of the formal banking system. Almost 40 per cent of the adult population of the country is unable to access mainstream financial products. The Reserve Bank of India has recently adopted a decentralised approach in this regard with close involvement of State Governments and banks and has used multiple channels to expand the outreach of banks. It is important to mention that the Union Bank has launched a new initiative called 'Village Knowledge Centres'. Here, technology is used to help the farmer improve his productivity. The Bank's staff at these village knowledge centres act as relationship managers, liaising between local authorities and farmers, facilitating the opening of accounts and ensuring that credit is provided to the needy. Such examples need to be followed by other banks.

- Secondly, commercial banks should change their marketing concept. Under the new concept of marketing, the task of management should not so much be skill in making the customer do what suits the rest of the business, as to be skilful in conceiving and making business do what suits the interest of the customers.
- Thirdly, stress should be laid on deposit mobilisation from the agricultural sector itself to finance its own credit requirements. Such a move will entail two steps—curtailment of unproductive expenditure and deposit of savings by the agriculturists in banks. It is common knowledge that villagers spend huge sums on unproductive social ceremonies, drinking, litigation, etc. Their outlook needs to be changed with the help of banking staff and utilising the services of the mass media. Villagers must be convinced that money spent on such social obligations is a waste and they themselves would gain in the long run if they would save and invest. The services of officers and staff of the community development projects may also be utilised for this purpose.
- Fourthly, the more important aspect of the whole drive is the deposit of savings by the agriculturist in the banks. Vast sums of money are lying idle even today in rural areas. We think that, in

spite of different agencies engaged in providing agricultural finance, the village moneylender continues to be a necessary evil. These moneylenders have great influence on the villagers. To mobilise the savings of the villagers, the services of these moneylenders—both professional and agricultural—can be utilised. The nationalised banks may appoint them as their agents. The banks should then ask them to encourage the villagers to deposit their money in the banks and approach the banks for loans through them. The banks may give them a sort of del-credere commission, depending upon the quantum of business done by them, as is done in the case of agents of the Life Insurance Corporation, General Insurance Corporation, National Savings Organisation, etc. Such a step would help in mobilising savings. The appointment of moneylenders as agents has an added advantage. These moneylenders have been living in villages for a long time and are, therefore, accustomed to the rural way of life. They know the local language and can, therefore, mix well with the villagers.This is not the case with the qualified, educated and sophisticated bank staff. Many a time, superiority complex on the part of the bank employees drives away the villagers. As a corollary to this, it is also suggested that, as far as possible, the staff to be deputed in the rural branches, should be drawn from the villages or semi-urban areas themselves and better living conditions be assured for the bank employees.

- Fifthly, there is need for a reorientation in the credit policy of banks. Priority sector landings should be restricted only to the core sector. Banks should provide credit not merely on the basis of collateral security such as land and buildings but they should also advance loans to the agriculturists after assessing the 'absorptive capacity' and the increase in productivity that is feasible with the help of such loans. Crops should also be accepted on a loan of security. To assess the 'absorptive capacity' of the farmers commercial banks should maintain a staff of agricultural experts.

- Sixthly, the commercial banks should also provide credit to the agriculturists on the basis of 'joint guarantee' given by the village panchayat or by a few well-known farmers of the village. The acceptance of such a basis will greatly help the farmers, particularly small farmers, in securing loans from commercial banks. This will also result in more purposeful advent of the commercial banks in the rural sector and will bring them into relationship with cooperative institutions. It will also ensure a fair understanding between them and encourage commercial banks to operate on the principle of collective service for a collective need.
- Seventhly, one problem experienced by banks is that, many a time, villagers divert the loans from productive to unproductive uses. This needs to be stopped and it needs to be ensured that the credit is used for the purposes for which it is meant. Banks may think in terms of advancing credit to agriculturists in the form of agricultural inputs. While giving credit to farmers in the form of agricultural inputs, it should be

ensured that inputs are supplied in adequate quantities and in time and complementary and supplementary facilities are also available.

- Finally, it needs to be remembered that stray attempts would not solve the problem of agricultural credit. The credit system as a whole government, commercial and cooperative must be so knit together that it does not suffer either from a gap or an overlap. It is only then that the real fruits of credit facilities will be enjoyed by the country at large in the form of agricultural development which still the key to India's prosperity in future.

## 5.3. Concluding remarks regarding Basel

The Capital Accord of 1988, which set global standards for regulation and supervision, has emerged as one of the most significant developments in strengthening the soundness and stability of the international financial system. The biggest contribution of the Basel Accord has been to arrive at a common definition of capital. Though the capital adequacy norms have been adopted in different countries with certain country-specific adaptations, the definition of capital given by the Basel Committee has been adopted almost uniformly across countries and has also been adopted in the new framework. Basel I served regulators and banks well for many years. However, for large and complex banking organisations, it increasingly failed to adequately align regulatory capital required with the underlying risks. There had been growing evidence of reduction in the Accord's effectiveness caused by financial innovations and some risks other than credit risk in the banking business, notably interest rate risk and the investment risk on securities, and operational risk. Subsequently, the Accord was fine-tuned to take in to account factors which were not considered initially for assessing overall capital adequacy. This, together with a better understanding of the conceptual shortcomings in the original Accord, led to a redesign of the framework which finally emerged as Basel II or the New Capital Adequacy Framework.

Basel II represents a fundamental shift in the regulatory capital framework by aligning the capital requirements with underlying risks through enhanced risk measurement techniques and encouraging banks to develop a more disciplined approach to risk management. Recognizing the need for a more broad-based and flexible framework, the new framework calls for better alignment of regulatory capital with underlying risks by replacing the earlier broad-brush approach with preferential risk weighting treatment. The framework provides for explicit capital charge for other risks viz., operational risk and interest rate risk in the banking book for banks where interest rate risks are significantly above average (outliers). The revised framework also aims at promoting the adoption of stronger risk management practices by the banking industry, and provide for a menu of options to be adopted by the banks and the regulators, the biggest challenge remains that of differential treatment to different groups of financial institutions, while at the same time preserving the benefits of a framework that can be applied as uniformly as possible at the national level.

The Basel II framework is a significant improvement over the Basel I rules in the incentives it provides for sound risk management practices, its alignment of minimum capital requirements with risks banks face, and its flexibility to be adapted to and address evolving risks from financial innovation. It is critical that the minimum capital requirements of the first pillar be accompanied by a robust implementation of the second, including efforts by banks to assess their capital adequacy and by supervisors to review such assessments. The second pillar is aimed at enabling early supervisory intervention if capital does not provide a sufficient buffer against risk. In addition, the disclosures provided under the third pillar of this Framework is intended to enhance the role of market participants in monitoring banks, and thereby ensuring that market discipline serves as an effective complement to the other two pillars. Supervisors should assess the need for additional capital buffers or supplementary measures of capital strength as a complement to risk-based measures. Basel II, therefore, would help in promoting the safety and soundness of the banking system. However, in view of the recent financial market turmoil, a number of modifications have been suggested in the Basel II framework. These measures need to be evaluated in terms of their ability to prevent future crises. Several countries have proposed or are considering such supplementary measures, including in the form of a balance-sheet leverage ratio, to better contain leverage in the system, guard against risk measurement errors and strengthen banks' overall shock absorption capacity. However, the insistence on holding higher capital by banks may lead to deepening of recession, as cautioned by Jean-Claude Trichet, the President of the European Central Bank at the World Economic Forum Meet, 2009. In this context, the observation of the Reserve Bank of India Deputy Governor 'understanding Basel II concepts is one step away from agreeing to it in principle. Implementing Basel II is another long step away from understanding it' appears to be pertinent. The recent turmoil in credit markets has displayed some of the deficiencies in the Basel II framework, and even after the changes recently announced by the Basel Committee are formalised, it is still uncertain whether the amendments could provide a complete solution for evaluating bank capital objectively. However, as Caprio and Honohan (1999) remind us, bank regulation must be seen as an evolutionary struggle and regulatory innovation will remain a constant challenge.

- Indian Banking sector is in transition phase i.e. from Basel II to Basel III.
- Commercial Banks have already adopted standardized approaches under Basel II.
- Large banks are in compliance mode of advanced approaches prescribed by enhanced Basel II i.e. Basel 2.5.
- Since the Basel III has mandated higher and better quality capital by explicitly defining components of Tier I and Tier II capital, relatively smaller banks will have to make necessary arrangement for augmenting their capital and also find innovative financial instruments capable of being defined as capital as per norms.

- Since the Basel III has mandated higher and better quality capital by explicitly defining components of Tier I and Tier II capital, relatively smaller banks will have to make necessary arrangement for augmenting their capital and also find innovative financial instruments capable of being defined as capital as per norms.
- With the introduction of Capital Conservation Buffer w.e.f.2015-16 in phased manner, banks are expected to experience shortfall in capital on account of building up capital buffer. The shortfall may become severe in the event of possible excessive credit growth.
- In case of Public Sector Banks, Government will have to infuse the shortfall in capital which, if financed through borrowings, may enlarge fiscal deficit.
- In the event of activation of Leverage Coverage Ratio w.e.f. April, 2015, banks will be required to deploy higher amount of funds in high quality but lower earning assets which shall cause the yield on assets to decline with negative effect on profitability.
- Indian banks will have to compensate the declining Return on Assets and Return on Equity, caused by the new Basel framework, by enhancing new avenues of non fund based income, curtailing the cost structure and such other appropriate measures.
- Basel III framework demands complex and sophisticated data collection and data analysis system in order to comply with various risk identification and risk management techniques such

as Duration Gap Analysis, VaR, and Stress Tests etc. Banks will have to put in place a robust MIS structure along with suitably trained manpower.

- Mr. Gobind Jain, Senior Vice-President, Kotak Mahindra Bank, argues that the challenges of Basel III implementation in India are more with regard to financing growth and enhanced credit demand. He articulates that once Basel III capital requirements are in place, banks can respond in one of three ways: - operational, tactical and strategic. An operational response will be on the lines of processes, methods and data. Banks could also look into increasing efficiency, strategic cost reduction, and reassessing risky processes so that operating costs will be reduced and productivity will simultaneously increase. A tactical response will be on the lines of pricing, funding, and asset restructuring. A strategic response will be along the lines of the business model, organisational structure, and equity. Such responses will be an active approach to balance sheet management, undertaking strategic cost reduction, including rationalization of branch structures, product rationalization or implementation of a shared services model.

**5.4. Recommendations Regarding Selected Nationalized Banks**

From my study I would like to suggest the entire selected 19 nationalized bank that banks should creates more deposits and attempt reduce the investments and credit policy as it was fluctuated in last few years. But if it is constantly reduce by the banks than it's create better future for the banks. As far as Gross

NPA Net NPA in the relation with total assets are concerned that were increased in the high proposition in last few years. That is not good for the banking industries. Banks should try to decreases in future for long term perspective for all the banks. Interest and other income create total income and it was increased during study period. Same way expenditure also increased with year's passed. However banks should try to make it double in compare with total expenditures in future. Operating profits was dived in to two parts one is provisions and contingency and second net profit all these increased with passes of years however banks should maintain level between both things because both are very essential for present and future operation of banks with its liquidity. Spread as percentage (%) of assets ratio show effective use of assets for generates net interest income. (Interest income –interest expenses)The higher the ratio shows good performance of bank. And it was fluctuated in last few years. All the banks should try to constant increase this ratio. Operating expenses as percentage to total expenses is decreases in last few years and that shows good performance for the banks and maintains the same level in future too. Return on assets was also deceased in last few years it was not good sign for the banks and try to constant increase it. Capital Adequacy Ratio - Basel –I and Basel- II Percentage **(%)** Capital adequacy was indicated by a minimum numerical ratio which the banks are expected to maintain to ensure stability and strength. As per RBI All banks must maintained 9 % rate for it. All banks have maintained this level and in last few years it was fluctuated however its contestant increase make good difference for banking industries. The ratio of “Net NPA to advance ratio” is a credit efficiency parameter if the ratio is lower, it is a sign of credit efficiency. There is a big problem of NPAs for all the banks. The high ratio of NPA is not good for any Bank or Business. In my study it was increased. However banks should try to continuous reduce it in future. Business per employee is an indicator of degree of employee’s productivity of banks. If the ratio is higher, it indicates more productivity of labour efficiency in banks. It also proves the managerial efficiency regarding staffing activities. And it was constant increased in study period and it’s good for all the banks and maintains constant increased in future year’s performance. Profit per Employee the labour productivity of banks with the angle of profit. Net profit per employee can be obtained in rupees. It indicates the profitability and productivity per employee for the bank positive and higher ratio indicates higher labour productivity. It was fluctuated in last few years. It should constant increased in futures by all the banks. With these entire things I have tried at my best level to represent banking scenario in India and concluding here my book. Thanks to all.

# BIBLIOGRAPHY


- A Chavez Irapta, Et Al. 2005. Introduction to Asia: History, Culture, and Civilization Rex Bookstore, Inc.,
- Agarwal M.R.2008 "Financial management" RBSA Publisher, Jaipur
- Agarwal O.P. 2008. "Modern banking in India" Himalaya Publication House, Mumbai, 1st edition,
- Altman, E. and A. Saunders,2001, 'An Analysis and Critique of the BIS Proposal on Capital Adequacy and Ratings', The Journal of Banking & Finance, Vol. 25, No.1, January.
- Austin, Granville. 1999. Working a Democratic Constitution – A History of the Indian Experience. New Delhi: Oxford University Press. ISBN 0-19-565610-5.
- Ayuso, J., D. Perez and J. Saurina. 2004, 'Are Capital Buffers Pro-cyclical? Evidence from Spanish Panel Data,' Journal of Financial Intermediation 13(2): 249-264.
- Bank for International Settlements, 1999, Credit Risk Modelling: Current Practices and Applications, Basel Committee on Banking Supervision, BIS: Basel, April.

- Bank for International Settlements,1999, Sound Policies for Loan Accounting, Credit Risk Disclosure and Related Matters, Basel Committee on Banking Supervision, BIS: Basel.
- Bank for International Settlements,2001, The New Basel Capital Accord: Consultative Document, BIS: Basel.
- Bank for International Settlements, 2004, Implementation of the New Capital Adequacy Framework in Non-Basel Committee Member Countries, FSI Occasional Paper 04, BIS: Basel, April.
- Bank for International Settlements, 2004, International Convergence of Capital Measurement and Capital Standards: A Revised Framework , Basel Committee on Banking Supervision, BIS: Basel.
- Bank for International Settlements, 2006, Basel II: International Convergence of Capital Measurement and Capital Standards: A Revised Framework - Comprehensive Version, Basel Committee on Banking Supervision, June.
- Bank for International Settlements, Annual Report, Various issues; BIS: Basel.
- Bardos, J.1988, 'The Risk-Based Capital Agreement: A Further Step towards Policy Convergence', FRB of New York Quarterly Review, Vol 12(4).
- Basotiya G.R. & Sharma K.K., 2002. "Research Methodology" Mangaldeep publication 1st edition,

- Bhalla V.K. 2014 “International Financial Management Text and cases” Anmol Publication House, New Delhi 3rd edition
- Bhattacharya & Agarwal, 2006. “Basics of banking and finance” Himalaya Publication House, Mumbai 1st edition
- Bhattacharya K.M. 2006.“Risk management in Indian Bank” Himalaya Publication House, Mumbai, 1st edition,
- Brigham Eugene F. & Gapenski Louis C. “Financial management theory & practice” Harcourt brace college publishers, 7th edition.
- Caruana, J. 2005, Basel II: Back to the Future, 7th Hong Kong Monetary Authority Distinguished Lecture, available at http://www.bde.es/prensa/intervenpub/gobernador/040205e.pdf.
- Computerization of banking sector".1988. "MICR technology". "Committee on Computerization in Banks.
- Cooke, Charles Northcote .1863. The rise, progress, and present condition of banking in India. Printed by P.M. Cranenburgh, Bengal Print. Co., pp.177-200.
- Cornford, A. (2006), ‘The Global Implementation of Basel II: Prospects and Outstanding Problems Policy Issues in International Trade and Commodities,’ Issues in International Trade and Commodities Study Series No. 34, United Nations Conference on Trade and Development.
- Desai Vasant 2006.“Banks and institutional management” Himalaya Publication House, Mumbai, 1st edition,

- Desai Vasant.2007 "Fundamental of the Indian financial system" Himalaya Publication House, Mumbai, 6th edition,
- Desai. M.A. & others. 2013-14 .Statistics Book, Sem. –V, B.Com., Shah B.S. Publication, Ahemedabad, pp 83-96 ISBN No. 81-8416-025-9
- Dewartipont, M. and J. Tirole (1994), The Prudential Regulation of Banks, MIT Press, Cambridge: MA.
- Gomez C. 2008. Financial Markets Institutions And Financial Services Prentice - Hall, ISBN 8120335376
- Gopinath, S. (2006), 'Approach to Basel II.' RBI Bulletin, June.
- Gordon & Natrajan.2006 "Banking theory law and practice" Himalaya Publication House, Mumbai, 20th edition,
- Gupta S.P., Statistical Methods. Sultan Chand and Sons, New Delhi
- Indian banking system.2006. I.K. International Publishing House Pvt. Ltd. ISBN 81-88237-88-4.
- Jain Gopal Lal, 2003. Research Methodology methods tools & techniques Mangal deep publication Jaipur, 2nd edition,
- Kaptan S. S., Chobey, N S, 2002 "Indian Banking in Electronic Era", Sarup and Sons Publication, New Delhi.
- Kaptan, S.S. 2002. "New Concepts in Banking", Sarup and Sons Publication, Edition, 2002 [10] New Delhi.

- Kashyap, A. and J. Stein,2004, 'Cyclical Implications of Basel II Capital Standards', Economic Perspectives, 28(1): 18–31, Federal Reserve Bank of Chicago.
- Kothari.C.R., 2011 Research Methodology methods & techniques. New age International (P) Limited, Publishers, New Delhi, 2nd Edition.
- Krishnaswami O.R., Methodology of Research in Social, Science. Himalaya Publishing House, Delhi
- Kroszner, R.2008, 'Improving Risk Management in Light of Recent Market Events.' speech delivered at the Global Association of Risk Management Professionals Annual Risk Convention, New York, February 25.
- Kroszner, R.2008, 'Liquidity-Risk Management in the Business of Banking,' speech delivered at the Institute of International Bankers, Washington, DC, March 3.
- Kupiec 2004, 'Capital Adequacy and Basel II', FDIC Centre for financial Research Working Paper No. 2004-02.
- Laurent, Balthazar. 2006, From Basel 1 to Basel 3: The Integration of State-of-the-Art Risk Modeling in Banking Regulation, Palgrave Macmillan.
- Leeladhar, V. 2006, 'Demystifying Basel II,' RBI Bulletin, October.
- Leeladhar, V. 2007, 'Basel II and Credit Risk Managment,' RBI Bulletin, October.

- Lowe, P. 2002, 'Credit Risk Measurement and Procyclicality,' BIS Working Papers No 116, Bank for International Settlements, September.
- M.Y. Khan & P.K. Jain,2006, Financial Management,Vikash Publishing House, New Delhi
- Maheshwari S.N.2006" Fundamentals of financial management" Sultanchand & sons publication, New Delhi
- Misra & Puri. 2007."Indian economy" Himalaya Publication House, Mumbai 24th edition 2007
- Nair Suja R.2005. "Marketing Research" Himalaya Publication House, Mumbai 1ST edition
- Narendra Singh.2007. "Advanced Financial management" Himalaya Publication House, Mumbai 1st edition,
- Pathak Bharti V.2003. "Financial system in India" Person education Singapore 1st edition.
- Pennacchi, G. 2004, 'Risk-Based Capital Standards, Deposit Insurance, and Procyclicality,' Department of Finance, University of Illinois.
- Proctor,C.2006, Basel II: credit Risk Mitigation, October, available on http://www.twobirds.com/english/publications/articles/Basel-II_Credit_Risk_Mitigation.cfm
- Report of the Financial Stability Forum on Enhancing Market and Institutional Resilience, April 2008.

- Srivastava P.K. 2008 "Banking theory and practice" Himalaya Publication House, Mumbai 10th edition,
- Srivastava R.M.2007. "Financial management and policy" Himalaya Publication House, Mumbai, 3rd edition,
- Tannan M.L., Banking Law & Practice in India" Indian Law House, New Delhi
- Wall, Larry D. 1989, Capital Requirements for Banks: A Look at the 1981 and 1988 Standards, Federal Reserve Bank of Atlanta Economic Review 74 (March/April): 14-29.
- Wellink, N. 2007, Basel II and Financial Institution Resiliency at the 'Risk Capital 2007' conference, Paris, June 27.
- White, W. 2000, 'What have We Learned from Recent Financial Crisis and Policy Responses?' BIS Working Paper No. 84, January.
- Wilkinson & Bhandarkar, 1993. "Methodology and techniques of social research" Himalaya Publication House, Mumbai, 9th edition.

**Websites:**

- http://currentaffairs.nirdeshak.com/rbi-extends-basel-iii-deadline-31-march-2019/ Date: 28/06/2014 time 5.12p.m.
- http://en.wikipedia.org/wiki/Bank#History
- http://en.wikipedia.org/wiki/Banking_in_India dated 21july,2014 time 5.15 pm
- http://en.wikipedia.org/wiki/Banking_in_India#Early_history

- http://en.wikipedia.org/wiki/Banking_regulation
- http://en.wikipedia.org/wiki/Regional_Rural_bank
- http://finance.indiamart.com/investmentinindia/Scheduled_commercial_banks.html
- http://www.iloveindia.com/finance/bank/nationalised-banks/allahabad-bank.html Accessed in June-July, 2014
- http://www.iloveindia.com/finance/bank/nationalised-banks/andhra-bank.html Accessed in June-July, 2014
- http://www.iloveindia.com/finance/bank/nationalised-banks/bank-of-baroda.html date 21july,2014 5.25 pm Accessed in June-July, 2014
- http://www.iloveindia.com/finance/bank/nationalised-banks/bank-of-india.html Accessed in June-July, 2014
- http://www.iloveindia.com/finance/bank/nationalised-banks/bank-of-maharashtra.html Accessed in June-July, 2014
- http://www.iloveindia.com/finance/bank/nationalised-banks/canara-bank.html Accessed in June-July, 2014
- http://www.iloveindia.com/finance/bank/nationalised-banks/central-bank-of-india.html Accessed in June-July, 2014
- http://www.iloveindia.com/finance/bank/nationalised-banks/corporation-bank.html Accessed in June-July, 2014
- http://www.iloveindia.com/finance/bank/nationalised-banks/dena-bank.html Accessed in June-July, 2014

- http://www.iloveindia.com/finance/bank/nationalised-banks/idbi-bank.html Accessed in June-July, 2014
- http://www.iloveindia.com/finance/bank/nationalised-banks/indian-bank.html Accessed in June-July, 2014
- http://www.iloveindia.com/finance/bank/nationalised-banks/indian-overseas-bank.html Accessed in June-July, 2014
- http://www.iloveindia.com/finance/bank/nationalised-banks/oriental-bank-of-commerce.html Accessed in June-July, 2014
- http://www.iloveindia.com/finance/bank/nationalised-banks/punjab-&-sind-bank.html Accessed in June-July, 2014
- http://www.iloveindia.com/finance/bank/nationalised-banks/punjab-national-bank. html Accessed in June-July, 2014
- http://www.iloveindia.com/finance/bank/nationalised-banks/state-bank-of- india.html Accessed in June-July, 2014
- http://www.iloveindia.com/finance/bank/nationalised-banks/syndicate-bank.html Accessed in June-July, 2014
- http://www.iloveindia.com/finance/bank/nationalised-banks/uco-bank.html Accessed in June-July, 2014
- http://www.iloveindia.com/finance/bank/nationalised-banks/union-bank-of-india.html Accessed in June-July, 2014
- http://www.iloveindia.com/finance/bank/nationalised-banks/united-bank-of-india.html Accessed in June-July, 2014

- http://www.iloveindia.com/finance/bank/nationalised-banks/vijaya-bank.html Accessed in June-July, 2014
- http://www.mainstreamweekly.net/article743.htmldate 30.08.2014 time 1.05 pm
- http://www.nabard.org/introduction.asp Accessed in June-July, 2014
- http://www.rbi.org.in/Scripts/bs_viewcontent.aspx?Id=2023 pp 6-30. date 28/06/2014 5.25. p.m.
- http://www.rbi.org.in/scripts/fun_urban.aspx
- http://www.scribd.com/doc/4569884/The-Reserve-Bank-of-India89
- http://www.scribd.com/doc/5434275/indian-banking-sector (ICBA), International Co-operative Banks Association
- ICICI's third eye: It's Indiatime. Indiatime.com. Retrieved 28 July 2010.
- India banking sector: http://www.scribd.com/doc/8361020/india-banking-sector
- www.asiatradehub.com
- www.banknetindia.com
- www.bcn.gob.ni
- www.blackwell-synergy.com
- www.business.mapsofindia.com
- www.fic.wharton.upenn.edu
- www.financeindiamart.com

- www.googleimage /logo/nationalizedbanks.com
- www.iba.org.in
- www.indianbank.in
- www.indiaonline.com
- www.info.ug.net
- www.internationalmonetaryfund.com
- www.rbi.org.in/scripts/publications
- www.researchandmarkets.com
- www.socserv.mcmoster.ca
- www.thehindubusinessline.com
- www.uninews.unicredit.it


**Notes:**


- RBI, Annual Report, 2006-07, p. 143. 2. RBI, Trend and Progress of Banking in India, 2005-06, p. 300. 3. RBI, Annual Report, 2006-07, p. 138. 4. Anil Kumar Jain, 'New Scheme of Deposit Mobilisation', Mainstream, January 30, 1971, pp. 17-18.
- Statistical Tables Related to Banks in India - Reserve Bank of India
- IBA Bulletins, Special Issues: March-2003, January-2005, August-2005
- RBI, Report on currency and Finance
- RBI, Report on Trend and Progress of Banking in India.
- Evolution of Payment Systems in India =Reserve Bank of India.

- ICICI personal loan customer commits suicide after alleged harassment by recovery agents. Parinda.com. Retrieved 28 July 2010.
- Karnataka / Mysore News: ICICI Bank returns tractor to farmer's mother. The Hindu (Chennai, India). 30 June 2008. Retrieved 28 July 2010.
- A Dissertation on "A Financial Performance of Indian Banking Sector A study of selected Nationalised Bank". By Mr. Purthvi Jadeja in the year 2007-08 at P.G. Department of Business studies, S.P. university. Vidyanagar use as reference for chapter 1.


**Notes Related to Chapter -4 Basel**

**1.)** It consisted of senior representatives of bank supervisory authorities and central banks from 13 countries, viz., Belgium, Canada, France, Germany, Italy, Japan, Luxembourg, the Netherlands, Sweden, Switzerland, the United Kingdom and the United States.

**2.)** Core Principles for Effective Banking Supervision, which the Basel Committee on Banking Supervision (the Committee)1 originally published in September 1997 was revised in October 2006 in view of the significant changes in banking regulation, experience gained with implementing the Core Principles in individual countries, and new regulatory issues, insights and gaps in regulation since 1997.

**3.)**The revised and updated document was released in 1998 and apart from the July 1988 text of the Basel Capital Accord contains five textual changes reflecting the November 1991 amendment (concerning general provisions);?the July 1994 amendment (concerning the qualification for the OECD risk weighting); ?the April 1995 amendment to Annex 3 (concerning certain off-balance-sheet items) and claims collateralised by securities issued by OECD non-central government public-sector entities; the April 1998 amendment(concerning the list of assets eligible for a 20 per cent risk weighting); and removal of references to transitional and implementation arrangements.

**4.)** The objective of the impact study is to assess whether the Committee has met its goals with regard to the New Basel Capital Accord.

**5.)** (Total capital) / (Credit risk + market risk + operational risk) >= 8 per cent minimum capital ratio.

**6.)** A forum of select senior representatives of national financial authorities including central banks, supervisory authorities and treasury departments, international financial institutions, international regulatory and supervisory groupings and committees of central bank experts.

**7.)** Kishori J. Udeshi, Deputy Governor, Reserve Bank of India at the World Bank/ IMF/US Federal Reserve Board 4th Annual International Seminar on Policy Challenges for the Financial Sector : Basel II at Washington on June 2, 2004.

**8.)** Prakash Anupam "Evolution of the Basel Framework on Bank Capital Regulation" Assistant Adviser in the Department of Economic Analysis and Policy of the Reserve Bank of India. Usual disclaimer applies. For the detail of Basel I & II

**9)** Academic Staff College, S.P. University, Vidyanagr lecture delivered on INDIAN BANKING SECTOR – ROAD TOWARDS BASEL III Lecture delivered by Dr. Ketan R. Upadhyay, Associate Professor, Department of Accounting & Financial Management, Faculty of Commerce, The Maharaja Sayajirao University of Baroda, Vadodara

www.ingramcontent.com/pod-product-compliance
Lightning Source LLC
Chambersburg PA
CBHW080801180526
45168CB00006B/2285

* 9 7 8 1 5 0 8 9 4 9 7 2 5 *